Mark H

G000127372

ONE J ___
AHEAD

THE TOP NH HORSES
TO FOLLOW FOR 2021/2022

THE AUTHOR

Mark Howard is 46 and graduated from Manchester University with a BA Honours Degree in History. For the last 28 years, he has written the National Hunt horses to follow book *One Jump Ahead*. He also writes the Flat racing equivalent, *Ahead On The Flat*. In addition, he appears as a pundit on *Racing TV* (Sky Channel 426) and, prior to that, *Attheraces*. He is also a regular contributor to sportinglife.com and has written for *The Irish Field, Sports Advisor and Racing & Football Outlook (Borderer & Trainer File)*. He is Ambassador for the successful syndicate ValueRacingClub.co.uk

FRONT COVER: *Top 40 Prospects* entry **BOB OLINGER** (Rachel Blackmore) wins the Grade 1 Ballymore Novices' Hurdle at the Cheltenham Festival by seven and a half lengths.

BACK COVER: Another of last year's *Top 40* **GALOPIN DES CHAMPS** (Sean O'Keeffe) wins the Martin Pipe Conditional Jockeys' Handicap Hurdle at the Festival by two and a quarter lengths.

Front & Back cover photographs supplied by FRANCESCA ALTOFT PHOTOGRAPHY.

Published by *Mark Howard Publications Ltd*. 69, Fairgarth Drive, Kirkby Lonsdale, Carnforth, Lancashire. LA6 2FB. Telephone: 015242 71826 Email: mark.howard@mhpublications.co.uk Website: www.mhpublications.co.uk

(Please note: If you are currently NOT on the *Mark Howard Publications* mailing list and you would like to be, and therefore receive all information about future publications then please post / email / phone your name and address to the above).

Printed by H&H REEDS. Southend Road, Penrith, Cumbria CA11 8JH. Telephone: 01768 864214. www.hhreeds.co.uk

All information correct at the time of going to press. Every care is taken with compilation of *One Jump Ahead*, but no responsibility is accepted by the publishers, for error or omissions or their consequences.

All rights reserved. Unauthorised duplication contravenes applicable laws.

ISBN: 978-1-9161259-2-6

CONTENTS

INTRODUCTION

Despite the fact Covid 19 has become part and parcel of our lives during the last eighteen months, the 2020/21 National Hunt season managed to take place without too much disruption even though very few people were able to witness the action first hand. Thankfully, crowds have returned and hopefully some form of normality will return this winter.

On the track, the Cheltenham Festival proved to be a complete Irish domination with 23 of the 28 races booked for export. Willie Mullins was crowned top trainer at the meeting for an eighth time with 6 winners, edging out compatriot Henry De Bromhead on the basis of having more seconds (7) and thirds (5). Indeed, it was a phenomenal year for the Closutton yard. Champion in his home country for a fifteen time, he sent out 16 winners over the Festive period, 9 winners at the Dublin Racing Festival in February, and 19 winners from 87 runners at the Punchestown Festival provided the icing on the cake. The aforementioned De Bromhead didn't do so badly himself with 10 Grade 1 winners throughout the season, plus the Grand National thanks to Minella Times. His half a dozen success at the Cheltenham Festival included the Champion Hurdle, Queen Mother Champion Chase and Cheltenham Gold Cup. The 48 year old has formed a formidable partnership with Rachel Blackmore who was top jockey at Cheltenham in March with six winners. Gordon Elliott returned from his six months ban in September and Cullentra House Stables is rumoured to contain in excess of 250 horses for the new season. The vice like grip Ireland currently has on the top National Hunt horses will loosen one day, but not in the immediate future.

On the domestic front, Paul Nicholls claimed his twelfth championship with a personal best 176 winners. The Ditcheat outfit enhanced their already outstanding record in the King George with Frodon providing the yard with their twelfth victory. However, arguably Nicholls' finest hour last season came with his handling of dual King George winner Clan Des Obeaux. The nine year old was beaten on his first three outings at Haydock, Kempton and Newbury. Fitted with cheekpieces for the first time in the Betway Bowl at Aintree in April, he claimed the third Grade 1 win of his career destroying his opponents by 26 lengths. Even better was to come 20 days later when the Kapgarde gelding provided the champion with his third win in the Punchestown Gold Cup. The fact he beat dual Cheltenham Gold Cup winner Al Boum Photo will have made the victory even more sweeter. Despite the fact his former assistant Dan Skelton is putting together a tremendous team of horses himself, the championship is not likely to be going anywhere soon. Nicholls has recruited heavily during the 'off season' and believes he has 'his strongest ever team'

Four times champion jockey Richard Johnson called time on his outstanding career after finishing third aboard Brother Tedd at Newton Abbot on Easter Saturday. The 43 year old, who was also runner-up seventeen times in the jockeys' title, partnered 3,819 winners (second in the all time jockey list). His first victory under Rules came in a hunter chase at Hereford on the 30th April 1994 steering Rusty Bridge to success. His personal best campaign came in 2015/2016 with 236 winners and he booted home 23 Cheltenham Festival wins. The weighing room has certainly changed in recent years with the departure of A.P.McCoy, Barry Geraghty, Ruby Walsh, Noel Fehily and now Johnson. It is the end of an era in many respects.

In terms of *One Jump Ahead*, the *Talking Trainers* section has been boosted by the return of Donald McCain who has assembled a strong bunch of youngsters, especially in the novice chase department. The Grand National winning trainer's near neighbour Olly Greenall is a new inclusion. Following an excellent season with 37 winners, the stable has been boosted by the significant investment from owners Tim Talbot (Ratkatcha Racing) and Steve Beetham. The latter paid £310,000 for Flat recruit Zinc White and the ex-French four year old Monte Igueldo. Greenall's best signing though is Josh Guerriero. The former amateur rider was assistant to Dan Skelton for three years and is set to be part of a joint licence for the start of the 2022/2023 campaign. Gary Moore has also been added to the roster for the first time. One of the finest dual purpose trainers on either side of the Irish Sea, the Sussex based handler had 61 winners last time around, including Graded success with stable star Goshen and Editeur Du Gite at Wincanton and Aintree respectively. Similar to Paul Nicholls, the stable have plundered the French market during the summer and I make no apology for including a quartet of Gary's horses in the *Top 40 Prospects*. Unlike his beloved Arsenal FC, he is set for an exciting season.

I am delighted to say *Bromley's Best Buys* is back in the fold after a year off. The purchaser of superstars Big Buck's, Kauto Star and Master Minded amongst others, Anthony Bromley has bought some of the best equine talent this century. In addition to his senior role at Highflyer Bloodstock alongside David Minton, the Newmarket based agent is also racing manager for high profile owners Simon Munir and Isaac Souede. His article includes a number of potentially smart youngsters who will sport the familiar two shades of green this winter.

Talking of high profile owners, *OJA* wouldn't be the same without an interview with Rich Ricci. Slightly different from previous years, the emphasis has been placed on the young, exposed horses – 10 of the 11 covered have yet to be seen in the 'pink and green.' One of which is described as "the most exciting horse we have purchased off the Flat since Galway Hurdle winner Saldier."

Aside from the two miles chase and novice chase divisions, I am particularly looking forward to the top juvenile hurdle races this season. Last term, Quilixos, Monmiral and, on occasions, Zanahiyr looked top notchers. However, I suspect the bar could be set even higher this year. The recruitment from France has been exceptional both in the UK and Ireland and they are all covered in the pages ahead.

Finally, thank you to all those who have helped with the production of *One Jump Ahead* – from owners, trainers, jockeys, bloodstock agents, secretaries, photographers, proof readers etc – and subscribers for your continued support, it is much appreciated.

Enjoy the winter.

Mark Howard

FOREWORD
by Nick Luck
8 times Broadcaster of the Year

I have lost count how many times Mark has asked me to write the *Foreword* to *One Jump Ahead* (and how many times he has had to chase me for the copy), but I wouldn't have it any other way. It is a rite of passage, a staging post - call it what you will, it has come to signify the changing of the seasons, the point at which the frenetic racing summer gives way to the mellow fruits of autumn jumping.

It is the week when the kids go back to school, the week when the *Racing Post* first crowbars in a story about Colin Tizzard's team for the upcoming season between the Ebor and the St Leger (did I use that one before?) and the week when - thanks to this pleasant task - I can remind myself who won the Fred Winter and the County Hurdle, though obviously there is no need to look up their country of origin.

And it is the Irish dominance of the last jumps season - and particularly the 23 - 5 drubbing meted out to the cowering Brits at the Festival - which continues to provoke so much agonising and hand wringing. It is a serious point, and a robust domestic jumping scene at all levels should rightly be high on the wish list of every fan, but it is equally a sad day if a sport that is so thrilling for its variety and relative complexity should be reduced to a scoreline.

As Mark Howard has recognised, this level of supremacy amongst the superstables in Ireland has long been coming and, as he has also recognised, you get paid no more or less at the windows based on the provenance of your horse. It's a good job, too, as regular subscribers to Mark's excellent *Updates* service will have been quietly taking advantage of some sneaky recommendations throughout last season.

And there was none sneakier than the November recommendation to back Galopin Des Champs at 25/1 for ANY race at the Festival. Given that the celebrated Mullins ordered chaos has pretty much bulldozed the last worthwhile remnants of ante-post betting, this counts as a seriously notable strike. In fact, the author made a habit of navigating the choppy waters of impossible handicaps as though he were Magellan mapping the East Indies: Minella Times (12/1), Milkwood (10/1) and Soaring Glory (12/1) beat 70 rivals between them in those three races, but they didn't beat Mark Howard.

Of course, you can have a pretty good stab at working out the well-handicapped horse, but much of Mark's methodology has relied on identifying the talent in the raw, drawing extensively on his network of contacts in France (James Reveley has been a smart addition in recent years), Ireland and the UK to bring you advance detail of the next cluster of stars. His *Top 40 Prospects* tend to be burgeoning talent rather than established names, and it was again pretty instructive that 20% of last year's crop went on to win Grade One races.

But like so much in racing, much of this is sales talk: you and I have been buying *One Jump Ahead* since we were at school and need little convincing. As we reach another Mark Howard Equinox, however, do tell your friends, because he remains the clear leader in a crowded field.

TYPE OF TRACK

AINTREE	National Course	Left-Handed, Galloping
	Mildmay Course	Left-Handed, Tight
ASCOT		Right-Handed, Galloping
AYR		Left-Handed, Galloping
BANGOR-ON-DEE		Left-Handed, Tight
CARLISLE		Right-Handed, Stiff / Undulating
CARTMEL		Left-Handed, Tight
CATTERICK BRIDGE		Left-Handed, Tight / Undulating
CHELTENHAM		Left-Handed, Stiff / Undulating
CHEPSTOW		Left-Handed, Stiff / Undulating
DONCASTER		Left-Handed, Galloping
EXETER		Right-Handed, Stiff / Undulating
FAKENHAM		Left-Handed, Tight / Undulating
FFOS LAS		Left-Handed, Galloping
FONTWELL PARK	Chase Course	Figure of Eight, Tight
	Hurdle Course	Left-Handed, Tight
HAYDOCK PARK	Chase Course	Left-Handed, Galloping
	Hurdle Course	Left-Handed, Tight
HEREFORD		Right-Handed, Tight
HEXHAM		Left-Handed, Stiff / Undulating
HUNTINGDON		Right-Handed, Galloping
KELSO		Left-Handed, Tight / Undulating
KEMPTON PARK		Right-Handed, Tight
LEICESTER		Right-Handed, Stiff / Undulating
LINGFIELD PARK		Left-Handed, Tight / Undulating
LUDLOW		Right-Handed, Tight
MARKET RASEN		Right-Handed, Tight /Undulating
MUSSELBURGH		Right-Handed, Tight
NEWBURY		Left-Handed, Galloping
NEWCASTLE		Left-Handed, Galloping
NEWTON ABBOT		Left-Handed, Tight
PERTH		Right-Handed, Tight
PLUMPTON		Left-Handed, Tight / Undulating
SANDOWN PARK		Right-Handed, Galloping
SEDGEFIELD		Left-Handed, Tight / Undulating
SOUTHWELL		Left-Handed, Tight
STRATFORD-UPON-AVON		Left-Handed, Tight
TAUNTON		Right-Handed, Tight
TOWCESTER		Right-Handed, Stiff / Undulating
UTTOXETER		Left-Handed, Tight / Undulating
WARWICK		Left-Handed, Tight / Undulating
WETHERBY		Left-Handed, Galloping
WINCANTON		Right-Handed, Galloping
WORCESTER		Left-Handed, Galloping

IRELAND

BALLINROBE	Right-Handed, Tight
BELLEWSTOWN	Left-Handed, Tight / Undulating
CLONMEL	Right-Handed, Tight / Undulating
CORK	Right-Handed, Galloping
DOWNPATRICK	Right-Handed, Tight / Undulating
DOWN ROYAL	Right-Handed, Tight / Undulating
FAIRYHOUSE	Right-Handed, Galloping
GALWAY	Right-Handed, Tight / Undulating
GOWRAN PARK	Right-Handed, Tight / Undulating
KILBEGGAN	Right-Handed, Tight / Undulating
KILLARNEY	Left-Handed, Tight
LEOPARDSTOWN	Left-Handed, Galloping
LIMERICK	Right-Handed, Galloping
LISTOWEL	Left-Handed, Tight
NAAS	Left-Handed, Galloping
NAVAN	Left-Handed, Galloping
PUNCHESTOWN	Right-Handed, Galloping
ROSCOMMON	Right-Handed, Tight
SLIGO	Right-Handed, Tight / Undulating
THURLES	Right-Handed, Tight / Undulating
TIPPERARY	Left-Handed, Tight
TRAMORE	Right-Handed, Tight
WEXFORD	Left-Handed, Tight

ACKNOWLEDGEMENTS

I would like to thank all the following Trainers who have given up their time, during the summer, to answer my inquiries:

Talking Trainers: Kim Bailey, Olly Greenall (Josh Guerriero), Philip Hobbs, Alan King, Tom Lacey, Gary Moore, Olly Murphy, Paul Nicholls, Jonjo O'Neill (plus Jonjo O'Neill jnr & Joe O'Neill), David Pipe and Nicky Richards. Plus, Nicky Martin, Dan Skelton, Jamie Snowden & Venetia Williams. Thank you also to the following secretaries for organising the appointments/answering queries: Sarah (Paul Nicholls), Jade (Jonjo O'Neill), James (David Pipe), Antonia Reid (Nicky Richards), Carolyn (Nicky Henderson).

Thank you also to Anthony Bromley, David Minton & Bernice Emanuel (Highflyer Bloodstock), Nick Luck (Foreword), Declan Phelan, James Reveley, Mags O'Toole, Rich Ricci, Joe Chambers (Racing Manager), Robcour (Brian), Mick Meagher, Michael Shinners & Dean Cracknell *(Skybet)*, Fran Berry *(Racing TV)*, Scott Salkeld, Kevin Blake, James Couldwell (ValueRacingclub.co.uk).

The TOP 40 PROSPECTS FOR 2021/2022

AMERICAN MIKE (IRE)

4 b g Mahler – American Jennie (IRE) (Lord Americo (IRE))
OWNER: NOEL & VALERIE MORAN
TRAINER: G.ELLIOTT. Longwood, Co.Meath.
CAREER FORM FIGURES: 1
CAREER WINS: 2021: Apr CORK Good/Yielding 4YO Mdn PTP 3m

Gordon Elliott, who had his licence suspended for six months in early March and fined £15,000, has stocked up heavily with Irish pointers whilst serving his ban. Ash Tree Meadow (£135,000), Au Fleuron (£220,00), Cool Survivor (£175,000), Curtain Tim (£100,000) and Happy D'Ex (£195,000) were all acquired for hefty sums. The unbeaten American Mike was also bought at the Cheltenham April Sale for £195,000 for Noel and Valerie Moran of Bective Stud. Expect the Mahler gelding to run in a bumper during the Autumn.

"A tall lanky unfurnished bay gelding with a white nose and spot on his forehead: his mother, American Jennie, was a jumps mare of real merit: she won five times, including a premier handicap chase (3m1f : Good) at the 2007 Punchestown Festival: she managed to place fourth and third in the 2006 and 2007 editions of the Irish Grand National. In a true run four-year-old maiden at Cork (Good/Yielding), American Mike jumped neatly and was anchored in the pack until set alight heading to the second last and he soon put his stamp on the race and galloped powerfully to the winning post, recording a twenty lengths win in the fastest time of the day. He was one of the most striking four-year-old maiden winners in the spring and it was inevitable that he would make good money when sold: the Morans paying £195,000 to add him to their squad at Gordon Elliott's. If he can maintain a clean bill of health, this youngster can not only match but exceed the 140 chase mark of his mother. Winning a bumper would be a formality, and he will be a more than competitive client in 2m 4f and upwards novice hurdles and one who will be mixing it at Graded level. When he bulks out his frame, he may mature into a fine staying novice chaser at a later date. He handled the good ground at Cork and I think he will operate on soft/heavy without a problem (as per his dam)," believes Irish point expert Declan Phelan.

POINTS TO NOTE:
Probable Best Distance   -   2m – 2m 4f
Preferred Going   -   Good/Soft
Connection's Comments: "He's very smart." Sean DOYLE at Cork (10/4/21)

GOING:	R	W	P	TRACK	R	W	P
Good/Yield	1	1	0	Right	1	1	0
				Galloping	1	1	0
TRIP:	R	W	P	JOCKEY:	R	W	P
3m	1	1	0	J.Scallon	1	1	0

ATHOLL STREET (IRE)

6 b g Jeremy (USA) – Allthewhile (IRE) (Old Vic)
OWNER: TREVOR HEMMINGS
TRAINER: P.F.NICHOLLS. Ditcheat, Somerset.
CAREER FORM FIGURES: 6 – 11P
CAREER WINS: 2020: Nov TAUNTON Good MH 2m; Dec TAUNTON Good/Soft 2m

Crowned champion trainer for a twelfth time, Paul Nicholls and Team Ditcheat enjoyed a magnificent campaign with a personal best tally of 176 winners (previous best of 171 in 2016/2017). Operating at a strike rate of 25%, the total included seven Grade 1 victories. There were numerous highlights along the way but Clan Des Obeaux's win in the Punchestown Gold Cup in late April must be near the summit. In an era of Irish domination, it must have given Nicholls immense satisfaction and, once again, proved he is the best in the business when it comes to staying chasers. It was the yard's third win in the race. Winning a twelfth King George at Kempton on Boxing Day courtesy of Frodon wouldn't have been too far behind either.

Not surprisingly, his squad appears to be strong in all departments once again for the winter ahead, especially in the novice chase ranks. Graded hurdle winners Bravemansgame and McFabulous are expected to be the headline acts, but it will be fascinating to see what the lightly raced Atholl Street can achieve over the larger obstacles. From the family of King George and Gold Cup winner Kicking King and another Grade 1 winning chaser Kalashnikov, the Jeremy gelding was an expensive store (€190,000). Well held in a bumper on his debut at Exeter on New Year's Day 2020, he had a wind operation soon afterwards. Returning to action over hurdles following an absence of 316 days, he was fitted with a tongue tie at Taunton in November and ran out a ready four lengths winner. Harry Cobden's mount travelled powerfully before taking over at the second last. Despite showing signs of greenness, he quickly settled the issue and was firmly on top at the finish. Returning to the Somerset track a month later, he made all under a penalty and never looked like relinquishing his advantage. A sixteen lengths scorer, he barely broke sweat. Two and a half months later, he was sent off 7/4 favourite for the Grade 2 Dovecote Novices' Hurdle at Kempton. However, the six year old was fresh and made mistakes early on before eventually pulling up before the second last. Found to have suffered a hairline fracture afterwards, Atholl Street has undergone surgery since and had a chip removed from a joint.

Back in work following his summer break, the 135 rated hurdler looks every inch a chaser in the making. Atholl Street has the option of starting off in a novices' handicap chase or a beginners' chase. Connections will be disappointed if he doesn't reach a higher mark over fences. He has the attributes to develop into a smart two mile chaser.

POINTS TO NOTE:

Probable Best Distance	-	2 miles
Preferred Going	-	Good/Soft

GOING:	R	W	P	TRACK	R	W	P
Soft	1	0	0	Right	4	2	0
Good/Soft	1	1	0	Stiff/Undul.	1	0	0
Good	2	1	0	Tight	3	2	0

TRIP:	R	W	P	JOCKEY:	R	W	P
2m	3	2	0	H.Cobden	3	2	0
2m 1f	1	0	0	Bryony Frost	1	0	0

AUTHORISED SPEED (FR)

4 b g Authorized (IRE) – Tangaspeed (FR) (Vertical Speed (FR))
OWNER: GALLAGHER BLOODSTOCK Limited
TRAINER: G.L.MOORE. Lower Beeding, West Sussex.
CAREER FORM FIGURES: 2

Authorized was a top-class horse who supplied Frankie Dettori with his first Epsom Derby winner in 2007. The son of Montjeu was brilliantly handled by Peter Chapple-Hyam winning 4 of his 7 races, including three Group 1 victories. He has proved equally successful as a stallion producing Group 1 winners on the Flat, namely Ambivalent, Complacent, Hartnell, Santiago and Seal of Approval, plus triple Group 3 winner Euchen Glen amongst others. Based in Turkey with a stud fee of €12,500, he hasn't done badly with his jumping stock either with dual Grand National Tiger Roll heading his roll of honour along with Grade 1 winning hurdlers Echoes In Rain and the ill-fated Nichols Canyon (8).

The 157 rated hurdler Goshen is another son of Authorized and the five year old was desperately unfortunate not to win the Triumph Hurdle at Cheltenham a couple of seasons ago. A wide margin winner of the Grade 2 Kingwell Hurdle at Wincanton last winter, his trainer Gary Moore is a huge fan of the sire and has another potentially smart youngster on his hands in the once raced Authorised Speed.

An expensive purchase (€155,000) at the Goffs Landrover NH Sales in August last year, his dam was a Listed winner over twelve furlongs in France and finished fifth behind the unbeaten Zarkava in the Group 1 Prix Vermeille in 2008. All the rage for his debut in a bumper at Market Rasen in May, he can be deemed an unlucky loser having met trouble in running in the homestraight. Close to the pace entering the final quarter of a mile, the 6/5 favourite went for a run along the far rail but was soon halted in his progress, which allowed the front running winner Grozni to stretch away. Once in the clear, Authorised Speed stayed on strongly to get within three lengths of the Denis Hogan trained victor. Josh Moore's mount had pulled seven lengths clear of the third. Admittedly, the form doesn't amount to much with the winner failing to score in four outings over hurdles since. However, a reproduction of that performance will see him win a bumper before tackling obstacles.

Gary Moore is eyeing a confidence boosting win in a bumper at one of the smaller track – Fontwell stage such an event on Saturday 2ⁿᵈ October, which is a possibility – before sending Authorised Speed over timber. Held in high regard at Cisswood Racing Stables, the four year old has the pedigree and talent to develop into a very useful performer.

POINTS TO NOTE:

Probable Best Distance	-	2m – 2m 4f
Preferred Going	-	Good/Soft

GOING:	R	W	P	TRACK:	R	W	P
Good/Soft	1	0	1	Right	1	0	1
				Tight/Undul.	1	0	1

TRIP:	R	W	P	JOCKEY:	R	W	P
2m	1	0	1	Josh Moore	1	0	1

BEAR GHYLLS (IRE)

6 br g Arcadio (GER) – Inch Princess (IRE) (Oscar (IRE))
OWNER: BRADLEY PARTNERSHIP
TRAINER: NICKY MARTIN. Withypool, Minehead, Somerset.
CAREER FORM FIGURES: 1 - 1114
CAREER WINS: 2020: Mar WARWICK Soft NHF 2m; Oct LINGFIELD Soft MH 2m 3f; Nov
FFOS LAS Soft NH 2m: 2021: Jan EXETER Soft HH 2m 2f

A wide margin bumper winner at Warwick in March 2020, Bear Ghylls had the likes of Guard
Your Dreams (rated 140), Bobhopeornohope (126) and Runswick Bay (118) in excess of
nineteens lengths in arrears on that occasion. The promise he showed that day was confirmed
over hurdles last winter with Nicky Martin's stable star developing into a high-class performer
winning three of his four races over obstacles.

Rated 147, the Arcadio gelding may have been found wanting at the Cheltenham Festival during
the spring, but he wasn't disgraced in fourth behind the brilliant Bob Olinger in the Ballymore
Novices' Hurdle. Beaten around a dozen lengths, he couldn't match Henry De Bromhead's
easy winner but was keeping on suggesting a step up to three miles wouldn't go amiss in
the future. Having contacted his trainer during the summer, Bear Ghylls is set to embark on a
chasing career and there is every reason to believe it will be a fruitful one. Bought for €22,000
as a three year old at the Tattersalls Derby Sale in Ireland, he impressed when winning by four
and a half lengths on his hurdles debut at Lingfield in October. Making virtually all, he stayed
on powerfully to beat subsequent Cheltenham winner and Grade 2 placed Make Me A Believer
(rated 138). Indeed, it proved to be an above average maiden hurdle with the second, third,
fourth, fifth, sixth, seventh (three times), eleventh and twelfth all winning since. Despite not
being suited by the drop back to two miles at Ffos Las over a month later, he edged out Gowel
Road (won twice since and is rated 136) conceding six pounds to Nigel Twiston-Davies' runner-
up. Back in action at Exeter in January, the six year old made the most of a lenient opening
mark on his handicap debut when beating Stormy Flight by five lengths. Matt Griffiths' mount
scored comfortably even though his jumping left something to be desired. Then, following an
absence of 66 days, the 15/2 shot lined up at the Cheltenham Festival and ran well behind
three Grade 1 winning novice hurdlers. Holding every chance after the second last, Bear Ghylls
was tapped for speed on the fastest ground he had encountered thereafter. His trainer said
afterwards: **"He's run a cracker, and if he'd jumped better I think he'd have been a lot
closer. He's never been that quick or in that sort of company - the first three are all Grade
One winners - and he just doesn't respect hurdles. He's big, rangy and raw, and he just
wants to get from one side to the other as quick as he possibly can. He came up the hill
well and I really can't complain. He'll probably have a couple of weeks off now and then
school over fences ready for next season."**

One would expect Bear Ghylls to commence his chasing career over two and a half miles
before possibly stepping up to three miles in due course. There were few better British staying
novice hurdlers last season and it is likely to be a similar story over fences this winter.

POINTS TO NOTE:

Probable Best Distance	-	2m 4f – 3 miles
Preferred Going	-	Soft/Heavy

Connection's Comments: "The horse has just got raw talent as he doesn't respect his hurdles and is a bit like a bull in a china shop. I think once he gets to see a fence, he will be better as it will help him respect the obstacles a bit more, plus he is built like a chaser." Nicky MARTIN, trainer.

GOING:	R	W	P		TRACK	R	W	P
Soft	4	4	0		Left Handed	4	3	0
Good/Soft	1	0	0		Right	1	1	0
					Galloping	1	1	0
					Stiff/Undul.	2	1	0
					Tight/Undul.	2	2	0

TRIP:	R	W	P		JOCKEY:	R	W	P
2m	2	2	0		M.Griffiths	5	4	0
2m 2f	1	1	0					
2m 3f	1	1	0					
2m 5f	1	0	0					

BLACK POPPY
5 b g Kayf Tara – Poppy Come Running (IRE) (Definite Article)
OWNER: WEST COAST HAULAGE Limited
TRAINER: KERRY LEE. Byton, Presteigne, Powys
CAREER FORM FIGURES: 1
CAREER WINS: 2021: Mar WARWICK Good NHF 2m

The seven year old Demachine developed into an above average novice chaser last season winning two of his four starts with his official rating rising from 122 to 142. Successful in novice handicaps at Uttoxeter and Ascot, he finished runner-up in the Grade 2 Reynoldstown Novices' Chase at the latter track in February. The Flemensfirth gelding is owned by West Coast Haulage Limited and the same patrons are responsible for unbeaten stablemate Black Poppy.

A five year old by Kayf Tara, he was bought at the Goffs Landrover Sale for €60,000 in June 2019 by Henrietta Knight. His dam won a bumper for Gary Moore and Black Poppy did likewise on his racecourse debut for Kerry Lee at Warwick in late March. Sent off 25/1, he was ridden by Brendan Powell and moved strongly throughout the two miles contest. Going well turning for home, he hit the front with a furlong to run before being pushed out for a length and a half victory. The runner-up Party Business had been placed twice in similar events at Newcastle and Doncaster, while the third Blairgowrie had filled the same position behind the highly thought of Might I over the same course and distance in December. The clock confirmed it was a decent performance, too, with the winning time being nearly five seconds quicker than the second division later on the card. Plus, it was almost ten seconds faster than the 0-115 handicap hurdle run seventy minutes earlier.

Time will tell whether Black Poppy needs a sound surface to show his best, but he couldn't have made a better start to his career and two and a half miles ought to be within his stamina range over obstacles. However, he is expected to reappear over the minimum trip for his hurdles debut. Kerry Lee has had eight Graded winners during her relatively short training career, which have all been over fences. This Kayf Tara gelding could provide her with her first over the smaller obstacles.

POINTS TO NOTE:

Probable Best Distance	-	2m - 2m 4f	
Preferred Going	-	Good/Soft	

Connection's Comments: "I'm very pleased with Black Poppy. That was a little unexpected but he had done a few nice pieces of work. He will improve for that." Kerry LEE at Warwick (30/3/21)

GOING:	R	W	P	TRACK	R	W	P
Good	1	1	0	Left Handed	1	1	0
				Tight/Undul.	1	1	0
TRIP:	R	W	P	JOCKEY:	R	W	P
2m	1	1	0	B.Powell	1	1	0

BOB OLINGER (IRE)

6 b g Sholokhov (IRE) – Zenaide (IRE) (Zaffaran (USA))
OWNER: ROBCOUR
TRAINER: H.DE BROMHEAD. Knockeen, Co.Waterford.
CAREER FORM FIGURES: 11 - 2111
CAREER WINS: 2019: Nov TURTULLA Yielding 4YO Mdn PTP 3m: 2020: Mar GOWRAN PARK Soft/Heavy NHF 2m 2f; Dec NAVAN Soft/Heavy MH 2m 4f: 2021: Jan NAAS Heavy Grade 1 NH 2m 4f; Mar CHELTENHAM Good/Soft Grade 1 NH 2m 5f

The novice chase division promises to be exceptional this winter with the likes of Appreciate It, Galopin Des Champs and My Drogo set to tackle fences for the first time. However, the most exciting of the whole lot is another Cheltenham Festival winner Bob Olinger. The former Pat Doyle trained winning pointer provided his owner Brian Acheson (Robcour) with his first Grade 1 winner when beating Blue Lord in the Lawlor's of Naas Novice Hurdle in January. Two months later, the Sholokhov gelding produced a stunning display to win the Ballymore Novices' Hurdle at Cheltenham by upwards of seven and a half lengths making Grade 1 winners Gaillard Du Mesnil and Bravemansgame look ordinary (he was one of 13 winners at the Cheltenham Festival who began their careers in Irish points). Rated 159 over timber, he was bought to be a chaser and looks every inch a future Gold Cup horse.

Bob Olinger's sole defeat during his career came on his hurdles debut at Gowran Park in November. Lining up in a two miles maiden hurdle, Rachel Blackmore's mount had the misfortune to cross swords with Festival bumper winner Ferny Hollow. The pair had an epic duel during the last half a mile with Willie Mullins' charge gaining the upper hand by a length. It was a distance back to the third. Grand National winning jockey David Mullins, who retired in January at the age of 24, commented: **"I've never been so amazed by two horses coming up a straight as I was when watching Ferny Hollow and Bob Olinger in a maiden hurdle at Gowran Park. They flew."** Stepped up in trip at Navan the following month, Bob Olinger never came out of second gear to win his maiden by a hard held fourteen lengths. He followed up with an authoritative display at Naas staying on strongly to win by six and a half lengths. His performance at Cheltenham will go down as one of the finest in recent years. Despite racing keenly, the six year old was still on the bridle rounding the hometurn and he readily left compatriot Gaillard Du Mesnil and Bravemansgame trailing in his wake. A superb jump at the last sealed his win and he bounded up the Prestbury Park Hill. **"He's very exciting. He's built like a chaser and jumps like one. He stays and he has got a hell of a lot of speed so he is extremely versatile in that sense, so it was a brilliant performance,"** enthused his trainer afterwards.

Henry De Bromhead's gelding missed the Punchestown Festival having been found to be coughing but it may prove a blessing in disguise. With only six career starts to his name, Bob Olinger has so much more to offer, especially over fences. The Grade 1 Drinmore Novices' Chase at Fairyhouse (28th November) looks an obvious first half of the season target with the Marsh Novices' Chase at Cheltenham in March his ultimate goal. I suspect it is unlikely he will tackle three miles this season with the 2023 Cheltenham Gold Cup the long-term aim.

POINTS TO NOTE:
Probable Best Distance   -   2m 4f +
Preferred Going   -   Good/Soft
Connection's Comments: **"We think he's good. Very, very good. We brought him away before he won his bumper to work with some of our Cheltenham horses and next thing I knew he was beside them and even in front of a few of them, in front of really good horses. This was before he even ran for us. He's just always looked very good. He's got gears and he stays." Henry De BROMHEAD (3/4/21)**

GOING:	R	W	P	TRACK	R	W	P
Heavy	2	1	1	Left Handed	3	3	0
Soft/Heavy	2	2	0	Right	3	2	1
Good/Soft	1	1	0	Galloping	2	2	0
Yielding	1	1	0	Stiff/Undul.	1	1	0
				Tight/Undul.	2	2	0

TRIP:	R	W	P	JOCKEY:	R	W	P
2m	1	0	1	R.Blackmore	4	3	1
2m 2f	1	1	0	P.W.Mullins	1	1	0
2m 4f	2	2	0	B.W.Harvey	1	1	0
2m 5f	1	1	0				
3m	1	1	0				

CITY CHIEF (IRE)
4 b g Soldier of Fortune (IRE) – Galant Ferns (IRE) (Bob Back USA))
OWNER: Mrs J.DONNELLY
TRAINER: N.J.HENDERSON. Lambourn, Berkshire.
CAREER FORM FIGURES: 1
CAREER WIN: 2021: May TRALEE Soft/Heavy 4YO Mdn PTP 3m

The two mile chase division promises to be a formidable one, too, this winter with Chacun Pour Soi, Energumene, Greaneteen and Shishkin amongst others going toe to toe. The last named is unbeaten over fences having won all five of his races as a novice last season. The Sholokhov gelding won the Arkle Trophy at Cheltenham by a dozen lengths before producing a more workmanlike display at Aintree less than a month later. The dual Festival winner was bought by

Highflyer Bloodstock for £170,000 in December 2018 on behalf of Joe and Marie Donnelly. The Newmarket based operation was also responsible for acquiring the unbeaten Irish pointer City Chief at the Tattersalls Cheltenham May Sale for £210,000 for the same patrons.

"Rangy bay gelding with white spot on his face and a couple of white socks: a €36,000 store in 2020: his dam was a five-times track winner (including a Listed bumper): his half-brother, Premium Package, a point and hurdle winner has been a flattering to deceive merchant for Henry de Bromhead. Saddled by Denis Murphy for a nine-runner maiden on the old racecourse circuit at Tralee (Soft/Heavy) in May. In a race run at a crawl for two miles, he dropped anchor in midfield, relaxing beautifully. When the inevitable last six furlongs injection of pace materialised, he was for a few strides after three out caught a little flat footed: soon back into rhythm, he was rolling at a fair lick heading to the second last: he winged the concluding fences and his jockey Luke Murphy, with a degree of confidence, dropped his head in front close to the winning post. There was plenty to admire about the style and nature of his success and it took a bid of £210,000 to ensure a transfer to the Henderson yard via Tattersalls May sales. He has loads of scope to bulk out his frame and he could easily adjust to a drop in trip. The slow time of the race prevents one from overegging his pudding: when French Dynamite won the corresponding maiden in 2019 (albeit on a sounder surface), he clocked 5.48, City Chief stopped the timer at 6.38...that 50 seconds differential highlights the lack of a proper gallop in the 2021 version of the Tralee maiden. City Chief is liable to be fertile raw material for Nicky Henderson to nurture and winning a bumper on his track debut can be achieved and he is liable to figure amongst the upper-class novice hurdlers in his yard in 2021/22: my hunch is it may take eighteen months or more before he is the complete physical package and his novice chase campaign at around that time will be an exciting one," reports Declan Phelan.

POINTS TO NOTE:
Probable Best Distance   -   2m – 2m 4f
Preferred Going   -   Good/Soft
Connection's Comments: "He's a very green horse that has a savage engine and he's one of the nicest horses we've run this year." Jockey Luke MURPHY at Tralee (23/5/21)

GOING:	R	W	P	TRACK	R	W	P
Soft/Heavy	1	1	0	Left Handed	1	1	0

TRIP:	R	W	P	JOCKEY:	R	W	P
3m	1	1	0	L.J.Murphy	1	1	0

Please see pages 183-194
for details of the
One Jump Ahead Updates

CLASSIC GETAWAY (IRE)

5 br g Getaway (GER) – Classic Magic (IRE) (Classic Cliché (IRE))
OWNER: CHEVELEY PARK STUD
TRAINER: W.P.MULLINS. Bagenalstown, Co.Carlow.
CAREER FORM FIGURES: 1 - 1
CAREER WINS: 2020: Nov BORRIS HOUSE Yielding 4YO Mdn PTP 3m: 2021: May TIPPERARY Heavy NHF 2m 4f

Cheveley Park Stud enjoyed another magnificent Cheltenham Festival with three winners, two seconds from only six runners. Ironically, Envoi Allen had looked their strongest chance over the four days but the previously unbeaten five times Grade 1 winner hit the deck at the fourth fence in the Marsh Novices' Chase. The Newmarket based operation were active at the Cheltenham December Sale buying Grangeclare West (£430,000), Guily Billy (£310,000) and, seven days later, they secured the once raced Classic Getaway for £570,000 at the Goffs UK December PTP Sale at Yorton Farm. The trio joined Gordon Elliott but departed Cullentra Stables three months later without running for the triple Grand National winning trainer.

Classic Getaway and Grangeclare West joined Willie Mullins, while Henry De Bromhead took over the tutelage of Guily Billy. It was a huge blow for Elliott, who returned from his six months ban in September. The trio are terrific prospects for the season ahead and beyond with each harbouring hopes of Cheltenham Festival success next spring. Expert Declan Phelan elaborates on this five year old gelded son of Getaway. **"Elegant virtually black gelding from an ordinary Irish jumps family: cost Monbeg €65,000 as a store in 2019 and, due to Covid, they had to wait until Borris (Yielding) in November to introduce the horse to pointing. In the first three from the start of the race and jumping with confidence, he picked up the lead on landing over four out, he soon asserted for minimum encouragement and sauntered clear to win by eight lengths in a respectable time. In that point to point, he was a horse with real presence and there was more than a whiff of class and elegance about the performance. When he turned up at the sales in December, it was inevitable he would become a sought-after commodity and the hammer dropped on a price of £570,000 and at the time Cheveley Park signed for him and then posted the horse with Gordon Elliott. When the troubles arose at Cullentra in the spring, this five-year-old was removed and Willie Mullins was selected as his new master. To give the horse some extra experience, Mullins saddled him to win a modest 2m 4f bumper at Tipperary (Heavy) in May. He again powered away inside the last quarter mile for a fifteen lengths triumph. At the death, I did notice he hung a little in the last hundred yards, it could have been greenness or a possible flaw in his character (something to monitor in the future). In his two victories, he has dominated weak rivals, we have yet to see how he will respond to a proper challenge and if he possesses battling assets in his arsenal. Likely to travel down the novice hurdle route in 2021/22, the middle distance, 2m 4f, may be his optimum for now, and he will certainly be a leading light in that division. His two outings to date have been on flat tracks, we have no idea how he will function on a stiffer circuit. He is one of the budding talents from the 2020/21 Irish point season with prospects of winning a race at Cheltenham 2021, currently he is fertile raw material, until avenues such as different tracks, ground and trips are examined, one cannot be definite on the question of whether he is either top class or simply above average. My hunch is that he will attain superior results as a chaser in due course, rather than in the hurdling sphere."**

Rob James, who rode his first Cheltenham Festival winner aboard Milan Native in March 2020, partnered the five year old in his point and said afterwards: **"It's easy to ride those proper ones. He jumped like a buck, travelled like a dream everywhere. He just quickened away from his rivals going to the second last. He was only in second gear. He's one of the best four year olds this season that Donnchadh (Doyle) had to come out. He is something special."** Cheveley Park Stud won the Grade 1 Ballymore Novices' Hurdle at Cheltenham with the aforementioned Envoi Allen in 2020 and Classic Getaway is expected to develop into their number one challenger this time around.

POINTS TO NOTE:

Probable Best Distance	-	**2m 4f**
Preferred Going	-	**Soft**

Connection's Comments: "He's a beautiful horse with a great walk. He was a bit more expensive than a Rolls-Royce Phantom, but I'm pretty sure Mrs Thompson will get more fun out of him than a Rolls Royce. This horse is a big baby for a five-year-old with a point-to-point run and that's why I was keen to teach him to stride out. He's not really a bumper horse and I'd imagine he'll go jumping. When the ground was so wet, we thought we'd get a run into him. Willie hasn't rushed him and let him settle in. I think he'll continue to improve mentally." Patrick MULLINS at Tipperary (25/5/21)

GOING:	R	W	P	TRACK	R	W	P
Heavy	1	1	0	Left Handed	2	2	0
Yielding	1	1	0	Tight	1	1	0

TRIP:	R	W	P	JOCKEY:	R	W	P
2m 4f	1	1	0	P.W.Mullins	1	1	0
3m	1	1	0	R.James	1	1	0

DREAMS OF HOME (IRE)

5 b g Jet Away – Knocktartan (IRE) (King's Ride (IRE))
OWNER: COLIN TAYLOR & Miss KAY WILDING
TRAINER: D.McCAIN. Cholmondeley, Cheshire.
CAREER FORM FIGURES: 1111
CAREER WINS: 2020: Oct MOIRA Yielding/Soft 4YO Mdn PTP 3m: 2021: Jan WETHERBY Heavy MH 2m; Feb CARLISLE Heavy NH 2m 1f; Mar NEWCASTLE Good/Soft NH 2m

Grand National winning trainer Donald McCain enjoyed an excellent winter with 66 winners and total prize-money just shy of £600,000. A handful of those victories came in Pattern events, including a second Grade 2 victory for Navajo Pass in Champion Hurdle Trial at Haydock in January. Bankhouse Stables has assembled a strong team of youngsters and they will be spearheaded this term by two exciting novice chase prospects. The 143 rated Minella Drama won the rescheduled Listed Sidney Banks Novices' Hurdle at Market Rasen in February before chasing home My Drogo in Grade 1 company at Aintree. The Flemensfirth gelding began his career in Irish points and that comment also applies to the unbeaten stablemate Dreams of Home. A gelding by Jet Away, the five year old is rated 134 over timber but is predicted to reach a much loftier figure now his attentions are turned to the larger obstacles. A length winner of his point at Moira in October, he beat Bill Baxter (won and finished fourth in a Listed bumper) and Banbridge (won three times for Joseph O'Brien since). His partner Rob James remarked afterwards: **"He's a lovely horse. He jumped like a buck everywhere. He winged the second** last, quickened away down the hill, winged the last and just galloped to the line. He's a good staying horse with a big engine."

Expert Declan Phelan comments: **"Medium sized bay gelding with a white stripe on his face: Monbeg unearthed him as a €20,000 store and he raced for that team at Moira (Yielding/ Soft) in October. To the fore in a true run race from the beginning, the race reduced to a match between this lad and Bill Baxter and, to his credit, he was always finding too much for his rival to land the maiden by a length: he appealed as a youngster with a high cruising speed, slick jumper and prepared to battle if required. Bought privately by Donald McCain, he then hit the ground running in the UK, as he racked up a hat trick of wins over hurdles at Wetherby, Carlisle and Newcastle: he made all to easily win the first two, it was more laboured at Newcastle (despite the nine lengths winning margin). McCain made a wise move to pull the plug on the campaign in early March, as this is certainly the best young pointer he has plucked out of Ireland since Peddlers Cross. Dreams Of Home is versatile (won from two miles to three miles), a fine athlete with excellent natural springs, and capable of coping with heavy or good ground. Plus, he enjoys the winning feeling. He closed his stint novice hurdling with an official mark of 134 over timber: the fact he was not pitched into Graded class may have placed a ceiling on his rating. With maturity and development, he will become a 140+ chaser and, if novice chasing is the chosen route this season, he will be a leading northern player in the division: time may relate his optimum trip, it could become 2m 4f. His half-brother, Minellacelebration is a 140 chaser and Dreams of Home can supplant him as the king of the clan."**

Dreams of Home was particularly impressive on his first couple of runs under Rules winning by a dozen lengths at Wetherby in January and then following up at Carlisle a month later (inner track didn't really suit him). Workmanlike in victory at Newcastle last time, he had been on the go for sometime by that stage of the season. All three wins were gained over the minimum trip and he is expected to improve still further once upped in distance – his half-brother Minellacelebration is a three times winner at Aintree over three miles one. He looks a proper one.

POINTS TO NOTE:

Probable Best Distance	-	2m 4f
Preferred Going	-	Soft

Connection's Comments: "He's still just learning his job. He was walking around down at the start like he was half asleep, but he jumps like a buck. He is still weak and immature, but is related to a few good staying chasers so what he's doing for us now is all really positive. I bought him because of the way he jumped fences in his point-to-point. We are really excited about him." Donald McCAIN at Carlisle (16/2/21)

GOING:	R	W	P	TRACK	R	W	P
Heavy	2	2	0	Left Handed	3	3	0
Yield/Soft	1	1	0	Right	1	1	0
Good/Soft	1	1	0	Galloping	2	2	0
				Stiff/Undul.	1	1	0

TRIP:	R	W	P	JOCKEY:	R	W	P
2m	2	2	0	B.Hughes	3	3	0
2m 1f	1	1	0	R.James	1	1	0
3m	1	1	0				

DUSART (IRE)

6 b g Flemensfirth (USA) – Dusty Too (Terimon)
OWNER: R.A.BARTLETT
TRAINER: N.J.HENDERSON. Lambourn, Berkshire.
CAREER FORM FIGURES: 13
CAREER WIN: 2020: Nov NEWBURY Good NH 2m

Simonsig was a hugely talented horse winning 10 of his 16 races. Trained in Northern Ireland by Ian Ferguson, the grey won a couple of point-to-points and a Fairyhouse bumper before joining Nicky Henderson. The Fair Mix gelding was a dual Cheltenham Festival winner for the Seven Barrows team producing a scintillating performance in the Neptune Investment Novices' Hurdle in 2012. He won his first two races over fences by an aggregate of 84 lengths before taking the Arkle Trophy in 2013. That proved to be his last win with injury plaguing the rest of his career before he suffered a fatal fall in the Shloer Chase at Cheltenham in November 2016. On his day, he was a brilliant horse.

His half-brother Dusart has plenty to live up to, but he is a highly promising horse in his own right. Like his older sibling, the gelded son of Flemensfirth is owned by Ronnie Bartlett and was bought for €85,000 as a three year old. Nicky Henderson's charge didn't make his debut until November but it was worth the wait as he justified strong market support to win a two miles novice hurdle at Newbury. Keen early on, he soon settled into a good rhythm before making his move in the home straight. Leading two out, he stayed on strongly to beat the subsequent *Betfair* Hurdle winner Soaring Glory by two and a half lengths. His trainer commented afterwards: **"He is very nice and Nico (De Boinville) was mad about him."** Unfortunately, he suffered a freak accident at home which meant Dusart was sidelined until the spring. Thrown in at the deep end, he contested the Grade 1 Top Novices' Hurdle at Aintree's Grand National meeting. However, he acquitted himself very well finishing third behind the County Hurdle winner Belfast Banter. Racing prominently, he held every chance but couldn't match the winner's turn of foot on drying ground. Beaten two and a half lengths, his trainer explained afterwards about the injury which had restricted his first season over hurdles: **"He escaped and got a stake stuck through the middle of his chest. You could have put your whole arm into the hole. He is very lucky to be here and I certainly didn't think he would be running again this season. He wants two and a half miles, but this was only his second run over hurdles. He'll be going over fences next season."** Nico De Boinville added: **"He probably wants an extra half mile and he probably already wants a fence. To go down by only a couple of lengths in a race as good as that was a very good effort."**

Given his lack of experience and match practice, Dusart emerged from his run at Aintree with his reputation enhanced (rated 141) and he looks a fine chasing prospect for the winter. His brother was arguably at his best over two and a half miles and the six year old looks like following suit. Provided he stays in one piece, Ronnie Bartlett and Nicky Henderson have another terrific prospect on their hands.

POINTS TO NOTE:
Probable Best Distance   -   **2m 4f**
Preferred Going   -   **Good/Soft**
Connection's Comments: "He's just a real standout animal – a proper horse. I loved the way he jumped the last. He's very different to Simonsig – this horse is a proper National Hunt type." Nico De BOINVILLE at Newbury (5/11/21)

GOING:	R	W	P	TRACK	R	W	P
Good/Soft	1	0	1	Left Handed	2	1	1
Good	1	1	0	Galloping	1	1	0
				Tight	1	0	1

TRIP:	R	W	P	JOCKEY:	R	W	P
2m	2	1	1	N.De Boinville	2	1	1

DYSART DYNAMO (IRE)

5 b g Westerner – Dysart Dancer (IRE) (Accordion (IRE))
OWNER: Ms ELEANOR MANNING
TRAINER: W.P.MULLINS. Bagenalstown, Co.Carlow
CAREER FORM FIGURES: 11
CAREER WINS: 2021: Mar CLONMEL Soft NHF 2m 2f; Apr PUNCHESTOWN Yielding NHF 2m

Willie Mullins became champion jumps trainer in Ireland for the fifteenth time last season and crowned another superb campaign with a memorable Punchestown Festival. The Closutton handler won 19 of the 34 races (for 14 different owners and 11 different jockeys) over the five days. In total, he ran 87 horses during the meeting and 9 of the 19 victories came in Grade 1 events. The fact his son and assistant Patrick rode 5 of those winners was the icing on the cake for Team Mullins.

Five of the 19 wins came on the final day of the Festival, including Dysart Dynamo's emphatic success in the bumper. Despite pulling hard, the Westerner gelding beat a decent field by upwards of seven and a half lengths under Mullins junior. Leading on the hometurn, he stretched clear inside the final furlong to win with authority. It is a race the stable have won with Yorkhill (2015) and Invitation Only (2016) and his trainer said afterwards: **"I don't think I've seen a horse pull as hard as he did and finish the race the way he did in a long time. He looks quite exciting and its lovely to have one like him in the yard."**

His victory at Punchestown also proved his versatility in terms of ground conditions because it was testing when Dysart Dynamo made a winning start to his career at Clonmel a month earlier. An eight and a half lengths winner on that occasion, he is a half-brother to 131 rated stablemate Dysart Diamond but has considerably more potential than his older sister. Provided he consents to settle in his races, the five year old will have no trouble staying at least two and a half miles over hurdles this season. He looks very much a Graded horse in the making who should be competing at the major spring Festivals in 2022.

POINTS TO NOTE:
Probable Best Distance - 2m 4f – 3 miles
Preferred Going - Soft
Connection's Comments: ""I thought Dysart Dynamo was awesome in winning the bumper. To pull Patrick around for two miles like he did and still finish at the end means he must have a huge engine. He's one I'm really looking forward to." Willie MULLINS – sportinglife.com (30/4/21)

GOING:	R	W	P		TRACK:	R	W	P
Soft	1	1	0		Right	2	2	0
Yielding	1	1	0		Galloping	1	1	0
					Tight/Undul.	1	1	0

TRIP:	R	W	P		JOCKEY:	R	W	P
2m	1	1	0		P.W.Mullins	2	2	0
2m 2f	1	1	0					

ELLE EST BELLE

5 b m Fame And Glory – Katalina (Hernando (FR))
OWNER: Mrs SUZANNE LAWRENCE
TRAINER: D.SKELTON. Shelfield Green, Warwickshire.
CAREER FORM FIGURES: 1132
CAREER WIN: 2020: Oct AINTREE Soft NHF 2m 1f; Nov CHELTENHAM Soft Listed NHF 2m

Last season couldn't have gone much better for the Skelton family. Harry was crowned champion jockey for the first time with 152 winners, which left him ten clear of former title holder Brian Hughes. Older sibling Dan didn't do too badly either breathing down the neck of his mentor Paul Nicholls in the trainers championship. Runner-up with 148 winners and total prize-money of £1,857,464, the yard were responsible for four Grade 1 victories during the 2020/2021 campaign.

Elle Est Belle proved herself a high-class bumper mare last term and the stable harbour high hopes she will develop into a leading player for the Dawn Run Mares' Novices' Hurdle at Cheltenham in March. A daughter of Fame And Glory who cost €42,000 as a three year old, she couldn't have won any easier on her debut in a mares' bumper at Aintree's Old Roan Chase meeting in late October. Making smooth headway in the homestraight, she barely came off the bridle to win by over five lengths. She then dead-heated with Harry Fry's Ishkhara Lady in a Listed event at Cheltenham's November meeting. Run in atrocious conditions, she was joined on the line by an opponent two years her elder with the pair nearly five lengths clear of the third. Despite suffering defeat for the first time, Elle Est Belle ran a storming race against the geldings in the Festival bumper at Cheltenham. Set an impossible task, she was too far back but stayed on strongly to finish third behind the Willie Mullins trained pair Sir Gerhard and Kilcruit. Beaten seven lengths, her rider said: **"It was a really good run. We probably could have done with a stronger gallop as she likes to be settled, but she's very exciting for next year and we've always thought a lot of her."** The five year old completed her bumper career with another excellent performance at Aintree when a length and a half runner-up behind Arthur Moore's Me Too Please in a Grade 2 event. Her high cruising speed was in evidence once more, but she was unable to reel in the Rachel Blackmore ridden winner. The Listed winner and 96 rated Flat filly Eileendover was five lengths back in fourth. The champion jockey remarked: **"She's a good mare. I was about two lengths down on Rachael (Blackmore) with a furlong and a half to go and I just couldn't get by her, but she's very exciting for next season and we're looking forward to that."**

Winning mares' novice hurdles will prove a formality for Elle Est Belle and it won't be long before she is heading down the Pattern route once again. The Skelton's have trained some very good mares, including Maire Banrigh, Rene's Girl, Roksana and Stephanie Frances and this one threats to be equally as good, if not better.

POINTS TO NOTE:

Probable Best Distance	-	**2m – 2m 4f**
Preferred Going	-	**Soft**

Connection's Comments: "She's brilliant. She's run in the two Championship races and she's placed in both so I'm very proud of her. She was last off the bridle there today and has got loads of class, so I can't wait to go hurdling with her." Dan SKELTON at Aintree (8/4/21)

GOING:	R	W	P	TRACK:	R	W	P
Soft	2	2	0	Left Handed	4	2	2
Good/Soft	2	0	2	Stiff/Undul.	2	1	1
				Tight	2	1	1

TRIP:	R	W	P	JOCKEY:	R	W	P
2m	2	1	1	H.Skelton	4	2	2
2m 1f	2	1	1				

FONTAINE COLLONGES (FR)
6 b m Saddler Maker (IRE) – Saturne Collonges (FR) (Dom Alco (FR))
OWNER: P.DAVIES
TRAINER: Miss V.M.WILLIAMS. King's Caple, Herefordshire.
CAREER FORM FIGURES: 26 – 115 - 31
CAREER WINS: 2019: May LE LION-D'ANGERS Soft AQPS 1m 4f: 2020: Jan LUDLOW Soft NHF 2m: 2021: Jan LEICESTER Heavy NH 2m

Venetia Williams has excelled with the horses she has purchased from France. Royale Pagaille was another very good example last season with the Rich and Susannah Ricci owned gelding winning three times over fences, including a sixteen lengths demolition job in the Grade 2 Peter Marsh Chase at Haydock in January. The seven year old's official rating rose from 135 to 166 in three months.

The Herefordshire handler has added to her already strong team with more purchases from across the English Channel – some of which are featured in the *French Revolution* section – during the spring/summer. The lightly raced Fontaine Collonges joined the yard in May 2019 having been acquired for €180,000 at the Arqana Sale. Previously trained by Fabrice Foucher (previously handled Un De Sceaux), the daughter of Saddler Maker won one of her three starts in bumpers in her native country. A bumper winner at Ludlow in January 2020 on her first start for her new connections, she was restricted to a couple of outings over hurdles last winter. Absent for 309 days (had a wind operation in the interim), she was beaten less than five lengths in a mares' novice hurdle at Wincanton on Boxing Day, staying on well in the process. Back in action less than three weeks later, she produced a gutsy display to beat the 125 rated No Risk

Des Flos (won next time) at Leicester, making virtually all the running. In receipt of thirteen pounds, Fontaine Collonges rallied well on the run-in having been briefly headed to prevail by a neck with seventeen lengths back to the third. A non runner at Wetherby and Exeter, she is crying out for a step up in trip and a switch to fences.

There are few, if any, better placers of their horses than Venetia Williams and, with that in mind, there is every possibility Fontaine Collonges will rattle up a sequence of wins once contesting handicap chases over two and a half miles this season. A mare with size and scope, she looks attractively treated off 116. Former stablemate Pepite Rose began her chasing career off 111 on 29th February 2012. By 12th April the same year, she finished fourth in the Grade 1 Manifesto Novices' Chase at Aintree off 150. It would be nice to think this six year old, who is from the family of Grand National winner Neptune Collonges, could do something similar.

POINTS TO NOTE:
Probable Best Distance - 2m 4f +
Preferred Going - Soft
Connection's Comments: "Fontaine Collonges is a lovely horse and she was our strongest chance. I was going to step her up in trip but we thought testing conditions and the uphill finish might compensate for it here. When she was headed halfway up the run-in I was cursing myself, but she showed plenty of resolve and stamina is her forte. The real excitement with her will be when she goes chasing." Venetia WILLIAMS at Leicester (13/1/21)

GOING:	R	W	P	TRACK	R	W	P
Heavy	2	1	0	Left Handed	2	1	0
Soft	5	2	2	Right	5	2	2
				Galloping	1	0	1
				Stiff/Undul.	1	1	0
				Tight	1	1	0
				Tight/Undul.	1	0	0

TRIP:	R	W	P	JOCKEY:	R	W	P
1m 3f	1	0	0	C.Deutsch	4	2	1
1m 4f	2	1	1	A.Bourgeais	2	1	1
2m	3	2	1	A.Roussel	1	0	0
2m 3f	1	0	0				

FRONTIER GENERAL (IRE)
4 b g Mahler – Lady Zephyr (IRE) (Toulon)
TRAINER: H.DE BROMHEAD. Knockeen, Co.Waterford.
CAREER FORM FIGURES: 1
CAREER WINS: 2021: May DROMAHANE Yielding/Soft 4YO Mdn PTP 3m

Sixty five year old Pat Doyle, who saddled his first pointer over forty years ago, has been associated with some top-class horses. The County Tipperary trainer was responsible for Grade 1 winners Bacardys, Brindisi Breeze, Death Duty, First Lieutenant, No More Heroes and Shattered Love. In March, he watched Appreciate It, Bob Olinger and Coolreevy score at the Cheltenham Festival. Doyle played no small part in that trio, either.

Based at Suirview Stables, he trained Frontier General to win his only point-to-point in May and Declan Phelan feels the Mahler gelding is set to develop into a high-class horse under Rules: "Tall sturdy bay gelding: purchased by Henry de Bromhead for a value €20,000 as a three-year-old store in 2020. His dam Lady Zephyr won five races for Nigel Twiston Davies and he was farmed out to Pat Doyle to gain some experience in the pointing world. He left his calling card as a talented individual on his sole appearance, at Dromahane (Yielding/Soft) in May. The race was run in miserable conditions, driving rain and a howling wind, it was easy for a faint-hearted animal to down tools, not this guy. Jumping with aggression, he led the field of ten runners, facing the worst of the elements, whilst the rest shielded behind him. When the race got serious from three out, he was almost knocked over when a rival barged into him attempting to slip up his inner: this tough cookie, quickly regained his balance and retained a narrow lead. When he got a kick in the belly heading to the last fence, he found more and asserted to win by a non-flattering length and a half. The time was the joint fastest on the card, all the more commendable as the race was run in the worst of the weather. This may be a Cheltenham Festival class horse: the outing at Dromahane identified that he had no trouble staying three miles, and he possesses the gears to drop down in trip: moreover, he will fight for a win, if required, and he served notice that he has the appetite for a fight. He found the testing ground to his taste. He moves back to Henry de Bromhead for a track career and with loads of physical scope, ambitious targets such as Graded hurdles/chases will be in his pipeline."

POINTS TO NOTE:
Probable Best Distance - **2m 4f – 3 miles**
Preferred Going - **Soft**
Connection's Comments: "He was very green and he will be a nice horse and one to really look forward to after a summer's grass." Pat DOYLE at Dromahane (9/5/21)

GOING:	R	W	P	TRACK	R	W	P
Yield/Soft	1	1	0	Left Handed	1	1	0

TRIP:	R	W	P	JOCKEY:	R	W	P
3m	1	1	0	P.A.King	1	1	0

GAELIC WARRIOR (GER)
3 b g Maxios – Game of Legs (FR) (Hernando (FR))
OWNER: Mrs S.RICCI
TRAINER: W.P.MULLINS. Bagenalstown, Co.Carlow
CAREER FORM FIGURES: 6 - 33

"I like him a lot. A laid horse and very much a staying chaser in the making, he will improve with age. He has progressed with each start and it wouldn't surprise me if he developed into a Triumph Hurdle contender. Long-term, I think he will be top-class," commented James Reveley when I spoke to the former French champion jump jockey in August about the thrice raced Gaelic Warrior, who has been bought by Rich and Susannah Ricci and joined Willie Mullins.

Ironically, his sire Maxios was responsible for the Triumph Hurdle winner in March, namely Quilixios, plus Aramax, who won the Boodles Juvenile Handicap Hurdle at the Cheltenham

Festival in 2020. Trained in France by Hector de Lageneste and Guillaume Macaire, he made his jumping bow in the Listed Prix Wild Monarch at Auteuil in April. Held up, he was outpaced before staying on in sixth behind Paradiso (won another Listed and Grade 3 hurdle since). Reappearing over the same course and distance less than a month later, he was much sharper and made good headway at the end of the backstraight. Holding every chance at the second last, Gaelic Warrior wasn't fluent at the final hurdle before keeping on at the one pace. Beaten a length in third, the runner-up has won since. His third outing also came at the Parisian track in a conditions hurdle in June and, once again, James Reveley's mount claimed the bronze medal. Six and a half lengths in arrears of Sans Bruit (fourth won next time), the experience he gained in France will stand him in good stead.

Graded winners Burrows Saint, Kalkir, Let's Dance and the mighty Vautour all began their careers with Guillaume Macaire before being bought for the Ricci family to join Mullins. Gaelic Warrior looks set to continue that trend and is a youngster with a bright future.

POINTS TO NOTE:

Probable Best Distance	-	2 miles (long-term 3 miles)
Preferred Going	-	Soft

GOING:	R	W	P	TRACK:	R	W	P
Heavy	2	0	2	Left Handed	3	0	2
Very Soft	1	0	0	Galloping	3	0	2

TRIP:	R	W	P	JOCKEY:	R	W	P
1m 7f	3	0	2	J.Reveley	3	0	2

GALOPIN DES CHAMPS (FR)

5 bl g Timos (GER) – Manon Des Champs (FR) (Marchand De Sable (USA))
OWNER: Mrs AUDREY TURLEY
TRAINER: W.P.MULLINS. Bagenalstown, Co.Carlow.
CAREER FORM FIGURES: 12P61 - 1
CAREER WIN: 2020: May AUTEUIL Very Soft Hdle 2m 2f: 2021: Mar CHELTENHAM Good/
Soft HH 2m 4f; Apr PUNCHESTOWN Yielding Grade 1 NH 3m

Another superb chasing prospect, it is hoped Willie Mullins and his team at Closutton elect to send the ex-French gelding over fences rather than pursue the Stayers' Hurdle route. Featured in last year's *Top 40 Prospects*, he justified his inclusion by coming good in the spring, making a mockery of an opening handicap mark in the Martin Pipe Conditional Jockeys' Hurdle at Cheltenham before trouncing a smart field in the Grade 1 Irish Mirror Novice Hurdle at the Punchestown Festival. Cheltenham Gold Cup winner Minella Indo won the same event in 2019 and it is not inconceivable the Timos gelding follows a similar path one day.

Trained in France by Arnaud Chaille-Chaille (same source as dual Gold Cup runner-up Djakadam), he won comfortably on his debut at Auteuil in May and was purchased soon afterwards by Mullins. Significantly, the five year old made his Irish debut in the same two miles novice hurdle at Gowran Park the stable had won with subsequent Grade 1 winners Douvan (2014), Sharjah (2017) and Franco De Port (2019) in previous years. Having held every chance, he was outsprinted after the last by the Arthur Moore trained Sea Ducor (rated 135). Found to be suffering with 'abnormal irregularities' when pulled up in a Grade 2 hurdle at Limerick over Christmas, he belied his odds of 100/1 when finishing a highly respectable sixth in a Grade 1 novice hurdle over two miles at the Dublin Racing Festival at Leopardstown in February. Mikey Fogarty's mount couldn't match stablemate Appreciate It's turn of foot but was still in contention when making a mistake at the last. Granted a rating of 142, Galopin Des Champs hasn't looked back since stepping up in trip. Sean O'Keeffe took over in the saddle at the Cheltenham Festival and he wasn't hard pressed to see off the Imperial Cup winner Langer Dan to win going away by two and a quarter lengths. He produced an even better display at Punchestown relishing the further step up in distance to three miles. Jumping fluently and travelling powerfully, he sauntered clear after the second last. A twelve lengths scorer, four times champion jockey Paul Townend said afterwards: **"That was very straightforward and he has a lovely temperament for that type of race. He jumps super and will jump a fence, if you want him to. It went like clockwork. The race worked out the way I thought it might, and it was just a case of staying on his back."** The 31 year old booted home 5 winners from only 9 rides at the Festival, four of which came in Grade 1 races.

Expect Galopin Des Champs to begin his chasing career over two and a half miles before returning to three miles later in the season. There is every chance the five year old will provide Willie Mullins with his sixth win in the Grade 1 Brown Advisory Novices' Chase at Cheltenham in March. He is top-class.

POINTS TO NOTE:
Probable Best Distance   -   **3 miles**
Preferred Going   -   **Good/Soft**
Connection's Comments: "He looked very smart. He just looked fantastic at three miles. When Paul (Townend) gave him a squeeze going to the third last, he just took off and the race was over coming into the last bend. He's very slick over hurdles and Paul said he could be a Stayers' candidate next season. However, I like going chasing quickly. I wouldn't mind going chasing with him anyhow." Willie MULLINS at Punchestown (28/4/21)

GOING:	R	W	P	TRACK:	R	W	P
Heavy	2	0	1	Left Handed	3	2	0
Soft/Heavy	1	0	0	Right	3	1	1
Very Soft	1	1	0	Galloping	4	2	0
Good/Soft	1	1	0	Stiff/Undul.	1	1	0
Yielding	1	1	0	Tight/Undul.	1	0	1

TRIP:	R	W	P	JOCKEY:	R	W	P
2m	3	0	1	P.Townend	2	1	1
2m 2f	1	1	0	S.O'Keefe	1	1	0
2m 4f	1	1	0	M.Fogarty	1	0	0
3m	1	1	0	D.E.Mullins	1	0	0
				T.Coutant	1	1	0

GENTLEMAN JOE

3 b g Authorized (IRE) – Bella Lulu (Iffraaj)
OWNER: ROBCOUR
TRAINER: H.DE BROMHEAD. Knockeen, Co.Waterford.
CAREER FLAT FORM FIGURES: 8 - 163
CAREER FLAT WIN: 2020: Mar KEMPTON Standard Mdn 1m

Henry De Bromhead took charge of the previously unbeaten Quilixios last spring on the eve of the Cheltenham following Cheveley Park Stud's decision to remove their horses from Gordon Elliott. The change of scenery didn't prevent the Maxios gelding from making it five wins from as many starts when taking the Triumph Hurdle by three and a quarter lengths.

The same handler will be thinking in terms of the same event for his high-class Flat recruit Gentleman Joe. Rated 92 on the level when trained by Joseph Tuite, the son of Authorized has been gelded since joining De Bromhead and spent time at Paul Power's livery yard during the summer. A 43,000gns foal, he is a half-brother to John and Thady Gosden's unbeaten 98 rated four year old Faisal. Eighth on his only run as a two year old at Kempton in November, Gentleman Joe has left that form behind this term. Well supported on his reappearance at the same track in March, he won a mile maiden by nearly four lengths stretching clear inside the final furlong. Elevated in class a month later, he wasn't disgraced in finishing sixth in the Listed Feilden Stakes over nine furlongs at Newmarket's Craven meeting. The winner Highland Avenue has subsequently finished sixth in the Group 1 St James's Palace Stakes and fourth in a Group 2 event in France. He rounded off his Flat career with a most respectable third in the Listed Cocked Hat Stakes at Goodwood. Stepping up to eleven furlongs, he couldn't match the first two, namely Lone Eagle (runner-up in the Irish Derby) and Yibir (won the Group 2 Great Voltigeur Stakes) but was keeping on in the closing stages. Both the fourth (Listed win) and fifth (rated 89) have scored subsequently. It is top-class three year old form.

Bought privately afterwards by agent Alex Elliott on behalf of Robcour, I spoke to Oisin Murphy (rode him at Goodwood) at York in August and the champion jockey was complimentary about Gentleman Joe. Suited by ease in the ground, he stays well and has the ingredients to make a very good hurdler. There is a possibility he will make his jumping bow at Gowran Park (20th November). Otherwise, his new connections may elect to wait for Leopardstown's prestigious Christmas fixture.

POINTS TO NOTE:
Probable Best Distance   -   2 miles
Preferred Going   -   Good/Soft
Connection's Comments: "He's a horse we like very much." Joseph TUITE (13/4/21)

GOING:	R	W	P	TRACK	R	W	P
Standard	2	1	0	Right	4	1	0
Soft	1	0	0	Galloping	1	0	0
Good	1	0	0	Tight	2	1	0
				Tight/Undul.	1	0	0

TRIP:	R	W	P	JOCKEY:	R	W	P
1m	2	1	0	R.Clutterbuck	1	1	0
1m 1f	1	0	0	Hollie Doyle	1	0	0
1m 3f	1	0	0	James Doyle	1	0	0
				O.Murphy	1	0	0

GRANGECLARE WEST (IRE)

5 b g Presenting – Hayabusa (Sir Harry Lewis (USA))
OWNER: CHEVELEY PARK STUD
TRAINER: W.P.MULLINS. Bagenalstown, Co.Carlow.
CAREER FORM FIGURES: 1 - 1
CAREER WINS: 2020: Nov LINGSTOWN Soft 4YO Mdn PTP 3m: 2021: May PUNCHESTOWN Soft NHF 2m

Cheveley Park Stud have won the Festival bumper at Cheltenham for the last three years, with both Ferny Hollow (2019) and Sir Gerhard (2020) being trained by Willie Mullins. The latter's victory in March provided Ireland's champion trainer with his eleventh success in the Grade 1 contest. It will be interesting to see if the twice raced Grangeclare West is aimed at the race next spring, having been acquired for £430,000 in December following an easy win 'between the flags' the previous month for Denis Murphy.

A Punchestown bumper winner in late May on his first start for his new connections, it is possible the Presenting gelding will embark on a hurdling career instead. It is worth recalling the recently retired and eleven times Grade 1 winning former stablemate Faugheen won a bumper at the same track during the same month in 2013 before going straight over timber the following Autumn. Either way, the five year old is a top-class prospect.

Declan Phelan takes up the story: "**David Thompson was the brains and financier behind the successful English stud Cheveley Park. The business focussed on Flat stallions and offspring. David himself loved the National Hunt game: in previous decades as a treat he purchased Grand National contenders such as Party Politics and Character Building for some fun. In the last four or five years as he advanced in years, Thompson injected plenty of capital into his passion for the jumping game and elected to run his jumps team in the famous red and blue Cheveley Park Stud silks. The team led by David invested in expensive pointers and some French recruits. The fruits of the selection process are borne by the results: the last three editions of the Cheltenham Festival bumper have been won by pointers sourced in Ireland by Cheveley Park: Envoi Allen, Ferny Hollow and Sir Gerhard. Thompson pulled out the chequebook again in late 2020 and purchased more pointers from the Autumn 2020 academy, personally turning up at the December sales to supervise the transactions. Alas, David passed away a month later in January, and the signs are that the current troop sporting the Cheveley Park colours will see out their racing careers for said stud, no further additional National Hunt purchases are likely. Grangeclare West is a strong muscled bay gelding with a white spot on his crown and a white nose: his dam was 0/4 in her four bumpers for Willie Mullins, said lady from the family of Gunner Welburn and she has produced previous track winners, including Coeur Joyeux. Joey Logan, a long-time supporter of trainer Denis Murphy, paid €62,000 for this youngster from the 2019 Derby Store sale and he bagged a chunky profit following one** outing in a point. He competed in a slowly run four year old maiden at Lingstown (Soft) in November. With five to jump the 9-runner field were bunched, covered by a handful of lengths due to the early crawl. Three out he was positioned in a close second by Jamie Codd: during the last four furlongs the race developed into a late sprint: this fellow quickened up from two out, was eyeballed by a rival heading to the last, fought him off and pinged the final fence to win going away. He jumped the fences like a natural and was exemplary at the final fence when in top gear. The style of victory forced Mr Thompson to pay £430,000 at the December sales. The horse was initially rehomed with Gordon Elliott, however following the Gordongate incident and the withdrawal of the Cheveley Park stock, the horse switched to Willie Mullins. He produced a smart bumper win at Punchestown (Soft) in May routing modest rivals. He has Grade 1 potential and, judged on his two wins, he appears to be the number one seed for the owners, if they wish to extend their winning sequence in the Cheltenham Festival bumper. Long term, he may be a mirror image of Vautour in that middle distances may be his happiest hunting territory over hurdles/fences."

POINTS TO NOTE:

Probable Best Distance	-	2m – 2m 4f
Preferred Going	-	Soft

Connection's Comments: "He's a gorgeous horse but still quite green and I'd say he would have been more impressive if he'd had something to race with him." Jody TOWNEND at Punchestown (29/5/21)

GOING:	R	W	P	TRACK	R	W	P
Soft	2	2	0	Right	2	2	0
				Galloping	1	1	0
TRIP:	R	W	P	JOCKEY:	R	W	P
2m	1	1	0	J.Townend	1	1	0
3m	1	1	0	J.Codd	1	1	0

HARMONIE STAR (FR)

4 b f Boris De Deauville (IRE) – Tulipe Star (FR) (East of Heaven (IRE))
OWNER: SHANAKIEL RACING SYNDICATE
TRAINER: W.P.MULLINS. Bagenalstown, Co.Carlow
CAREER FORM FIGURES: 51111
CAREER WIN: 2020: Jun CRAON Very Soft AQPS 1m 4f; July LE LION D'ANGERS Good/Soft Grade 3 AQPS 1m 4f; Aug VICHY Good/Soft Grade 3 AQPS 1m 4f; Sept CRAON Good AQPS 1m 4f

The Henry De Bromhead trained Tellmesomethinggirl ended Willie Mullins' monopoly on the Grade 2 Dawn Run Mares' Novices' Hurdle at the Cheltenham Festival in March. The Closutton trainer had won the previous five renewals and he will be keen to reclaim the crown next spring. French import Harmonie Star is expected to develop into a major contender having won four of her five outings in bumpers in her native land.

Purchased for the Shanakiel Racing Syndicate, who have tasted Grade 1 success twice with Bacardys (placed a couple of times at the Festival), the four year old was trained in France by Nicolas Payson. Sporting a noseband on each occasion, she invariably raced handily and showed a will to win when tackled late on during her races. She raced five times in less than four months and, having finished fifth on her debut at Vichy in May, she racked up a sequence of wins, including twice in Grade 3 company. A length and a half scorer from Hotel Dieu (won four times since) at Craon the following month, she was always holding her rival. She then dead-heated with Holly (subsequently bought by J.P.McManus and has joined Jonjo O'Neill) in a Grade 3 at Le Lion D'Angers having been joined on the line by Erwan Grall's filly. A more comfortable success in similar grade at Vichy swiftly followed with jockey Tristan Baron waving his stick to the crowd in the closing stages. The fourth (Henares) has won twice over hurdles at Auteuil since, while the fifth (Hurrick Des Obeaux) has done likewise (including a Listed hurdle) and finished second in a Grade 3 hurdle at the Parisian track. Harmonie Star rounded off her French career with another cosy win at the expense of old rival Hotel Dieu at Craon in September.

Effective on soft and good ground, she has size and scope and ought to develop into a high-class hurdler for her new connections. She is one to very much look forward to.

POINTS TO NOTE:

Probable Best Distance	-	**2 miles**
Preferred Going	-	**Good/Soft**

Connection's Comments: "I'll be really disappointed if she doesn't turned out to be very good. I really like her physically. She is strong and was very good in her bumpers, which is normally good enough for them to perform over the jumps. It's a bit like with Gaillard Du Mesnil, as he was a good bumper horse. She's the same and I liked her the first time I saw her at Nicolas Paysan's yard." Agent PIERRE BOULARD who sourced her in France.

GOING:	R	W	P	TRACK:	R	W	P
Very Soft	1	1	0	Left Handed	1	1	0
Soft	1	0	0	Right	4	3	0
Good/Soft	2	2	0				
Good	1	1	0				

TRIP:	R	W	P	JOCKEY:	R	W	P
1m 4f	5	4	0	T.Baron	4	4	0
				A.Pouchin	1	0	0

HARTUR D'OUDAIRIES (FR)

4 b g Kapgarde (FR) – Brise D'Oudairies (FR) (Califet (FR))
OWNER: J.P.McMANUS
TRAINER: D.SKELTON. Shelfield Green, Warwickshire.
CAREER FORM FIGURES: 1
CAREER WIN: 2020: Nov LE MANS Soft AQPS 1m 7f

Dan Skelton is another trainer who has been busy acquiring fresh talent from France. They include a trio of potentially useful juvenile hurdlers, namely In This World, Message Personnel and Rocky Man.

Fourteen times champion British owner J.P.McManus has sent another French recruit Hartur D'Oudairies to Paul Nicholls' former assistant. A four year old by Kapgarde, he is a half-brother to Fumut D'Oudairies, who won a couple of hunter chases this spring for Tom Ellis. Previously owned by M.L.Bloodstock, he made a winning start to his career in an AQPS Flat race for Daniela Mele at Le Mans (Left-Handed) in November. A tall powerful looking gelding, he made all the running and was taken wide for much of the race. Ridden along turning for home, the Kapgarde gelding responded well and powered clear to win comfortably by two and a half lengths. The further he went, the better he looked. The third and sixth have lost their maiden tags since and the seventh has finished runner-up at Auteuil and joined Willie Mullins afterwards.

Given plenty of time since being bought by the legendary Irish owner, he joined Dan Skelton in the late summer/early Autumn and his new trainer describes Hartur D'Oudairies as **'a lovely horse.'** The plan is to start him off in a two miles maiden/novice hurdle but there is every chance he will improve when stepped up to two and a half miles. He is a smashing prospect who will jump fences, too.

POINTS TO NOTE:

Probable Best Distance	-	**2m 4f**
Preferred Going	-	**Soft**

GOING:	R	W	P	TRACK:	R	W	P
Soft	1	1	0	Left Handed	1	1	0
				Tight	1	1	0

TRIP:	R	W	P	JOCKEY:	R	W	P
1m 7f	1	1	0	T.Bachelot	1	1	0

HENN SEE (FR)

4 b g Slickly Royal (FR) – Onvavoir (FR) (Diableneyev (USA))
OWNER: BRUTON STREET PARTNERSHIP
TRAINER: W.P.MULLINS. Bagenalstown, Co.Carlow
CAREER FORM FIGURES: 72

As discussed, Galopin Des Champs was one of the success stories of the *Top 40 Prospects* last season winning at the Cheltenham and Punchestown Festivals, including at Grade 1 level. The lightly raced Henn See has arrived from France with a similar profile and is the type to develop into a high-class novice hurdler once stepping up in distance later in the campaign. Ultimately, his future lies over fences though because he looks a lovely big scopey four year old.

Purchased for the Bruton Street Partnership, who tasted Grade 1 success last season with Franco De Port, the Slickly Royal gelding is a half-brother to new stablemate Gjoumi. Under the guidance of Yannick Fouin (same source as Min), Henn See made his racecourse bow in the same AQPS Flat race won by the aforementioned Hartur D'Oudairies at Le Mans in November. In rear for the majority of the contest, he made late headway in seventh without being a threat to the easy winner. Beaten around twenty lengths, he went jumping next time and proved a different proposition. Ridden by Jeremy Da Silva in a conditions hurdle at Auteuil in mid March, he was held up before being taken wide down the backstraight. Creeping into contention, he stayed on well in second behind Halo Des Obeaux (joined Paul Nicholls). A length and three quarters separated the pair with twelve lengths back to the third. He looked a natural jumper who travelled well and will come into his own over longer trips.

It is not beyond the realms of possibility that Henn See could emerge as a contender for something like the Martin Pipe Conditional Jockeys' Handicap Hurdle at the Cheltenham Festival. Capable of winning a two miles maiden hurdle on his stable debut, he will get better as the season goes on. He is a long-term project and very much one to keep an eye on.

POINTS TO NOTE:

Probable Best Distance	-	2m 4f – 3 miles
Preferred Going	-	Good/Soft

GOING:	R	W	P	TRACK:	R	W	P
Very Soft	1	0	1	Left Handed	2	0	1
				Galloping	1	0	1
				Tight	1	0	0

TRIP:	R	W	P	JOCKEY:	R	W	P
1m 7f	1	0	0	S.Maillot	1	0	0
2m 1f	1	1	0	J.Da Silva	1	0	1

HOUKA D'OUDAIRIES (FR)
4 gr f Gris De Gris (IRE) – Quinine (FR) (Network (GER))
OWNER: BARONESS S.NOAKES
TRAINER: G.L.MOORE. Lower Beeding, West Sussex.
CAREER FORM FIGURES: 11
CAREER WINS: 2021: Apr DURTAL Soft APQS 1m 6f; May VICHY Good/Soft APQS 1m 5f

On the recommendation of Nicolas Bertrand de Balanda, this unbeaten filly was acquired for €110,000 during the spring and has joined Gary Moore. Successful in both her AQPS Flat races in France when trained by Daniela Mele, she has settled in well and her new connections are looking forward to campaigning her in mares' novice hurdles this season.

Out of a mare who won twice over fences, including at Auteuil, she made her debut in an eight runner bumper at Durtal in April. Racing handily, she joined the leader turning for home before staying on well to win cosily by a length and a half (eighth has won over fences since). She then produced an even better display at Vichy less than a month later. A length and three quarters winner from the Lord Daresbury owned Heritier (joined Olly Greenall since), she was in receipt of weight from the runner-up but was firmly on top at the finish. The time was good, too. Reported to have schooled well over hurdles, Gary Moore is very keen on her prospects this season and she is a potentially smart addition to his team.

POINTS TO NOTE:

Probable Best Distance	-	2 miles
Preferred Going	-	Good/Soft

GOING:	R	W	P	TRACK:	R	W	P
Soft	1	1	0	Right	2	2	0
Good/Soft	1	1	0	Galloping	2	2	0

TRIP:	R	W	P	JOCKEY:	R	W	P
1m 5f	1	1	0	M.Androunin	2	2	0
1m 6f	1	1	0				

HUBRISKO (FR)
4 b g Doctor Dino (FR) – Ubriska (FR) (Apsis (FR))
OWNER: Mrs S.RICCI
TRAINER: W.P.MULLINS. Bagenalstown, Co.Carlow
CAREER FORM FIGURES: 1
CAREER WIN: 2020: Aug LE LION D'ANGERS Good/Soft AQPS 1m 4f

The once raced Hubrisko has yet to make his Irish debut for Willie Mullins but is hopefully a four year old with a big future. Highlighted in the *French Revolution* section in *One Jump Ahead* last season, the Doctor Dino gelding spreadeagled a small field in an AQPS Flat race in France during the summer of 2020.

Having viewed his eight lengths win at Le Lion D'Angers (1m 4f : Good/Soft) in August last year, the former Alain Couetil trained gelding looked star material. Contesting a field made up of five debutants, Hubrisko raced in fourth position for much of the contest but was produced on the outside in the home straight before streaking clear. It was a performance which oozed class. In terms of form, the second has finished runner-up three times at Auteuil (hurdles and fences), the third (Haddex Des Obeaux) won a similar event next time before scoring over hurdles at Auteuil in April. He is now in training with Gary Moore. The fourth has won a bumper, over hurdles and fences, while the fifth has won his only start since over fences.

Half-brother to stablemate Grand Bornand, who won on his chasing debut at the Galway Festival in July, Hubrisko will hopefully be in action in November/December in a two miles maiden hurdle. Fingers crossed, he is another star for Rich and Susannah Ricci.

POINTS TO NOTE:

Probable Best Distance	-	2 miles
Preferred Going	-	Soft

GOING:	R	W	P	TRACK:	R	W	P
Good/Soft	1	1	0	Left Handed	1	1	0
				Galloping	1	1	0

TRIP:	R	W	P	JOCKEY:	R	W	P
1m 4f	1	1	0	L.Poggionovo	1	1	0

IRON BRIDGE (IRE)

5 b g Milan – Chit Chat (Bob Back (USA))
OWNER: TREVOR HEMMINGS
TRAINER: J.J.O'NEILL. Temple Guiting, Gloucestershire.
CAREER FORM FIGURES: 1
CAREER WIN: 2021: Mar TIPPERARY Soft NHF 2m 3f

Trevor Hemmings and Jonjo O'Neill combined to win the Ladbrokes Trophy at Newbury in late November with Cloth Cap, the Beneficial gelding making all and scoring by ten lengths. It was a tremendous result for two legends of National Hunt racing. Unfortunately, things didn't go to plan in the Grand National for the nine year old but he progressed from an official rating of 138 to 157 nevertheless during the 2020/2021 season.

The same combination are responsible for the once raced Iron Bridge who arrived at Jackdaws Castle during the summer. A five year old by Milan out of a mare who won over hurdles for O'Neill in 2011, he was bought for €58,000 at the Tattersalls Ireland Derby Sales in 2019. Sent into training with Damian Murphy in Ireland, he was due to contest a point-to-point but the season was delayed due to the pandemic. He made his debut in a point-to-point bumper at Tipperary in March instead and scored by three lengths from the more experienced Colin Bowe trained Casey West, who had finished second in a maiden hurdle at Punchestown the previous month. Ridden patiently early on, he made headway with a circuit to run before moving into contention rounding the hometurn. Leading over a furlong out, he overcame greenness before being driven out by Johnny Barry.

Speaking to racing manager Mick Meagher at the beginning of September, he is described as **"a lovely model and very much a three miles chaser in the making."** Don't expect him to be a star over hurdles but is considered capable of winning a couple of staying novice events before embarking on his chasing career in twelve months time. That's when Iron Bridge is expected to come into his own.

Mick also kindly mentioned **FAMOUS BRIDGE** who has joined Nicky Richards. A former stablemate of Iron Bridge, he is a five year old by Fame And Glory who was third in a pointers bumper at Punchestown in March. Bought for €84,000 as a three year old, he is a half-brother to Cheltenham Festival winner Tellmesomethinggirl. Expect him to be a similar type over hurdles before going over fences next season.

POINTS TO NOTE:
Probable Best Distance   -   3 miles
Preferred Going   -   Soft
Connection's Comments: **"He was ready for point-to-pointing, he has jumped but has no galloping done and this is different training. That's a lot of pressure off me thank god because I've always loved this horse and was stone mad about him." Damian MURPHY at Tipperary (24/3/21)**

GOING:	R	W	P	TRACK	R	W	P
Soft	1	1	0	Left Handed	1	1	0
				Tight	1	1	0

TRIP:	R	W	P	JOCKEY:	R	W	P
2m 3f	1	1	0	J.C.Barry	1	1	0

JONBON (IRE)

5 b g Walk In The Park (IRE) – Star Face (FR) (Saint Des Saints (FR))
OWNER: J.P.McMANUS
TRAINER: N.J.HENDERSON. Lambourn, Berkshire.
CAREER FORM FIGURES: 11
CAREER WINS: 2020: Nov DROMAHANE Yielding/Soft 4YO Mdn PTP 3m: 2021: Mar NEWBURY Good/Soft NHF 2m

Eight times Grade 1 winner Douvan achieved the rare feat during the spring of 2016 by winning at Cheltenham, Aintree and Punchestown in the space of 44 days. Many will argue he is the finest horse to have sported the famous pink and green silks of Rich and Susannah Ricci. Victorious in 14 of his 17 races while under the care of Willie Mullins, he suffered his first defeat for the Closutton outfit in the Queen Mother Champion Chase at Cheltenham in 2017 and was never quite the same again. He was an outstanding horse though.

Jonbon is a full-brother to the dual Cheltenham Festival winner and therefore has a lot to live up to. Irish point expert Declan Phelan believes: **"One of the star turns of the 2020/21 Irish point campaign: naturally as a full brother to Douvan and coming at a cost of €140,000 as a store, there was a fair degree of hype and speculation prior to his debut. Prepared by Ellmarie Holden, he lined up for his four-year-old maiden at Dromahane (Yielding/Soft) in the hands of Derek O'Connor, and it was akin to an armchair ride as Jonbon coasted along and took control landing over three out and drew away, changing gears on the run in for a fifteen lengths success. He defeated a modest cast, yet he beat the six minutes on the clock around Dromahane, which is decent on winter terrain. A fine athletic bay gelding with a white face, he is not as physically imposing as Douvan. The win prompted much interest when he sold at Goffs UK November sales and Derek (O'Connor) encouraged J.P. McManus to stump up the winning bid of £570,000. His track debut at Newbury (Good/ Soft) enhanced his standing with Jonbon exciting in recording a silky four and a quarter lengths win. He undoubtedly has pure speed and sheer class and the potential is rich. He will warrant serious attention as a candidate for either the Supreme or Ballymore championship novice hurdles at the 2021 Cheltenham Festival and he may be Arkle material when he begins his chasing career in due course, his natural hunting territory may be between 2m and 2m 5f rather than 3 miles tests of stamina."**

A smooth winner on his hurdles debut at his local track, there must be every chance Jonbon will return to the same venue for his hurdles debut at the Ladbrokes Trophy meeting (26th November) – the Seven Barrows team have won the two miles maiden hurdle four times in the last seven years, including with Buveur D'Air (2015). Nicky Henderson has been fortunate to train Sprinter Sacre, Altior and Shishkin during the last eleven years and Jonbon could be his latest superstar.

POINTS TO NOTE:
Probable Best Distance   -   2 miles
Preferred Going   -   Good/Soft
Connection's Comments: "Jonbon relaxed, raced beautifully and quickened up well. I think he is a bit special. He's a gorgeous horse who has the looks and pedigree. I spoke to Derek O'Connor, who rode him in his point this morning and he came with big recommendations. It's only the first step of what I hope will be a long and successful

career - he's something to look forward to. He's a bit of a fidget at home and wouldn't stand still for long, but he looks magnificent on it and is not a horse who worries about it. He can anticipate things a bit, but I was pleased with how he relaxed in the race and got on with the job. We've not had to gallop or train him too much, but he's done three or four bits of work and they've very clearly been of a high standard; he's in no way wound up to do this. It was nice to get that run under his belt and it's holiday time." Nicky HENDERSON at Newbury (27/3/21)

GOING:	R	W	P	TRACK	R	W	P
Yielding/Soft	1	1	0	Left Handed	2	2	0
Good/Soft	1	1	0	Galloping	1	1	0

TRIP:	R	W	P	JOCKEY:	R	W	P
2m	1	1	0	N.De Boinville	1	1	0
3m	1	1	0	D.O'Connor	1	1	0

JOURNEY WITH ME (IRE)
5 ch g Mahler – Kilbarry Demon (IRE) (Bob's Return (IRE))
OWNER: ROBCOUR
TRAINER: H.DE BROMHEAD. Knockeen, Co.Waterford.
CAREER FORM FIGURES: 11
CAREER WINS: 2020: Nov BALLINDENISK Soft 4YO Mdn PTP 3m: 2021: Mar GOWRAN PARK Heavy NHF 2m 2f

Henry De Bromhead won the Grade 1 Albert Bartlett Novices' Hurdle at the Cheltenham Festival in 2019 courtesy of his subsequent Gold Cup winner Minella Indo. The County Waterford trainer has a prime candidate for the 2022 version in the unbeaten Journey With Me. Widely available at 25/1 for the three miles event, he makes plenty of appeal and ought to give ante-post backers plenty of fun during the winter months.

Irish expert Declan Phelan comments: **"Rangy athletic chestnut gelding: his unraced dam is a half-sister to Racing Demon and has produced three track winners, including the 130+ chaser Yorkist. Running for Wexford handler Mick Murphy, this gelding produced a striking twelve lengths win on his debut at Ballindenisk (Soft) in late November. Jumping like a seasoned veteran, he led the field at a fair clip: challenged on the approach to the second last, in a few strides he brushed away his main threat and proceeded to gallop right to the line and triumph by a dozen lengths in a commendable time. A six-figure transfer culminated in him next lining up for Henry De Bromhead and Robcour in a pointers' limited bumper at Gowran (Heavy) in March over 2m 2f, and he won that race without jockey Paddy Mullins moving a muscle: to be honest, what he beat were modest and he had more of a test in his point victory. He is an exciting staying project as his long stride and appetite to please will be best harvested in races when a premium is placed on stamina. This winter he will be a contender for the major novice staying hurdles and he may follow the path set by stablemate Minella Indo and over time become a high-class novice and senior staying chaser. He enjoys racing with dig in the ground and we do not know if he is blessed with the versatility to function on a drier terrain."**

The point-to-point bumper at Gowran Park in March, which he landed by thirteen lengths, has been won by subsequent Cheltenham Festival winners First Lieutenant (2010), Yorkhill (2015) and Bob Olinger (2020). Don't be surprised if the twice raced Journey With Me stars at Prestbury Park in the spring, too.

POINTS TO NOTE:
Probable Best Distance   -   3 miles
Preferred Going   -   Soft
Connection's Comments: "Bob Olinger would have more gears than this horse, this fellow is more of a galloper and he'll be a lovely horse to go jumping next season." Henry De BROMHEAD at Gowran Park (12/3/21)

GOING:	R	W	P	TRACK	R	W	P
Heavy	1	1	0	Right	2	2	0
Soft	1	1	0	Tight/Undul.	1	1	0

TRIP:	R	W	P	JOCKEY:	R	W	P
2m 2f	1	1	0	P.W.Mullins	1	1	0
3m	1	1	0	S.Staples	1	1	0

KYNTARA
5 b g Kayf Tara – Speed Bonnie Boat (Alflora)
OWNER: Lady DULVERTON
TRAINER: K.C.BAILEY. Andoversford, Gloucestershire.
CAREER FORM FIGURES: 11
CAREER WIN: 2020: Oct BISHOPS COURT Soft Mdn 4&5YO PTP 3m: 2021: Feb WARWICK Heavy NHF 2m

One of the real success stories in recent years amongst the training ranks has been the resurgence of Kim Bailey. The Grand National/Cheltenham Gold Cup and Champion Hurdle winning trainer sent out a personal best 86 winners during the 1993/1994. While he has yet to recapture those glory days, the stable sent out their fifth Cheltenham Festival winner in 2020 and First Flow provided Bailey with his first Grade 1 winner since 1995 when capturing the Clarence House Chase at Ascot in January.

Happygolucky, who featured in the *Top 40 Prospects* last season, won three times over fences, including the Grade 3 handicap chase at Aintree's Grand National meeting. Unfortunately, the seven year old is currently sidelined and will miss the season. However, his owner Lady Dulverton still has plenty to look forward to with the unbeaten former English pointer Kyntara, who was bred by Henry Daly. From the family of Dublin Flyer, he cost €30,000 as a three year old having been purchased at the Tattersalls Derby Sales in Ireland. Trained by Phil and Mel Rowley, he was an easy winner of a maiden point at Bishops Court in October pulling away under Alex Edwards to score readily. He subsequently joined Bailey and made his Rules debut nearly four months later. Making all in a Warwick bumper, he bounded clear inside the final half a mile to record a seventeen lengths win (third has won since). Twelve months earlier, Sizable Sam (rated 131) beat Cadzand (138) in the same contest.

Set to go novice hurdling, Kyntara will start off over two miles but will have no trouble staying further, if necessary. Yet to race on ground quicker than soft, he has already proved he can jump and is an exciting prospect for Lady Dulverton and Kim Bailey.

POINTS TO NOTE:

Probable Best Distance	-	2 miles
Preferred Going	-	Soft

GOING:	R	W	P	TRACK:	R	W	P
Heavy	1	1	0	Left Handed	2	2	0
Soft	1	1	0	Galloping	1	1	0
				Tight/Undul.	1	1	0

TRIP:	R	W	P	JOCKEY:	R	W	P
2m	1	1	0	D.Bass	1	1	0
3m	1	1	0	A.Edwards	1	1	0

MATTERHORN (FR)

3 b g Martaline – Sacarine (FR) (Turgeon (USA))
OWNER: Mrs JOHNNY DE LA HEY
TRAINER: P.F.NICHOLLS. Ditcheat, Somerset.
CAREER FORM FIGURES: 3

Champion trainer Paul Nicholls has recruited the likes of Dolos (3rd in 2016), Hinterland (won in 2011) and San Benedeto (2nd in 2014) from the Listed Prix Wild Monarch at Auteuil during the last ten years. Team Ditcheat is the home of the once raced Matterhorn, who finished third in the 2021 renewal in April. Previously trained by Gabriel Leenders, the Martaline gelding was unlucky not to make a winning debut following a bad mistake at the final hurdle. Subsequently bought on behalf of patron Johnny De La Hey, he looks a terrific prospect.

Both Footpad (7th in 2015) and Long Run (2nd in 2008), who won a dozen Grade 1 races between them, also made their debuts in the Prix Wild Monarch and fifteen runners assembled for the latest edition last spring. Positioned on the rail, Matterhorn was never too far off the pace before making his move on the approach to the second last off the hometurn. Leading at the penultimate hurdle, he was switched to the stands side and was still in front when losing his hind legs after the last. Handing the advantage to Paradiso, his chance soon disappeared but he rallied well to regain third position. Beaten eleven lengths, the form is strong with the David Cottin trained winner landing Listed and Grade 3 hurdles at the same track in May and June respectively. The eighth Issam has also won since. James Reveley rode the aforementioned Gaelic Warrior to finish sixth and when I spoke to him in August, he said: **"Matterhorn looks a very nice horse because Gabriel Leenders horses weren't running well at the time."**

Paul Nicholls was responsible for arguably the best juvenile hurdler last season in Monmiral, who also began his career in a three year old hurdle at Auteuil. Don't be surprised if this gelded son of Martaline follows a similar programme – low key to begin with before a tilt at the Grade 2 Summit Juvenile Hurdle at Doncaster (11th December). The stable have won three of the last five runnings and Town Moor will play to Matterhorn's strengths. Adrien Du Pont, Diego Du Charmil, Irish Saint and Solo all won Graded juvenile hurdles for the De La Hey family and expect this exciting three year old to do likewise this winter.

Probable Best Distance			-	2 miles			
Preferred Going			-	Good/Soft			

GOING:	R	W	P	TRACK:	R	W	P
Very Soft	1	0	1	Left Handed	1	0	1
				Galloping	1	0	1

TRIP:	R	W	P	JOCKEY:	R	W	P
1m 7f	1	0	1	A.Chitray	1	0	1

MONTE IGUELDO (FR)

4 b g Cokoriko (FR) – Petite Nany (FR) (Green Tune (USA))
OWNER: STEPHEN BEETHAM
TRAINER: O.GREENALL. Oldcastle, Malpas, Cheshire.
CAREER FORM FIGURES: 2

These are exciting times for everyone concerned with Stockton Hall Farm in Cheshire. Oliver Greenall enjoyed a personal best season during 2020/21 with 37 winners and the yard has received a huge shot in the arm during the spring/summer with the acquisition of some high quality equine talent. Emma Blue (£82,000), Jet of Magic (£75,000) and Zinc White (£310,000) are a trio of expensive recruits, plus a number of additions from France who belonged to the trainer's son Lord Daresbury.

Monte Igueldo was trained across the English Channel by Francois Nicolle and made his debut in a conditions hurdle at Auteuil in June. A big scopey gelding by Cokoriko, he was held up for the first half of the race by Angelo Zuliani. Making headway down the backstraight (jumped the path before the third last), he held every chance turning for home. Having hit the front after the last, he was worn down by the long time leader Sonigino (joined Paul Nicholls) who had the benefit of experience (two runs beforehand) and the stands rail. A length and a quarter separated the pair with three and a half lengths back to the third (Listed placed).

The four year old went through the race like an above average performer jumping very well throughout. He will make a cracking chaser one day but is more than capable of winning his share of hurdle races beforehand. Two miles on a galloping track ought to suit but there is a suspicion he will be even better over further. Bought by Stephen Beetham since, he is a tremendous prospect for his upwardly mobile stable.

POINTS TO NOTE:

Probable Best Distance			-	2m - 2m 4f			
Preferred Going			-	Soft			

GOING:	R	W	P	TRACK:	R	W	P
Heavy	1	0	1	Left Handed	1	0	1
				Galloping	1	0	1

TRIP:	R	W	P	JOCKEY:	R	W	P
2m 1f	1	0	1	A.Zuliani	1	0	1

MR INCREDIBLE (IRE)

5 b g Westerner – Bartlemy Bell (IRE) (Kalanisi (IRE))
OWNER: STEPHEN E. McCARTHY
TRAINER: H.DE BROMHEAD. Knockeen, Co.Waterford.
CAREER FORM FIGURES: 221
CAREER WIN: 2021: Jan NAAS Heavy MH 2m 3f

Lightly raced, Mr Incredible is another first rate novice chase prospect for Henry De Bromhead. Indeed, it will be disappointing if the Westerner gelding doesn't make an impact in Graded events this winter over two and a half miles plus.

The five year old began his career in point-to-points with Colin Bowe. Expert Declan Phelan explains: **"Rangy bay gelding, a €75,000 store. Travelled by Colin Bowe to Dromahane (Good/Yielding) for his sole point in October: in a tactical affair, most of the field were still bunched clearing the third last fence: than in a dash over the last two furlongs, Mr Incredible manoeuvred his path into second place jumping the last: he then mounted a challenge on the inside of the more experienced Carroll's Cottage and was forced to snatch up when the door closed, and had to be content with the runner up spot: given a clear passage on the run in, it would have been a close call. Bought to join Henry De Bromhead, he produced an excellent track debut, earning second to a future Grade 1 winner in an upper class 2m 4f maiden hurdle at Leopardstown (Soft). It was third time lucky, as he secured a fair scalp by handing Glens Of Antrim a four and a half lengths beating, whilst conceding the mare five pounds: the pair drawing 33 lengths away from the remainder in a Naas (2m3f : Heavy) maiden hurdle in January. Parked up for the rest of the season, he remains a horse with exciting potential. He has the size and scope to advance as a quality novice chaser and he will be competitive at distances from 2m 4f to 3 miles and has proven his versatility on contrasting terrain. One can certainly entertain the notion that he is capable of winning Graded chases as his career develops, under-estimate him at your peril."**

Nine and a half lengths runner-up behind Gaillard Du Mesnil (dual Grade 1 winner) at Leopardstown over Christmas, it was an excellent first run under Rules. Stablemate and Cheltenham Festival runner-up Magic Daze was a further eight and a half lengths back in third. He then beat another decent mare, Glens of Antrim, at Naas galloping strongly to the line in the process. The sort his trainer excels with, Mr Incredible will stay three miles and could develop into Brown Advisory Novices' Chase contender.

POINTS TO NOTE:

Probable Best Distance   -   2m 4f – 3 miles
Preferred Going   -   Soft
Connection's Comments: **"He's a lovely big chasing prospect, still a big baby and very raw. Colin Bowe recommended him to us."** Henry De BROMHEAD at Naas (31/1/21)

GOING:	R	W	P	TRACK	R	W	P
Heavy	1	1	0	Left Handed	3	1	2
Soft	1	0	1	Galloping	2	1	1
Good/Yield	1	0	1				

TRIP:	R	W	P	JOCKEY:	R	W	P
2m 3f	1	1	0	R.Blackmore	1	1	0
2m 4f	1	0	1	S.Flanagan	1	0	1
3m	1	0	1	B.O'Neill	1	0	1

MY DROGO

6 b g Milan – My Petra (Midnight Legend)
OWNER: Mr & Mrs R.KELVIN-HUGHES
TRAINER:.D.SKELTON. Shelfield Green, Warwickshire.
CAREER FORM FIGURES: 21111
CAREER WIN: 2020: Nov NEWBURY Good MH 2m; Dec ASCOT Soft Grade 2 NH 2m: 2021:
Mar KELSO Good/Soft Grade 2 NH 2m 2f; Apr AINTREE Good/Soft Grade 1 NH 2m 4f

"I think he is exceptional," were the words of Dan Skelton when inquiring about My Drogo a few days after the Milan gelding had finished runner-up on his debut in a bumper at Cheltenham. That assessment proved unerringly accurate as he won his next four starts over hurdles, including a Grade 1 at Aintree in April and he is now one of the hottest properties in British jump racing. Rated 155, the six year old has been brilliantly handled by the Skelton team and threatens to reach an even loftier figure over fences.

Out of a Grade 2 winning chaser, he belied his odds of 50/1 when chasing home the highly regarded I Am Maximus at Cheltenham in October before switching to obstacles. Despite his share of jumps errors, My Drogo quickened up well on the run-in to win a two miles maiden hurdle at Newbury's Winter Festival in late November. Grade 1 winners Buveur D'Air (2015) and Lostintranslation (2017) feature on the events roll of honour. His jumping was much more polished next time as he stayed on strongly to lift the Grade 2 Kennel Gate Novices' Hurdle at Ascot by nearly three lengths. The subsequent *Betfair* Hurdle winner Soaring Glory was six lengths back in third. **"My Drogo didn't surprise me because he's high-class, but the improvement with his jumping from Newbury to today has surprised me. We'd done loads of schooling with him but the improvement from that to today was incredible,"** commented his trainer afterwards. His connections purposely skipped the Cheltenham Festival and the Richard Kelvin-Hughes owned gelding returned to action following a break of 78 days defying a penalty in the Grade 2 Premier Novices' Hurdle at Kelso. Appreciating the step up in trip, he conceded five pounds and handed out a nine and a half lengths beating to the 136 rated Do Your Job. The best was yet to come though with My Drogo announcing himself a top-class novice hurdler when winning the Grade 1 Mersey Novices' Hurdle at Aintree by the same margin. With the exception of avoiding the stricken Lucky One who fell at the fourth last, Harry Skelton never had an anxious moment as his partner took over at the third last and defeat was never an option thereafter. Pulling away, he proved in a different league to his eleven opponents.

Chasing is very much on his radar this Autumn and, having spoken to Dan Skelton in August, he suggested that he wouldn't mind taking My Drogo to Carlisle for his chasing debut – there are a couple of two and a half miles novice chases at the Cumbrian track on Thursday 21st October and Monday 8th November. Grade 1 winning stablemate Protektorat won on his chasing bow at the same venue last season. Either way, he is very much one to look forward to over fences with the Marsh Novices' Chase likely to be his spring target. A clash with Bob Olinger would be something to savour.

POINTS TO NOTE:

Probable Best Distance - 2m – 2m 4f

Preferred Going - Soft

Connection's Comments: "It is a very exciting moment to be involved with a horse like him as he has got it all. The idea was to get through this season novice hurdling and next season go chasing and nothing will change. Despite the lure of better hurdles there has to be a point where you have to decide whether they are a hurdler or a chaser and given his breeding, size and jumping you have to go now or never. He has to have a good novice chase career to make it into a top class horse." Dan SKELTON at Aintree (10/4/21)

GOING:	R	W	P	TRACK:	R	W	P
Soft	2	1	1	Left Handed	4	3	1
Good/Soft	2	2	0	Right	1	1	0
Good	1	1	0	Galloping	2	2	0
				Stiff/Undul.	1	0	1
				Tight	1	1	0
				Tight/Undul.	1	1	0

TRIP:	R	W	P	JOCKEY:	R	W	P
2m	3	2	1	H.Skelton	5	4	1
2m 2f	1	1	0				
2m 4f	1	1	0				

PORTICELLO (FR)

3 b g Sholokhov (IRE) – Chinawood (FR) (Chichcastenango (FR))

OWNER: Mr O.HARRIS

TRAINER: G.L.MOORE. Lower Beeding, West Sussex.

CAREER FORM FIGURES: 1

CAREER WIN: 2021: Apr AUTEUIL Very Soft Hdle 1m 7f

The vast majority of Gary Moore's top notch jumpers have either been French bred or began their career's across the English Channel. Grade 1 winners Ar Mad and Sire De Grugy, plus Baron Alco (Grade 3), Camping Ground (Grade 2), Editeur Du Gite (Grade 3), Goshen (Grade 2) and Traffic Fluide (Grade 2) all fitted into that bracket. The West Sussex handler has excelled with juvenile hurdlers over the years and, as discussed, came very close to winning the Triumph Hurdle a couple of seasons ago.

The same trainer may have another live contender for the four year old event next spring in French recruit Porticello. A €20,000 foal, the son of Sholokhov was under the guidance of David Cottin in his native country. Making his debut in the Prix Grandak, a conditions hurdle at Auteuil in early April, he made a striking impression in a contest which was won by dual Grade 1 winner Frodon in 2015. He looked a strong stayer at the Parisian track picking up well after the second last before leading on the run-in and pulling away from stablemate Magistrato, who has joined Paul Nicholls since. A three lengths winner, the form has been boosted with the third (twice, including a Listed hurdle) and seventh winning subsequently. James Reveley rode in the race and says **"it is always a very good race and this year's renewal felt no different."** Bought privately soon afterwards, Porticello has settled in well to his new surroundings according to Moore. Indeed, he is described as **'a great big horse and I can't believe he has run already.'** Given his style of racing, one can envisage him being effective at tracks such as Cheltenham and Chepstow, which means something like the Grade 1 Finale Juvenile Hurdle at the latter venue (27th December) may come under consideration. Ironically, We Have A Dream, who won that event in 2018 beating the Moore trained Sussex Ranger, also made his racecourse debut in the Prix Grandak at Auteuil.

Given a summer break, Porticello will jump fences in time and is a tremendous addition to a yard which is blessed with a plethora of promising youngsters.

POINTS TO NOTE:

Probable Best Distance			-	**2 miles**			
Preferred Going			-	**Soft**			

GOING:	R	W	P	TRACK:	R	W	P
Very Soft	1	1	0	Left Handed	1	1	0
				Galloping	1	1	0

TRIP:	R	W	P	JOCKEY:	R	W	P
1m 7f	1	1	0	F. De Giles	1	1	0

SAINT FELICIEN (FR)
4 b g Saint Des Saints (FR) – In Race (FR) (Sageburg (IRE))
OWNER: ROBCOUR
TRAINER: G.ELLIOTT. Longwood, Co.Meath
CAREER FORM FIGURES: 1
CAREER WIN: 2021: Mar AUTEUIL Very Soft Hdle 2m 1f

Leading owner Brian Acheson and his Robcour team have assembled a formidable team of National Hunt horses with Cheltenham Festival winner Bob Olinger spearheading his challenge. That squad has been further bolstered during the spring/summer with new recruits Gentleman Joe (Henry De Bromhead), Jumping Jet (Gordon Elliott), Noche Negra (full-brother to Champion Chase runner-up Nube Negra) and the once raced Saint Felicien.

A four year old, Saint Felicien has joined Gordon Elliott and looks a Graded hurdler/chaser in the making having been bought by agent Alex Elliott. Trained in France by David Cottin, he made his debut in a conditions hurdle at Auteuil in March and created quite an impression winning hard held by eight lengths. Ridden by James Reveley, he raced handily before taken wide. Racing against the hedge down the backstraight, he struck the front approaching the second last before being pushed clear. Eased down close home, his rider was most impressed saying: **"He felt very good and one of the nicest horses I have ridden this year. In fact, he felt something else. I am not surprised he won because I had ridden work against him and knew he was very good. A chaser in the making, I think he will be top-class."**

The runner-up Gallipoli won next time at the same track before finishing third in a Grade 2 hurdle at Auteuil in April, while the third, fourth, fifth and ninth have also entered the winners' enclosure since. It will be interesting to see how Saint Felicien is campaigned this season. Still a novice until the end of November, he could be aimed at the Grade 1 Royal Bond Novice Hurdle at Fairyhouse (28th November) – Elliott has won three of the last four renewals, including with four year old Mengli Khan in 2017. Thereafter, the Saint Des Saints gelding will have to compete in open company and is likely to contest conditions/Graded hurdles. Given his age, chasing is unlikely to be on the agenda until next season.

Regardless of his immediate plans, Saint Felicien is a horse with a big future and another budding star for his high profile owner. Remember the name.

POINTS TO NOTE:

Probable Best Distance	-	**2m – 2m 4f**
Preferred Going	-	**Soft**

GOING:	R	W	P	TRACK:	R	W	P
Very Soft	1	1	0	Left Handed	1	1	0
				Galloping	1	1	0

TRIP:	R	W	P	JOCKEY:	R	W	P
2m 1f	1	1	0	J.Reveley	1	1	0

SAM BARTON

6 b g Black Sam Bellamy (IRE) – Bartons Bride (IRE) (Anshan)
OWNER: TREVOR HEMMINGS
TRAINER: EMMA LAVELLE. Ogbourne Maizey, Wiltshire.
CAREER FORM FIGURES: 3 - 5214
CAREER WINS: 2021: Jan DONCASTER Soft MH 2m 4f

It was announced in May that 26 year old Tom Bellamy will be the new stable jockey for Emma Lavelle, although Aidan Coleman retains the ride on four times Grade 1 winner Paisley Park. Bellamy will be looking forward to partnering a number of promising youngsters, including the Trevor Hemmings owned Sam Barton. Purchased for £12,000 as a yearling, the Black Sam Bellamy gelding has been brought along slowly and his connections' patience is expected to be rewarded now he switches to fences.

Having shown promise in an Exeter bumper the previous season, the six year old wasn't disgraced when fifth on his hurdles debut at Chepstow in October. Beaten thirteen lengths by the subsequent Grade 2 winner Star Gate, he was then a close second at Hereford the following month. Given a break of 65 days, Sam Barton showed what he is capable of when beating the well regarded The Edgar Wallace by two and a quarter lengths at Doncaster in late January. Overcoming a mistake at the second last, Adam Wedge's mount was in control thereafter and always holding the runner-up with the pair eighteen lengths clear of the third (subsequent dual winner Up For Parol was fourth). His trainer said the following month: **"He is a lovely horse that is clearly going to be a chaser. The race at Doncaster has worked out well and he has come on for that mentally and physically. I was impressed how easily he travelled through the race. Though he was clearly green when he got to the front, I loved how he went about it through the race."** He completed his education over hurdles by finishing a respectable fourth in the EBF Final at Sandown in mid March. Ridden with restraint, he made steady headway on the hometurn before moving into contention at the second last. Keeping on, he was beaten nearly twenty lengths in testing conditions.

With his rating of 132, he looks tailormade for a two and a half miles novices' handicap chase this Autumn. His connections feel he will be even better once stepped up to three miles for the first time and encounters better ground – he has only raced on soft and heavy. Reportedly to have schooled well over fences, Sam Barton is the type to be contesting a race such as the *Sky Bet* Chase at Doncaster one day.

POINTS TO NOTE:

Probable Best Distance	-	**3 miles**
Preferred Going	-	**Good/Soft**

Connection's Comments: "I was confident even though we hit the front too soon, which I couldn't do much about as Sam Barton took me there. He's a fine horse, who's still a big baby, and he'll make a lovely chaser." **Adam WEDGE at Doncaster (29/1/21)**

GOING:	R	W	P	TRACK	R	W	P
Heavy	1	0	1	Left Handed	2	1	0
Soft	4	1	1	Right	3	0	2
				Galloping	2	1	0
				Stiff/Undul.	2	0	1
				Tight	1	0	1

TRIP:	R	W	P	JOCKEY:	R	W	P
2m 1f	1	0	1	T.Bellamy	1	0	0
2m 3f	3	1	1	J.Bowen	1	0	1
2m 4f	1	0	0	A.Coleman	1	0	0
				A.Wedge	2	1	1

SHALLWEHAVEONEMORE (FR)

4 b g Authorized (IRE) – Princess Roseburg (USA) (Johannesburg (USA))
OWNER: STEVEN PACKHAM
TRAINER: G.L.MOORE. Lower Beeding, West Sussex.
CAREER FORM FIGURES: 1
CAREER WIN: 2021: Mar KEMPTON Good NHF 2m

Owner Steven Packham and trainer Gary Moore are responsible for the high-class hurdler Goshen who could be a very interesting proposition stepping up in trip this season. Still only five, he ploughed through the mud to win the Grade 2 Kingwell Hurdle at Wincanton by 22 lengths in February. Most effective when racing right handed and when the ground is testing, the gelded son of Authorized looks tailormade for something like the Grade 2 Coral Ascot Hurdle (20th November) over two miles three. It is not inconceivable he could return to the Berkshire track for the Grade 1 Long Walk Hurdle over three miles before Christmas.

The same connections are understandably excited about another gelded son of Authorized in the unbeaten Shallwehaveonemore. A cheap yearling (€7,000), his dam was a dual winner on the Flat in France and Listed placed over a mile. He appears to have inherited plenty of speed judged on his debut win in a bumper at Kempton in March. The two miles event has been dominated by former champion trainer Nicky Henderson in recent times with the Seven Barrows outfit winning five of the previous eight renewals, including with Mister Fisher (2018) and Shishkin (2019). Their representative last spring was the well bred Walking On Air. However, the 11/8 favourite was put firmly in his place with the Moore trained runner winning decisively by four and a half lengths. Held up in the early stages, Josh Moore's mount moved smoothly into contention turning for home before taking charge with a furlong to run. Shallwehaveonemore quickly settled the issue pulling away in the manner of an above average performer. The form has yet to be tested with the second, third and fourth not seen again.

Reported to have schooled well at home, Gary Moore is considering another bumper before embarking on his hurdling career. Blessed with a turn of foot, Shallwehaveonemore may always prove at his best on level tracks and one could envisage him returning to the Sunbury track for the two miles novice hurdle on Boxing Day – it has been won by subsequent Graded winners Altior (2015), If The Cap Fits (2017) and Mister Fisher (2018). This once raced four year old looked every inch a similar type last spring. Longer-term, it will be interesting to see if he is aimed at the *Betfair Hurdle* at Newbury in February. Novices have won 9 of the last 12 renewals and Moore is seeking his fourth win in the race – he has won it twice with five year olds – plus, Fifty Ball was runner-up as a novice last season.

POINTS TO NOTE:
Probable Best Distance - **2 miles**
Preferred Going - **Good/Soft**
Connection's Comments: "Shallwehaveonemore has gone through the race well and when I've gone to pick him up, I'm still on the bridle. He was having a bit of a look when he hit the front, but he's galloped out and through the line well. He's done everything nicely and hopefully he can keep coming forward." Josh MOORE at Kempton (20/3/21)

GOING:	R	W	P	TRACK:	R	W	P
Good	1	1	0	Right	1	1	0
				Tight	1	1	0

TRIP:	R	W	P	JOCKEY:	R	W	P
2m	1	1	0	Josh Moore	1	1	0

SOFT RISK (FR)
5 b g My Risk (FR) – Douce Ambiance (FR) (Kouroun (FR))
OWNER: JAMES WESTOLL
TRAINER: N.G.RICHARDS. Greystoke, Cumbria.
CAREER FORM FIGURES: 1
CAREER WIN: 2021: May AYR Soft NHF 2m

Former Carlisle racecourse chairman James Westoll tragically lost the 149 rated Glingerburn when suffering a fatal injury when falling at the third last in the Tennent's Cup Handicap Hurdle at Ayr in October 2015. The King's Theatre gelding won four times over hurdles, including the Grade 2 Premier Kelso Hurdle when beating Bristol De Mai by over three lengths.

The same owner is responsible for the unbeaten Soft Risk who, ironically, made a winning start to his career on the West coast of Scotland in May. Lining up in an eight runner bumper at Ayr in early May, he had reportedly caught the eye in a racecourse gallop at Carlisle beforehand and a bold introduction was expected. Confidently ridden by Brian Hughes, the My Risk gelding made smooth headway in the homestraight before taking over passing the two marker. Pushed clear, he wasn't hard pressed to score by nine lengths. His win impressed the former champion jockey and an exciting future over hurdles is anticipated. Bought for £40,000 as a three year old at the Goffs UK Spring Sale, he has been given plenty of time to mature.

Soft Risk possesses plenty of speed and will start his hurdles career over the minimum trip. Expect to see him line up at either Ayr, Carlisle or Newcastle and it is hoped James Westoll has another smart young horse on his hands. One of the nicest people in the sport, he deserves another good 'un.

POINTS TO NOTE:

Probable Best Distance			-		**2 miles**		
Preferred Going			-		**Soft**		

GOING:	R	W	P	TRACK:	R	W	P
Soft	1	1	0	Left Handed	1	1	0
				Galloping	1	1	0

TRIP:	R	W	P	JOCKEY:	R	W	P
2m	1	1	0	B.Hughes	1	1	0

SONIGINO (FR)

4 b g It's Gino (GER) – Soniador (FR) (Legolas (JPN))
OWNER: Sir A.FERGUSON, G.MASON, J.HALES & L.HALES
TRAINER: P.F.NICHOLLS. Ditcheat, Somerset.
CAREER FORM FIGURES: 4 - 11
CAREER WINS: 2021: May MOULINS Very Soft Hdle 2m 1f; Jun AUTEUIL Heavy Hdle 2m 1f

Paul Nicholls had the misfortune to lose two promising juvenile hurdlers during the spring/summer. Sadly, both Good Ball and Houx Gris are no longer with us. The former was owned by Sir Alex Ferguson, Ged Mason and John and Lisa Hales and the partnership has purchased the dual hurdles winner Sonigino as a replacement. Bought by Anthony Bromley, the four year old remains a novice for this season and brings a strong level of form from France with him.

By the same stallion as new stablemate Lalor, he raced three times over hurdles for David Cottin. Beaten around six lengths on his debut at Pau in December, he returned to action nearly six months later and was a comfortable winner at Moulins. Raced prominently, he jumped neatly and took over leaving the backstraight. Pushed clear after the second last, his rider Damien Mescam gave him a couple of reminders on the run-in but he crossed the line six and a half lengths in front (fourth has won over fences since). Thirteen days later, Sonigino produced an even better effort to win at Auteuil. Conceding weight all round, he led with a circuit to run and jumped beautifully. Having got in tight at the last, he handed the initiative to the aforementioned Monte Igueldo before rallying to win going away by a length and a quarter.

Snapped up during the summer, he has been campaigned exclusively over trips around two miles, but Sonigino is related to stayers and is expected to improve over longer trips. Something like the Grade 2 Winter Novices' Hurdle at Sandown (3rd December) could be a target. The champion trainer has won the race four times. Either way, he is another smart addition to Team Ditcheat.

POINTS TO NOTE:

Probable Best Distance	-	**2m – 2m f**
Preferred Going	-	**Soft**

GOING:	R	W	P	TRACK	R	W	P
Heavy	2	1	0	Left Handed	1	1	0
Very Soft	1	1	0	Right	2	1	0
				Galloping	2	2	0
				Tight	1	0	0

TRIP:	R	W	P	JOCKEY:	R	W	P
2m 1f	3	2	0	K.Nabet	2	1	0
				D.Mescam	1	1	0

STATE MAN (FR)

4 ch g Doctor Dino (FR) – Arret Station (FR) (Johann Quatz (FR))
OWNER: Mrs J.DONNELLY
TRAINER: W.P.MULLINS. Bagenalstown, Co.Carlow
CAREER FORM FIGURES: 2

Footpad could only finish a remote seventh in the Listed Prix Wild Monarch at Auteuil in April 2015 when trained by Robert Collet. Runner-up the following month at the same track, he was purchased soon afterwards on behalf of Simon Munir and Isaac Souede and subsequently won six Grade 1 races, including the Arkle Trophy at Cheltenham in 2018.

The Creachadoir gelding was trained by Willie Mullins and Ireland's champion trainer is in charge of the once raced State Man who finished runner-up in the same Listed contest at the Parisian track last year. Owned by M.L.Bloodstock and trained by Daniela Mele, he was towards the rear of the nineteen strong field for the majority of the contest. Overcoming a mistake in the backstraight, he made headway after the third last but was still in eleventh position turning for home. Staying on well, the Doctor Dino gelding got to within two lengths of Busselton (runner-up in a Grade 2 and third in a Grade 1 for Joseph O'Brien last season). The third Bimbo Has won a Grade 3 chase at Auteuil in June this year, while the fourth Hades has won over fences and finished third in a Grade 1 chase at France's number one jumping track.

Willie Mullins, via agent Pierre Boulard, snapped up State Man and the four year old now belongs to high profile owner Joe Donnelly. Despite being given an entry in the Triumph Hurdle last spring, Mullins purposely didn't run him last term in order to protect his novice status for this winter. The Doctor Dino gelding left the impression he stays well and it wouldn't be a surprise to see him ridden from the front over two miles for his new connections. The *Sky Bet* Supreme Novices' Hurdle at Cheltenham in March looks a realistic target. Mullins is seeking his eighth win in the Festival opener (Vautour (2014), Douvan (2015) and Klassical Dream (2019) won it as five year olds), while the Donnelly's claimed the prize courtesy of Shishkin in 2020.

POINTS TO NOTE:

Probable Best Distance	-	2m – 2m 4f		
Preferred Going	-	Soft		

GOING:	R	W	P	TRACK:	R	W	P
Very Soft	1	0	1	Left Handed	1	0	1
				Galloping	1	0	1

TRIP:	R	W	P	JOCKEY:	R	W	P
1m 7f	1	0	1	C.Lefebvre	1	0	1

THREE STRIPE LIFE (IRE)

5 br g Leading Light (IRE) – Hirayna (Doyoun)
OWNER: K.HAUGHEY & LAURA HAUGHEY & KIERAN T BYRNE
TRAINER: G.ELLIOTT. Longwood, Co.Meath.
CAREER FORM FIGURES: 14
CAREER WINS: 2021: Jan NAVAN Heavy NHF 2m

There is every reason to believe the first three home in the Cheltenham Festival bumper in March will develop into top-class novice hurdlers this term. That comment is also likely to apply to the fourth, Three Stripe Life, who belied his lack of experience to get within eight and a quarter lengths of Sir Gerhard. Bred to stay well, the five year old is expected to make his mark in the leading two and a half miles plus novice events in Ireland this winter for Gordon Elliott.

Purchased for €40,000 as a three year old, the Leading Light gelding is a half-brother to three miles winners Ballyshannon Rose and Sealous Scout. Well touted on his debut in a bumper at Navan in late January, Jamie Codd's mount moved strongly throughout before hitting the front approaching the two marker. Lengthening clear in the testing conditions, Three Stripe Life booked his ticket to Gloucestershire with a nine lengths win. Sent off 10/1 at the Festival, his 'stand in' trainer Denise Foster commented beforehand: **"Three Stripe Life is a lovely horse. He looked very impressive at Navan and everybody here is excited about him for the future. They all think he's a horse with real potential."** Ridden by Jack Kennedy, he still look babyish beforehand and raced keenly during the early stages. However, once settled he travelled well and held every chance coming down the hill. Keeping on without quickening inside the final quarter of a mile, he left the impression he will come into his own once stepped up in distance over obstacles. A tall rangy gelding, he was reportedly still weak last season.

Gordon Elliott has won the Grade 3 Monksfield Novice Hurdle at Navan (21st November) six times in the last ten years and the two and a half miles event looks an ideal target. Then, we will see the best of Three Stripe Life over three miles.

POINTS TO NOTE:

Probable Best Distance	-	2m 4f – 3 miles	
Preferred Going	-	Soft	

Connection's Comments: **"We think a good bit of him and he's done everything right at home. He was a big, backward horse last year and we didn't get to run him but we think he's a proper horse." Gordon ELLIOTT at Navan (29/1/21)**

GOING:	R	W	P	TRACK	R	W	P
Heavy	1	1	0	Left Handed	2	1	0
Good/Soft	1	0	0	Galloping	1	1	0
				Stiff/Undul.	1	0	0

TRIP:	R	W	P	JOCKEY:	R	W	P
2m	2	1	0	J.J.Codd	1	1	0
				J.Kennedy	1	0	0

VAUBAN (FR)

3 ch g Galiway – Waldfest (Hurricane Run (IRE))
OWNER: Mrs S.RICCI
TRAINER: W.P.MULLINS. Bagenalstown, Co.Carlow
CAREER FLAT FORM FIGURES: 4411
CAREER WINS: 2021: Jun LYON Soft 1m 3f; July VICHY Soft Listed 1m 4f

Rich Ricci is understandably excited about his latest purchase from France, Vauban and it is hoped the progressive three year old will develop into a leading contender for the Triumph Hurdle. Trained overseas by Philippe Decouz, he is from the family of St Leger winner and stallion Masked Marvel.

Unraced at two, the Galiway gelding shaped well on his first two starts at Longchamp and Chantilly during the spring finishing fourth on both occasions. He was beaten three and a quarter lengths by the subsequent German Derby runner-up Alter Adler at the latter venue. Vauban confirmed the promise of that run by running out an easy four and a half lengths winner at Lyon in late June. Held up, he made smooth headway on the outside in the homestraight before streaking clear to win decisively (second and third have won since). Less than a month later, he produced an even better display when overcoming traffic problems to win the Listed Prix Frederic De Lagrange at Vichy. Even though there were only six runners, the Jules Mobain's mount found himself hemmed in on the far rail and was forced to pull his mount wide. With ground to make up, Vauban showed good acceleration to lead close home and win by a short head from the Coolmore owned Friendly Face. His victory proved he possesses speed, stamina and determination, which will hold him in good stead for his future over timber.

Rated 104 on the Flat, Vauban is likely to return to the level at some stage but he has been bought with a hurdling career in mind, too. His jumping bow is eagerly anticipated.

POINTS TO NOTE:
Probable Best Distance	-	2 miles
Preferred Going	-	Soft

GOING:	R	W	P	TRACK:	R	W	P
Soft	3	2	0	Left Handed	1	1	0
Good	1	0	0	Right	3	1	0
				Galloping	4	2	0

TRIP:	R	W	P	JOCKEY:	R	W	P
1m 2f	1	0	0	Jules Mobain	3	2	0
1m 3f	1	1	0	R.Thomas	1	0	0
1m 4f	2	1	0				

SWITCHING STABLES

Gordon Elliott has taken charge of two exciting bumper performers. **JUMPING JET** was a 29 lengths winner at Gowran Park (Heavy) in March under 17 year old Kieran Callaghan when trained by Barry Fitzgerald. A five year old mare by Getaway, who cost €4,500 as a three year old, she powered away from Choice of Words who subsequently won a similar event at Punchestown by 13 lengths before finishing runner-up in a Grade 3 mares' bumper at the same track's Festival in late April. Bought privately since on behalf of Robcour, she is an exciting prospect for mares' novice hurdles.

Similarly, the triple Grand National winning trainer has acquired the dual winner **LEVEL NEVERENDING**. A four year old by Flemensfirth, he has been bought out of Joseph O'Brien's yard and is a horse with a bright future. Third on his debut at Tipperary in July, he then battled on gamely to win a bumper at the Galway Festival (Good) by half a length. However, the best was yet to come as he beat seven opponents, including three previous winners, by upwards of fifteen lengths at Killarney (Good) in August. His jockey Tom Hamilton said afterwards: **"He was very impressive as it looked a very strong race. He has improved from each run and is a very exciting horse going forward."** Given his age and the fact he is most effective on decent ground, it is possible he is kept to bumpers this season and aimed at the Cheltenham Festival championship event.

Don't forget to read my Diary @
www.mhpublications.co.uk

Please see pages 183-194
for details of the
One Jump Ahead Updates

OWNERS' ENCLOSURE
RICH & SUSANNAH RICCI
CHELTENHAM FESTIVAL WINNERS: 18

Saldier provided leading owners **Rich and Susannah Ricci** with their second win in the Galway Hurdle in the last four years during the summer. The Grade 1 winning hurdler shouldered 11st 10lb and a rating of 155 under Patrick Mullins, who was landing the valuable prize for a third time during the same period. The famous pink and green silks were carried to Grade 1 glory on eight occasions during the 2020/2021 campaign. 28 domestic winners in Ireland, plus a further five in the UK, including Monkfish's six and a half lengths success in the Brown Advisory Novices' Chase at the Cheltenham Festival in March, ensured it was another highly successful year for the Ricci's.

Once again, Chacun Pour Soi, Monkfish and Royale Pagaille (back to full fitness following a nasty injury sustained in the Cheltenham Gold Cup) will spearhead their challenge over fences this winter. However, following the retirement of Douvan, Faugheen and Benie Des Dieux – who won 23 Grade 1 races between them, including five at the Cheltenham Festival – it is very much a transition period for Rich and Susannah. Therefore, different to the interviews in the past, this article concentrates on their young horses, ten of which have yet to be seen in public wearing the 'pink and green.' Racing manager **Joe Chambers** has kindly run through these, including some exciting recruits from France. With that triumvirate of superstars enjoying their retirement, this could be 'the changing of the guard.'

ALLEGORIE DE VASSY was trained in France by Marcel Rolland and has plenty of experience having raced four times over hurdles. Runner-up at Compiegne in April, she was then a staying on third in a conditions hurdle at Auteuil later the same month. Beaten around two lengths, the winner Belle Promesse has subsequently won Listed and Grade 3 hurdles at the same track. A four year old, her sire No Risk At All has done well, including with former Champion Hurdle winner Epatante, and she looks a nice filly for mares' novice hurdles.

FEU DU BRESIL is a six year old who finished runner-up on his only start over hurdles in France. Second at Auteuil in October 2018, he has yet to run for us but is a very good looking horse by Blue Bresil. The form of his race at Auteuil worked out well and we are hoping we have a clearer run with him this season and he can make up for lost time.

FIGAROC is a similar type in that he was second over hurdles in France. Beaten less than a length at Compiegne in May 2019, he was unable to run last season but is back in training and it is a case of so far so good. A six year old by Masterstroke, his work at Willie's (Mullins) has always been good.

GAELIC WARRIOR ran three times over hurdles at Auteuil for Nicolas De Lageneste and Guillaume Macaire in France. We have bought some very good horses from the latter, including Vautour, and this is a three year old by Maxios. Sixth on his debut in a Listed hurdle in April, he was third on his next two outings. Beaten a length on his penultimate start, his form looks decent and he will hopefully do well in juvenile hurdles.

HA D'OR won a French bumper by six and a half lengths last year and he raced twice for us last winter. A promising third on his hurdles debut in a Grade 2 at Leopardstown on St Stephen's day, he was then too keen when contesting a Grade 1 at the Dublin Racing Festival at the same track in February. We have minded him since and purposely kept him as a novice for this season. We still harbour high hopes for him.

HORANTZAU D'AIRY is a half-brother to Venetia Williams' dual winning chaser Enzo D'Airy and he won an APQS Flat race by three parts of a length at Fontainebleau in September. The runner-up Hurrick Des Obeaux has won twice over hurdles at Auteuil since, including a Listed event. Previously trained by Hugo Merienne, he only arrived at Willie's in October and is very much a chasing type for the future. Only four, he is by Legolas and will be going straight over hurdles.

HUBRISKO hasn't raced since winning an APQS Flat race at Le Lion D'Angers in France during the summer of last year. Given plenty of time since joining Willie, it was always the plan to leave him off until this season. He looked impressive when winning and we are looking forward to seeing him over hurdles. A half-brother to Grand Bornand, who won on his chasing debut for us at the Galway Festival in July, he looks an exciting prospect.

MERCUREY is unraced and due to have his name changed shortly. A three year old by Muhtathir, the same sire as Envoi Allen, he has done some nice pieces of work and is one for bumpers in the New Year.

PAUL MARVEL is an interesting horse by Masked Marvel. A nice athletic four year old, he was previously owned by Walter Connors and was due to run in a point-to-point for Pat Doyle. However, he never ran and we bought him. He will start off in a bumper.

VAUBAN is a horse we are excited about having acquired him during the summer. Formerly trained in France by Philippe Decouz, he only raced four times on the Flat progressing with each start. Unraced at two, he shaped promisingly on his first two outing before winning by four and a half lengths at Lyon in June. He then produced a very good performance to win a Listed contest over a mile and a half at Vichy the following month. By Galiway, who has had very few jumpers to date, he is from a German family and has been bought to go hurdling. Rated 101, we haven't been as excited about a horse we have purchased off the Flat since Saldier.

Unnamed 3 b g Saint Des Saints (FR) – Jahra (FR)
We don't purchase many stores but he was bought at the Tattersalls Ireland Derby Sale in June (Lot 67). He will be given time but will hopefully make his debut during the second half of the season.

> **RICH'S HORSE TO FOLLOW: ALLEGORIE DE VASSY**
> **RACING MANAGER JOE CHAMBERS' HORSE TO FOLLOW: HUBRISKO**

TALKING TRAINERS
Kim BAILEY
Stables: Thorndale Farm, Withington Road, Andoversford, Cheltenham, Gloucestershire.
2020/2021: 59 Winners / 313 Runners 19% Prize-Money £669,714
www.kimbaileyracing.com

AJERO (IRE) 6 b g Red Jazz (USA) – Eoz (IRE)
A half-brother to Charbel, he enjoyed a very good season over hurdles winning four times. Following his victory at Kempton in November, we operated on his wind and that made a difference because it made it easier for David (Bass) to ride him. Having won at Market Rasen and Huntingdon, we ran him in the Grade 1 novice hurdle at Aintree, but he had had enough by that stage of the season. He is a nice horse who I hope will continue to be progressive off his mark 139. We will be aiming him at the decent two miles handicap hurdles and, although he didn't perform well at Aintree, I don't think racing left-handed will be a problem. He doesn't want the ground too soft though.

BALLETICON (IRE) 7 br g Arakan (USA) – Miss Garbo (IRE)
Lightly raced, he came back from a spell on the sidelines to win on his hurdles debut at Southwell in December. He had another couple of runs at Ludlow and Wetherby and the plan is to send him chasing this season. Yet to race beyond two miles, he will stay further.

BOBHOPEORNOHOPE (IRE) 6 b g Westerner – Bandelaro (IRE)
A winning Irish pointer, he had a good season over hurdles winning at Exeter and Doncaster before pulling up on his final two runs. We have operated on his wind since his run at Ffos Las in May and we are hoping that will make a difference. Set to go novice chasing, he stays well and I think he improve over fences.

CHARMING GETAWAY (IRE) 4 b g Getaway (GER) – Charming Leader (IRE)
Unraced, he did a couple of nice pieces of work last season and is hopefully one to look forward to. In all likelihood, he will start off in a bumper before going hurdling.

CHIANTI CLASSICO (IRE) 4 b g Shantou (USA) – Ballinderry Lady (IRE)
A lovely horse we bought at the Cheltenham April Sale having won a point-to-point for Colin Bowe in Ireland. The form looks strong, too, with the fourth and sixth winning subsequently. There is a possibility he will run in a bumper, but his future lies over hurdles and fences. He looks a very nice horse who I like a lot.

DOES HE KNOW 6 b g Alkaased (USA) – Diavoleria
I was pleased with him last season winning three times, including a Grade 2 novice hurdle at Cheltenham in November. We then ran him in the Grade 1 Challow Hurdle at Newbury but he ran out and we don't know why. Well held in very bad ground at Exeter in February, we ran him there because we were trying to qualify him for the Pertemps Final. Even though it was a small field, I thought he ran well in the Ballymore Novices' Hurdle at the Cheltenham Festival. A winning English pointer, he will go novice chasing and, while we will start him off over two and a half miles, I am expecting him to stay three miles in time.

EL PRESENTE 8 b g Presenting – Raitera (FR)
Enjoyed a fantastic season winning four times, including the Listed Badger Beers Silver Trophy at Wincanton in November. A close fourth in the bet365 Gold Cup at Sandown, we then ran him in the Sam Moreshead Perth Gold Cup because we were keen to win it. Unfortunately, the plan backfired and he fell early on. The Becher Chase at Aintree (4th December) is a possible target, although he doesn't want the ground too soft.

EQUUS DREAMER (IRE) 6 ch g Getaway (GER) – Thornleigh Blossom (IRE)
Runner-up in two of his three English point-to-points before joining us, I thought he would struggle to win a novice hurdle last season, but he had a good season scoring at Hereford in February. Runner-up at Carlisle last time, he found the inner hurdles track too tight but wasn't disgraced. He goes novice chasing and I hope he will improve over fences.

ESPOIR DE ROMAY (FR) 7 b g Kap Rock (FR) – Miss Du Seuil (FR)
A very nice horse who developed into a high-class novice chaser last season. Twice a winner at Huntingdon and Leicester, he was still in front when falling at the second last in the Grade 1 Mildmay Novices' Chase at Aintree last time. Nobody knows what would have happened, but we are hoping he will progress again this winter. The King George at Kempton (26th December) is the race I would like to aim him at with the Listed Colin Park Memorial Chase at Carlisle (31st October) an option in the Autumn.

FAIR FRONTIERES (IRE) 6 ch g Sans Frontieres (IRE) – Cappawhite Lass (IRE)
He is a nice type of horse who has joined us. Narrowly beaten in a maiden hurdle at Navan in January, the winner (Gars De Sceaux) has scored again since so the form looks sound. He will continue over hurdles.

FIRST FLOW (IRE) 9 b g Primary (USA) – Clonroche Wells (IRE)
Had a fantastic season winning three times, including the Grade 1 Clarence House Chase at Ascot. Sixth in the Queen Mother Champion Chase at Cheltenham, he is not the easiest to place because he needs to go right-handed and is ground dependent – he wants it testing. He loves Ascot (2311) and we have got the Tingle Creek Chase at Sandown (4th December) in mind for him, too. I suppose the Haldon Gold Cup at Exeter (2nd November) is a possible early target but it will depend on the ground.

FLIRTATIOUS GIRL (IRE) 5 b m Flemensfirth (USA) – Another Gaye (IRE)
A lovely mare who didn't surprise us last season winning two of her three starts in bumpers. Indeed, the only surprise was when she was beaten on her second start. However, she made amends with a very good performance at Sandown winning a Listed mares' bumper. We thought beforehand that the track would suit her more than Huntingdon. Suited by soft ground, she has schooled well over hurdles and will be aimed at mares' events.

GETAWEAPON (IRE) 6 b m Getaway (GER) – Milan Serenade (IRE)
Started her hurdles campaign well with victory at Hereford and finishing second a couple of times at Ffos Las and Ludlow. She then had a few niggling little problems and hasn't run since. The summer break has done her good though and, being a former winning pointer, she should have no trouble jumping fences.

GLANCING GLORY (IRE) 5 br m Presenting – Littlemissthistle (IRE)
Bought at the Goffs UK December Point-to-Point Sale at Yorton Farm, she ran in two Irish points winning on the second occasion. We have given her plenty of time since and she looks very well. She will be running in mares' only novice hurdles.

HAMILTON DICI (FR) 4 b g Coastal Path – Umbria Dici (FR)
A winner over hurdles at Warwick in December for Jane Williams, we bought him shortly afterwards at the Cheltenham Sales with the intention of sending him novice chasing this season as a four year old. In fact, he will be my first ever four year old novice chaser. We have schooled him over fences and he looks a natural jumper.

HENDRA HOUSE (IRE) 5 b g Yeats (IRE) – Gold Strike (IRE)
He is a lovely unraced horse we bought at the Goffs Land Rover Sale as a three year old. He has had a few issues hence he is still to run but he's got plenty of ability.

HURLERONTHEDITCH (IRE) 5 ch g Shirocco (GER) – Maid of Malabar (IRE)
Having unseated his rider in an Irish point, he then won a point-to-point bumper at Wexford in March. We bought him later the same month at the Cheltenham March Sale at Newmarket. We haven't done much with him yet, but he looks a nice horse who will probably go straight over hurdles.

I SPY A DIVA 4 b f Telescope (IRE) – Molly's A Diva
We trained her dam to win seven races and she made a winning start to her career in a bumper at Worcester during the spring. It was a bit of a rush to get a run into her, but she did it well and we will aim her at mares' novice hurdles this season.

IMPERIAL AURA (IRE) 8 b g Kalanisi (IRE) – Missindependence (IRE)
Won the Listed Colin Parker Memorial Chase at Carlisle followed by a Grade 2 chase at Ascot last season. His big target was the Ryanair Chase at the Cheltenham Festival but unfortunately he bled. It was an extraordinary race because they went too quick and only five horses finished. He has never bled before and hopefully it won't happened again. The intention is to step him up in trip this season and he is under consideration for the Charlie Hall Chase at Wetherby (30th October). He has had a wind operation during the summer.

INCE ROSE 6 ch g Malinas (GER) – Cinderella Rose
From a family we know well, he has been unlucky not to have won a race before now. Runner-up in three of his four races, he has done a lot of growing and suffered with sore shins. However, I think he will progress and his day will come. He will continue over hurdles.

INFLAGRANTE (IRE) 5 ch g Getaway (GER) – Maggie Connolly (IRE)
A lovely big unraced horse, he has had a few issues, but his owners have been patient and he could develop into a very nice horse.

JAVA POINT (IRE) 6 b g Stowaway – Classic Sun (GER)
A winning Irish pointer, he won over hurdles at Warwick during the spring having finished second a couple of times. All set to go over fences, we will look for a suitable novices' handicap chase off his mark of 120. He stays well and should get three miles later on.

KYNTARA 5 b g Kayf Tara – Speed Bonnie Boat
He is a very nice horse who won a point-to-point for Melanie Rowley by eight lengths last Autumn. Bought privately afterwards, he didn't surprise us when winning a bumper at Warwick in February. He has always shown us plenty at home since arriving. We will start him off over hurdles at a low level and take our time. He has plenty of speed and is an exciting horse for the future.

MARTON ABBEY 5 br g Orientor – Naywye
He has an unusual pedigree being by a sprinter, but I liked him at the Cheltenham April Sale. Runner-up in his only point-to-point in the UK last season, he comes from the same source as Does He Know and I was guided by his trainer who recommended him. He is likely to go straight over hurdles.

MR GREY SKY (IRE) 7 gr g Fame And Glory – Lakil Princess (IRE)
A dual bumper winner a few seasons ago, he has a lot of ability but has had his fair share of problems, too. Third on both his outings over hurdles last season, he will continue over timber and hopefully we can have a clear run with him.

NEWTIDE (IRE) 8 br g Getaway (GER) – C'Est Fantastique (IRE)
Third on his reappearance at Haydock last season, he had a wind operation afterwards but burst a blood vessel next time at Ascot. A few of our horses weren't right at the time and hopefully there won't be a recurrence in the future. Rated 140, he stays well and handles soft ground and will follow a similar programme.

ONE FOR ROSIE 8 gr g Getaway (GER) – Whisky Rose (IRE)
A lovely horse who joined us last season having had a spell on the sidelines. Unbeaten in both his races over fences, he was impressive on his chasing debut at Leicester in February and followed up at Carlisle beating a decent rival in the process. The plan is for him to return to the Cumbrian track for the Listed Colin Parker Memorial Chase (31st October), a race we won last season with Imperial Aura. He goes well on soft ground.

PARC D'AMOUR (IRE) 4 b g Walk In The Park (IRE) – Mal D'Amour (IRE)
He is a nice big unraced horse who we bought at the Goffs Landrover Sale in August last year. We have purposely taken our time with him and he will start off in a bumper.

PARTY FUZZ 6 b g Great Pretender (IRE) – Very Special One (IRE)
Placed in a bumper and over hurdles at Uttoxeter and Warwick respectively last season, we are going to send him chasing. He is 16.2hh and jumps well and I am expecting him to develop into a better chaser. With his rating of 117, he will run in a novices' handicap chase. He likes soft ground.

PAY THE PILOT 4 b g Telescope (IRE) – Becky B
Runner-up in a point-to-point bumper at Punchestown during the spring when trained by Sean Doyle, we acquired him at the Cheltenham March Sale at Newmarket a couple of weeks later. He is a lovely big horse who has grown and filled his frame. We are going to take our time with him and he is therefore unlikely to be in action until Christmas time. He looks a very nice horse and one for the future.

PERCY VEERING 4 ch g Sir Percy – Saltpetre (IRE)
He is another who we purchased at the Goffs Land Rover Sale last summer. A big backward horse, he has benefited from his summer break and will start off in a bumper.

PHANTOM GETAWAY (IRE) 4 ch g Getaway (GER) – Belle Provence (FR)
Bought at the Goffs UK Spring Sale at Doncaster in May, he is a lovely young horse who won the second of his two Irish points for Donnchadh Doyle. It is early days, but he has come back in following his summer break looking well and is a big strong four year old. He is hopefully one to look forward to.

PIPESMOKER (FR) 6 b g Authorized (IRE) – Pisa (GER)
A new arrival during the summer, he has some very solid form during the last two seasons running well against Grade 1 winners Chantry House and Sporting John. Not an easy horse to train having had his issues, we will take it gently with him and see how he progresses. We have the option of remaining over hurdles or going chasing.

ROSE AND THISTLE 4 b f Blue Bresil (FR) – Cinderella Rose
An unraced half-sister to Inca Rose, we trained the dam to win four times and she is a lovely filly. She nearly ran last spring but the ground dried out, so we decided to leave her off and give her a break. I would expect her to run in a bumper and we will take it from there.

SAINT BIBIANA (IRE) 4 b f Sholokhov (IRE) – En Vedette (FR)
Similar to Rose And Thistle, she came close to making her debut in a bumper last season but the ground went against her. A half-sister to The Milan Girl, who won for us a couple of years ago, she looks a nice filly.

SAYADAM (FR) 4 b g Saint Des Saints (FR) – Catmoves (FR)
Unbeaten in both his runs winning a bumper on his debut at Kelso before following up over hurdles at Warwick in May. I thought he was going to be quite a small horse, but he has grown three inches since his last run and developed into a fine big four year old. He will spend this season over hurdles.

SHANTOU EXPRESS (IRE) 6 ch g Shantou (USA) – Spanker
Had a productive season over hurdles winning at Exeter and Sedgefield and was runner-up on three occasions. He appears to handle most types of ground and will go novice chasing over two and two and a half miles. He is a nice horse.

STARVOSKI (IRE) 6 b m Aizavoski (IRE) – Telstar (IRE)
She is a lovely mare and an out and out chaser in the making. A winning pointer, we thought she was going to be a stayer but benefited from dropping back to two miles over hurdles. Having won at Southwell in February, she was unlucky not to follow up at Sandown next time when making a mistake at the second last. A big strong mare, she will be running in mares' novice chases over two miles.

THE EDGAR WALLACE (IRE) 6 b g Flemensfirth (USA) – Annalecky (IRE)
Won nicely over hurdles at Uttoxeter in March and the form has worked out, too (runner-up won twice since). If we had known it was going to continue to rain during the spring we would have run him again but we put him away for the summer. He is going to be a chaser but remains eligible for novice hurdles until the end of October, so he will continue down that route for the time being. He is a decent horse who will make a nice chaser eventually.

THRUTHELOOKINGLASS 4 b g Kayf Tara – Amazing D'Azy (IRE)
Homebred, we trained the mother to win a couple of times and he is a nice type. A big strong horse, he ought to be running in a bumper around Christmas time.

TIME FOR HOLLIE 5 b m Black Sam Bellamy (IRE) – Any Pearl
Yet to run, we nearly ran her last season, but the ground wasn't suitable. I have been pleased with her during the summer and she looks a nice mare who will have a run in a bumper.

TWO FOR GOLD (IRE) 8 b g Gold Well – Two of Each (IRE)
He had a good season winning a decent handicap chase at Warwick and finishing runner-up in a Listed handicap chase at Wetherby. Third at Kempton and Kelso, too, we ran him in the Topham Chase at Aintree, but he missed the break which is never ideal for a horse who likes to race prominently. Rated 150 over fences, he isn't going to be the easiest to place but I hope he can win another nice handicap this season. Two and a half miles on soft ground are his optimum conditions.

VINNDICATION (IRE) 8 b g Vinnie Roe (IRE) – Pawnee Trail (IRE)
Runner-up in the Charlie Hall Chase at Wetherby, he then unseated his rider in the Ladbrokes Trophy at Newbury next time. Sixth in the Stayers' Hurdle at Cheltenham in March, we are going to send him back over fences this season. His first target is the Sodexo Gold Cup Handicap Chase at Ascot (30th October), which he won a couple of years ago.

YOUNEVERCALL (IRE) 10 b g Yeats (IRE) – Afarka (IRE)
A remarkable horse who won the Grade 2 Select Hurdle at Sandown in April for the second time. Fourth in the Grade 1 Long Walk Hurdle at Ascot, he wasn't disgraced in the Stayers' Hurdle at Cheltenham and that proved he can operate left-handed. With that in mind, he will reappear in the Grade 2 West Yorkshire Hurdle at Wetherby (30th October).

TRAINER'S HORSE TO FOLLOW: THRUTHELOOKINGLASS

Don't forget to read my Diary @
www.mhpublications.couk

Oliver GREENALL

Stables: Stockton Hall Farm, Oldcastle, Malpas, Cheshire.
2020/2021: 37 Winners / 329 Runners 11% Prize-Money £303,110
www.olivergreenall.co.uk

ADJOURNMENT (IRE) 5 b g Court Cave (IRE) – Cherry Eile (IRE)
One of the top rated five year old UK pointers last season, he finished second on both his starts for Francesca Nimmo before we bought him at the Cheltenham April sale. Runner-up at Maisemore Park in March conceding ten pounds to the winner, he is a lovely big horse and very much a chaser for the future. He shows speed in his work and travelled strongly in his races and will probably have a run in a bumper before going hurdling. Two and two and a half miles is likely to be his trip over hurdles. He looks promising.

ASK THE DOC (IRE) 5 b g Ask – Benedicta Rose (IRE)
A big chasing type with a massive stride, he finished fourth in a point-to-point bumper at Tipperary in March. He has settled in well since arriving and looks one for novice hurdles over two and a half miles this year.

BLACKWELL BOY (IRE) 4 ro g Carlotamix (FR) – Koochie Baby (IRE)
A huge horse, he still looked weak when arriving. Runner-up in a point-to-point for Tom Weston, he did well to finish so close and can only improve given his physique. A strong galloper, he will go novice hurdling over two and a half miles plus.

BLUE COLLAR GLORY (IRE) 4 b f Fame And Glory – Rosy De Cyborg (FR)
Only four, we have given her a break having raced three times in bumpers during the spring/ summer. Narrowly beaten on her penultimate start at Stratford in May, she won nicely next time at Worcester. The hood has helped and she has plenty of ability and will go mares' novice hurdling in the Autumn.

DONAIRE (IRE) 5 b g Califet (FR) – Grangeclare Lark (IRE)
A nice horse who finished runner-up in a bumper at Kelso in March when trained by Stuart Crawford. The form looks strong, too, with the winner scoring again over hurdles since. A good traveller, we will run him in another bumper in the Autumn before going hurdling. We haven't schooled him over jumps yet, but we don't envisage any problems.

DONDIAM (FR) 4 b g Diamond Boy (FR) – Nouvelle Donne (FR)
Purchased at the Cheltenham April Sale at Newmarket, we haven't done a lot with him yet. A winner at Chaddesley Corbett in his only point-to-point for Francesca Nimmo, he is a lovely horse with speed and class and we will try and win a bumper with him before sending him over hurdles.

DOOYORK (IRE) 5 b m Shantou (USA) – Hannah Rose (IRE)
A nice big mare who won the second of her two Irish points for Colin Bowe. Acquired at the Cheltenham May Sale at Newmarket, she is a full-sister to the useful Zero Ten and appears to be suited by decent ground. She seems to have plenty of speed, too, and will run in a mares' bumper in October.

DUKE OF DECEPTION (IRE) 4 b g September Storm (GER) – Mrs Peachey (IRE)
Still green when running in a couple of Irish points in May, he finished third last time. Bought a few days later, he is a big chasing type who could run in a bumper before sent hurdling. He looks a galloper who will benefit from racing over two and a half miles plus.

EMMA BLUE (IRE) 4 b f Mahler – Rhapsody In Blue (GER)
A very nice filly we purchased at the Cheltenham May Sale. She won her sole point-to-point in Ireland by three lengths only five days earlier and is a filly with plenty of quality. She has speed, too, and will start off in a mares' bumper in the Autumn. Her point win was gained on good ground.

EVANDER (IRE) 6 br g Arcadio (GER) – Blazing Belle (IRE)
Has been a star for us winning twice over hurdles and then he won a couple of times over fences last season. He struggled with his jumping initially but it got better and better and he won at Doncaster and Ludlow. Pulled up at Sandown in February, the ground was testing and he slithered on landing after the second last. We are hoping he will continue to improve and win a nice race over fences one day. Effective over two and a half miles, he will stay three miles in time. He doesn't want the ground too soft and is best suited by smaller fields.

FIVE BAR BRIAN (IRE) 7 br g Elusive Pimpernel (USA) – Vayenga (FR)
Previously trained by Tim Reed and Willie Mullins, he has only raced once for us finishing second in a maiden hurdle at Ayr in October. Unfortunately, he got a leg afterwards hence he hasn't run since. All being well, he will be back in action around December time. Two miles on very soft ground are his conditions. Indeed, the ground is the key to him.

GARETH CAEL (FR) 5 gr g Montmartre (FR) – Dallia (FR)
A winner of his second point-to-point at Mollington in May when trained by Bradley Gibbs, he will start off in a novice hurdle over two or two and a half miles. Expect him to improve once going handicapping.

GESSKILLE (FR) 5 b g Network (GER) – Nashkille (FR)
Arrived during the summer, he showed a good level of form over hurdles and fences in France. He won over hurdles at Toulouse in June before finishing third over fences at Auteuil next time. Fourth in a Listed chase at Dieppe on his latest start, he will go hunter chasing in the New Year and ought to be a real force in that sphere.

GOLD DESERT 4 ch g Mastercraftsman (IRE) – Tendency (IRE)
He's been a star for us since we bought him out of Richard Hannon's yard in August last year. He took well to jumping, winning juvenile hurdles at Sedgefield and Catterick before chasing home subsequent Grade 1 winner Monmiral in a Grade 2 event at Doncaster in December. Injured after finishing third on the Flat at Southwell in January, he will be back in action in the New Year. A tough horse who stays well, he handles easy ground and ought to be competitive in two and two and a half miles handicap hurdles.

HERBIERS (FR) 4 b g Waldpark (GER) – Quanlanke (FR)
A real stable star, he arrived from France in the Autumn and kept improving throughout last season. Well thought of in France, he wasn't right when disappointing on his British debut in a bumper at Huntingdon. However, he never looked back thereafter winning three of his five

races over hurdles. Successful in handicaps at Ascot and Sandown during the spring, two miles on good ground is ideal. The plan is for him to run in the four year old hurdle at Chepstow (8th October) and we are then likely to enter him in the Greatwood Hurdle at Cheltenham (14th November). Only four, he has always looked smart at home and is open to further improvement.

HERITIER (FR) 4 b g Fuisse (FR) – Toscane (FR)
Raced twice over obstacles in France but didn't fire over hurdles or fences. Switched to bumpers, he won at Lyon before finishing second at Vichy last time. He came over here soon afterwards and we have done a lot of schooling with him. We will aim him at two miles novice hurdles.

HOMME PUBLIC (FR) 4 b g Cokoriko (FR) – Uddy (FR)
Runner-up twice over hurdles at Auteuil when trained by Francois Nicolle, we ran him soon after he arrived from France and he finished second again at Catterick in February. Sean Quinlan rode him and felt he took a blow at the second last. He improved for that outing winning next time at Market Rasen. We then ran him in the Boodles Juvenile Hurdle at the Cheltenham Festival, but the ground went against him. He has grown during the summer and is one to look forward to in two miles handicap hurdles. Soft ground is ideal and we feel he is on a fair mark.

HORACIO APPLES (FR) 4 ch g Saddex – Apple's Noa (FR)
A big backward four year old who is owned by Highclere Thoroughbred Racing. We nearly ran him during the spring but the ground wasn't right, so we left him off. The break has done him good and he will go novice hurdling over two and a half miles in the Autumn. He jumps well.

JET OF MAGIC (IRE) 5 b g Jet Away – Ginandit (IRE)
He is a gorgeous big horse we bought at the Tattersalls Cheltenham March Sale at Newmarket. A four lengths winner of a heavy ground point-to-point bumper at Punchestown a fortnight earlier for Denis Murphy, he travelled strongly throughout. He has plenty of class and is an exciting prospect. We will start him off in a two miles novice hurdle before stepping him up in trip later on.

LETTHETRUTHBEKNOWN (IRE) 5 b m Shirocco (GER) – Pescetto Lady (IRE)
Half-sister to dual Punchestown Festival winner Burn And Turn, she is a former stablemate of Jet of Magic. Fourth in her only Irish point, she won a bumper by eight lengths at Cork in April. We brought her back into work earlier because she appreciates better ground and she will be aimed at a mares' bumper in September/October before going jumping. Two miles ought to suit her over hurdles.

MISS TARA MOSS 6 b m Kayf Tara – Brackenmoss (IRE)
Consistent over hurdles, she won over two and a half miles at Sedgefield in March and will improve again when stepping up to three miles later on. Indeed, she is crying out for that trip. She is capable of winning again over hurdles before going chasing later on.

MONTE IGUELDO (FR) 4 b g Cokoriko (FR) – Petite Nany (FR)
Probably as good as we have got, he looks very exciting and is one for the future. Trained in France by Francois Nicolle, he wasn't fully wound up for his debut over hurdles at Auteuil in June but still ran well in second. Showing signs of greenness, he stayed on well and is a proper big chasing type. He isn't short of speed though and will be suited by two miles novice hurdles on soft ground. We could start him off at a big galloping track like Wetherby.

PATAGONIA (FR) 4 b g Ballingarry (IRE) – Daramour (FR)
Unraced, he is a very well bred four year old being a full-brother to Diego Du Charmil. We have done plenty with him and he will make his debut in a bumper in the Autumn. We will then send him hurdling over two miles. He is likely to want some cut in the ground.

PHIL DE PAIL (FR) 4 gr g Silver Frost (IRE) – Dame De Pail (FR)
We really like him and feel he has improved during the summer. A big horse last year, he ran in three bumpers finishing third on his first start at Newcastle. Fourth at Wetherby last time, we were lucky to get so many runs into him. Very laid back, he is a galloper who will want a trip over hurdles. We may start him off over two miles but he will be suited by two and a half miles plus. Measuring over 17hh, he is a chaser for the future.

POST CHAISE (IRE) 4 b g Shirocco (GER) – Trazona Kit (IRE)
Still green and backward, he was an encouraging third in a point-to-point for Tom Weston during the spring. He will go novice hurdling but is another who will improve once going handicapping over two and a half to three miles.

PYM (IRE) 8 b g Stowaway – Liss Rua (IRE)
A Listed chase winner for Nicky Henderson, we bought him at the Goffs UK Spring Sale at Doncaster in May. He had his first run for us in the Summer Cup at Uttoxeter in June but came back sick. We switched him back to hurdles a month later at the same track and he really enjoyed it finishing second. It will have done his confidence a lot of good. He was bought to run in some nice races in the Autumn, but he doesn't want soft ground though and we will probably give him a mid season break before bringing him back in the spring.

THE QUESTIONER (IRE) 5 ch g Ask – Cush Bach (IRE)
Another we bought at the Doncaster Spring Sale, he didn't look the quickest when a staying on second in his only Irish point in April. A tough genuine type, he stays very well and will be at home in two miles six or three miles novice hurdles on soft ground this winter.

THE WILD WILD SEA 5 b m Gentlewave (IRE) – Sting In The Gale
Runner-up on her debut in a mares' bumper at Newbury in March, she was a bit disappointing on her next two starts but had probably had enough by the time she ran at Cheltenham and Southwell. Given a break since, she jumps very well and will contest mares' novice hurdles over two and two and a half miles. We are expecting her to improve over jumps.

TWOTWOTHREE (IRE) 8 b g Shantou (USA) – Sibury (IRE)
A three times winner over fences, he produced a very good performance to win at Wetherby on Boxing Day. The step up to two and a half miles suited him and, having began his career in point-to-points, we are expecting him to stay three miles eventually. We hope he will continue to improve.

WASASTYLEQUEEN 6 b m Schiaparelli (GER) – As Was
Half-sister to Welsh National runner-up The Two Amigos, she loves soft ground and jumps very well. A winning pointer, she was off the track for nearly two years prior to finishing third in a bumper at Carlisle in February. She ran a blinder that day and will appreciate stepping up in trip over hurdles. Two and a half to three miles mares' novice hurdles on soft ground will suit her.

ZINC WHITE (IRE) 3 gr g Vadamos (FR) – Chinese White (IRE)

An exciting prospect who was progressive on the Flat winning twice this year for Ralph Beckett. A wide margin winner at Wetherby and Salisbury, he loves soft ground and is ideal for juvenile hurdling. Bought at the Goffs London Horses in Training Sale in June on behalf of Stephen Beetham, he jumps brilliantly at home. We will start him off low key, possibly at Wetherby (13th October). We know he handles the track and he stays very well. The Grade 2 Summit Juvenile Hurdle at Doncaster (11th December) and the Grade 1 Finale Juvenile Hurdle at Chepstow (27th December) are options later on. Long-term, we will aim him at some good staying handicaps back on the Flat.

TRAINER'S HORSE TO FOLLOW: EMMA BLUE

TRAINER'S ASSISTANT (JOSH GUERRIERO) HORSE TO FOLLOW: MONTE IGUELDO

Philip HOBBS
Stables: Sandhill, Bilbrook, Minehead, Somerset.
2020/2021: 54 Winners / 464 Runners 12% Prize-Money £681,377
www.pjhobbs.com

AUBA ME YANG (IRE) 5 b g Fame And Glory – No Bodys Flame (IRE)

Yet to run for us, he was declared to run at Chepstow in February but was lame. Given time off since, he ran in a couple of bumpers for Jamie Snowden finishing third and fourth prior to joining us. He has schooled well over hurdles and, even though we will probably start him off over two miles, he will be suited by further.

BIG SHARK (IRE) 7 b g Vinnie Roe (IRE) – Castlelost (IRE)

A big strong horse, he missed the whole of last season due to a tendon problem but is back in work. Twice a winner over hurdles at Worcester and Hereford, he has some good form and is very much a chaser in the making. He stays three miles and appreciates soft ground. A horse who has struggled to hold condition in the past, we are hoping that will get better as he gets older.

CAMPROND (FR) 5 b g Lope De Vega (IRE) – Bernieres (IRE)

Ex-French, he has won twice over hurdles at Taunton and Market Rasen. He has run some good races in defeat, too, finishing runner-up at Aintree and third in the Swinton Hurdle at Haydock. Only beaten a length in fourth in the Summer Handicap Hurdle at Market Rasen in July, I think he would have won if he had jumped the last two hurdles better. Despite that, he is gradually getting his jumping together and it should continue to improve. He then finished second at Stratford in September. Keen when he first arrived, he is effective over two miles but will stay further in time.

CHALGROVE (FR) 5 b g Le Havre (IRE) – Exit To Derawlin (IRE)

He is enormous and the heaviest horse in the yard. His work prior to making his debut in a bumper at Kempton had been encouraging and he made a very good start to his career when winning narrowly. He jumps well at home and we will start him off in a two miles novice hurdle.

CROSSING THE BAR (IRE) 4 b g Poet's Voice – Ship's Biscuit
Well bred, he is a half-brother to Mekong who was Listed and Group 3 placed on the Flat. He has only just arrived having been bought at Tattersalls August Sale. Rated 83 on the Flat, he stays well having won over a mile and six at Carlisle in May. We will school him with a view to going hurdling.

DEFI DU SEUIL (FR) 8 b g Voix Du Nord (FR) – Quarvine Du Seuil (FR)
Disappointing in both his starts at Cheltenham and Ascot last season, we are hoping he can get back on track this year. He has had a wind operation since his run in the Clarence House Chase at Ascot and he has had a good break at Martinstown Stud during the spring/summer. We haven't made any plans yet but need to decide whether to keep him over two miles or step him up in distance. Having won the Grade 1 JLT Novices' Chase at Cheltenham a couple of years ago, we know he stays two and a half miles and I have always thought he will get even further. We kept him over two miles last season because it looked an open division. However, it looks a lot stronger this time around.

DEISE ABA (IRE) 8 b g Mahler – Kit Massini (IRE)
Inconsistent last year, he produced a good performance to win the same three miles handicap chase at Sandown in February which he had won the previous season. However, he pulled up in his three other starts. He doesn't like to be crowded in his races but has plenty of ability. Three miles plus on soft ground are his optimum conditions.

DEMOPOLIS (FR) 7 b g Poliglote – Princess Demut (GER)
Won over hurdles at Hereford in December and was then fourth and second over fences at Carlisle and Fontwell respectively. I view him as a genuine two mile chaser who is capable of winning more races. He appears to handle any ground.

DOSTAL PHIL (FR) 8 b g Coastal Path – Quiphile (FR)
A talented horse who won on his chasing debut at Newbury in January. He stayed on well to finish third in the Red Rum Handicap Chase at Aintree in April. While he possesses enough speed for two miles, I think he will be at his best over two and a half miles. He copes with soft ground and has the ability to win a decent handicap chase this season.

EARTH COMPANY (IRE) 5 bb g Arcadio (GER) – Lady Rhinestone (IRE)
He is a nice horse who ran well in his first couple of bumpers. Fourth at Wincanton on his debut, he then finished second at Kempton before disappointing last time at Stratford. We have operated on his wind since and we are looking forward to sending him novice hurdling.

EARTH LORD (IRE) 5 ch g Mahler – Glebe Beauty (IRE)
Full brother to the dual Grade 2 winner Sutton Place, he is very much a chaser in the making but will continue over hurdles for the time being. We tinkered with his wind after his first couple of runs and he improved finishing third at Wincanton and then a close second at Taunton. Two and a half miles is his trip and we are hoping he will progress this season.

FOR LANGY (FR) 6 b g Day Flight – Jubilee II (FR)
Missed last season due to a leg injury, he will be back this winter and is a horse with ability. A winner on the Flat and over hurdles in France, he has only raced once for us finishing third behind Masters Legacy at Taunton. Capable of winning races, he will go handicap hurdling.

GOSHEVEN (IRE) 8 b g Presenting – Fair Choice (IRE)
Has had breathing issues and benefited from a wind operation last year. He raced three times at Doncaster last season winning on his second outing before finishing runner-up last time. He has a good level of form and stays well. A big strong horse, he will go over fences and we will start him off in a novices' handicap chase.

GREAT OCEAN (FR) 5 b g Great Pretender (IRE) – Diamond of Diana (FR)
A new recruit, we bought him at the Goffs UK Spring Sale in May having run in three Irish points for Denis Murphy. Placed on his first two starts, he won by eight lengths last time. Recommended to us, I liked him at the sales and he will be suited by novice hurdles over two and a half miles plus.

GUERNESEY (FR) 5 gr g Martaline – Myrtille Jersey (FR)
Runner-up behind the subsequent Grade 2 winning novice chaser Ga Law over hurdles in France, he has only raced a handful of times for us. Placed at Wincanton and Warwick last season, he had an issue with his back, which has hopefully been rectified. He looks favourably treated and will continue in handicap hurdles for the time being. Long-term, he will jump a fence.

HEAD AND HEART 4 b f Mount Nelson – Don't Stop Me Now (FR)
Bought privately, she was runner-up in her only Irish point-to-point for Denis Murphy in April. She looks a nice filly and may have a run in a mares' bumper before going hurdling.

HONESTLYNTRUFULLY (IRE) 5 b g Getaway (GER) – Sixty Forty (IRE)
Another we acquired at the Doncaster Spring Sales in May, I don't know a lot about him yet. He had a couple of runs in bumpers for Pam Sly finishing third at Warwick last time. His form looks OK and, while we haven't schooled him, he looks athletic and will hopefully make his mark in novice hurdles.

HOPE YOU DO (FR) 4 b g Boris De Deauville (IRE) – Une Tournee (FR)
A bumper winner in France, he ran OK in three starts over hurdles finishing third at Chepstow last time. He is a typical French horse who has taken a while to acclimatise. We are therefore hoping he will improve this season and benefit from stepping up in trip. Rated 107, he will start off in a suitable novices' handicap hurdle.

ICEBURGH BAY (IRE) 5 b g Sageburg (IRE) – Aspelenie (IRE)
Ran in two Irish points for Sean Doyle winning easily on the second occasion. Bought on behalf of the Philip Hobbs Racing Club at the Cheltenham May Sale at Newmarket, he will probably go straight over hurdles over two and a half miles.

JATILUWIH (FR) 7 ch g Linda's Lad – Jaune De Beaufai (FR)
Narrowly beaten in a hunter chase at Worcester in May, he won a point-to-point during the Autumn but then had an issue with his eye. He will run in handicap chases during the first half of the season and then revert back to hunter chases in the New Year.

JERRYSBACK (IRE) 9 b g Jeremy (USA) – Get A Few Bob Back (IRE)
Despite the fact it's a while since he has won, he retains plenty of ability. Third behind subsequent Grade 1 winner Dashel Drasher at Ascot in January, he ran in the Irish National last time but I don't think it suited him. He will continue to run in the good staying handicap chases.

KALOOKI (GER) 7 gr g Martaline – Karuma (GER)
A big strong horse who has been backward and needed time. An impressive winner on his chasing debut at Newbury, he was third in a couple of Grade 2 novices at Newbury and Ascot before being narrowly beaten in a handicap at the former track last time. Rated 144, I think he will make his mark in two and a half miles handicap chases, although he stays further. He handles soft ground.

KEEP WONDERING (IRE) 7 b g Scorpion (IRE) – Supreme Touch (IRE)
Had an issue with his back which meant he missed last season. A winning pointer, he has only raced twice over fences winning in good style at Ffos Las. Two and a half miles on soft ground is ideal and we will be aiming him at handicap chase in such conditions.

LANGLEY HUNDRED (IRE) 4 b g Sholokhov (IRE) – Theregoesthetruth (IRE)
A nice unraced horse who has done everything right at home. He jumps and works well and we will start him off in a bumper in the Autumn.

LITTLE RIVER BAY (IRE) 6 b m Shirocco (GER) – Penneyrose Bay
Successful in her first three races last season gaining victories at Wincanton, Fontwell and Newbury, she produced a very good performance at the last named track. However, she was disappointing next time in a Grade 2 mares' novices' hurdle at Sandown and we don't know why. Rated 132 over hurdles, she jumps well and we are thinking of sending her over fences. She ought to do well in mares' novice chases over two and a half miles.

LONGSHANKS (IRE) 7 b g Scorpion (IRE) – Cash A Lawn (IRE)
Placed in an English point-to-point prior to joining us, he has been a difficult horse to keep condition on. We have given him a long break and he is a big horse who will be going over fences before too long. A winner over hurdles at Wincanton in February, he is rated 121 and will be one for novices' handicap chases.

LUTTRELL LAD (IRE) 5 b g Beat Hollow – Fairly Definite (IRE)
A very nice horse who isn't over big but has a lot of ability. A dual bumper winner at Market Rasen and Taunton, he ran a very good race at Aintree finishing fourth in a Grade 2 event. His schooling over hurdles has gone well and he will be in action in September/October because he prefers better ground. We will start him off over two miles because he isn't slow.

MASTERS LEGACY (IRE) 6 br g Getaway (GER) – Gently Go (IRE)
Twice a winner over hurdles a couple of seasons ago, he was a bit disappointing in his two outings last term. Admittedly, he needed the run on his reappearance at Taunton but we were expecting more from him next time at Newbury. Hopefully that was only a blip and he will be back to his best this time around. We will give him another run over hurdles before going chasing.

MONEY SPINNER (IRE) 4 b g Soldier of Fortune (IRE) – Floral Spinner
A nice youngster who was in training last year but has yet to make his debut. He has schooled well and I like him. His owners aren't overly keen on bumpers so I would imagine he will go straight over hurdles.

MUSICAL SLAVE (IRE) 8 b g Getaway (GER) – Inghwung
There is no doubt he is a horse with plenty of ability, but I was disappointed with him last season. Having run a promising race at Newbury on his reappearance, he failed to build on it and I don't know why. Three miles handicap chases will be on his agenda and the handicapper has given him a chance by dropping him a few pounds.

MY KEEPSAKE 5 br m Kalanisi (IRE) – Dudeen (IRE)
Showed ability in bumpers last season finishing third at Taunton and second at Wincanton. Disappointing last time at the latter track, we are hoping she can leave that run behind. A half-sister to Catherines Well who we trained to win over hurdles, she has been schooled and will contest mares' novice hurdles.

OFF THE PLANET (IRE) 6 ch g Presenting – Kings Diva (IRE)
I have always thought he was a nice horse and is open to improvement. Fourth over hurdles at Taunton during the spring, we were keen to run him again, but the ground wasn't suitable. A big horse, he will jump fences but will continue over hurdles for the time being.

ONE FOR YOU (IRE) 6 b g Yeats (IRE) – Tempest Belle (IRE)
Has had a few issues with a joint but came good in the spring winning twice at Ludlow and Market Rasen. A half-brother to Grade 1 winning chaser Monalee, he stays well and appreciated stepping up in trip. Raised five pounds since his last win, I hope he is better than his mark and will continue to progress. He has summered well.

ORBYS LEGEND (IRE) 5 b g Milan – Morning Legend (IRE)
A lovely horse who has won two of his three starts over hurdles. I was delighted with his performance at Sandown in March winning by a dozen lengths and he looks progressive. His only defeat over hurdles came at Exeter on his penultimate start when the ground was desperate. The Silver Trophy at Chepstow (9th October) is a possible target – we have won it three times in the past. Longer-term, he is a big strong horse who finished runner-up in an Irish point and jumping fences will be his game.

POL CROCAN (IRE) 6 br g Shirocco (GER) – She's All That (IRE)
Surprised us when he won over hurdles at Wincanton in December and then he followed up a couple of months later. Over the top by the time he pulled up at Sandown last time, he is open to more improvement and will stay over hurdles for now. He is a big strong horse though who will jump fences later on.

PULLING STUMPS (IRE) 4 b g Soldier of Fortune (IRE) – Pride of The Braid (IRE)
Purchased at the Goffs UK Spring Sale in May, he won a bumper at Ludlow for Phil and Mel Rowley earlier the same month. He still looked green and immature and the runner-up has won on the Flat since to give the form some substance. We haven't done a lot with him yet, but he has settled in well and hopefully one to look forward to in novice hurdles this season.

SHARP SHADOW (IRE) 5 br m Fame And Glory – Sharps Express (IRE)
Bought at the Cheltenham May Sale at Newmarket on behalf of Joanna Peppiatt, she won her only Irish point-to-point for Denis Murphy earlier the same month. She has summered well and looked a strong stayer when winning, suggesting two and a half miles mares' novice hurdles will suit her.

SMARTY WILD 7 b g Fair Mix (IRE) – Blaeberry
Big, powerful horse, he won at Kempton and ran some good races in defeat last season. Still lightly raced over fences, he should progress and, while two and a half miles is his trip at the moment, he will stay further.

SPORTING JOHN (IRE) 6 bb g Getaway (GER) – Wild Spell (IRE)
It was fantastic to win the Grade 1 Scilly Isles Novices' Chase at Sandown. Unfortunately, he didn't back it up in his subsequent two starts at Cheltenham or Aintree. He was a high-class novice hurdler a couple of seasons ago and when he is at his best, he is a very good horse. He spent the summer in Ireland and we haven't made any plans for him. I suppose Graduation chases would be an option because he has only won once over fences. In terms of trip, he stayed well at Sandown but isn't short of speed either.

ST BARTS (IRE) 7 b g High Chaparral (IRE) – Lindeman (IRE)
A dual winner over hurdles the previous season, he looked very good when winning over fences at Newbury in December. Only fifth next time at Uttoxeter, he found the ground too quick. He is at his best on testing ground – it was desperate conditions when he won over hurdles at Ascot one day. A strong stayer, we are likely to give him one run before aiming him at the Welsh National at Chepstow (27th December).

STELLAR MAGIC (IRE) 6 b g Arctic Cosmos (USA) – Inter Alia (IRE)
Looked useful when winning his first two starts over hurdles at Taunton, including when beating a subsequent Grade 2 winner on the second occasion. Pulled up next time at Warwick, it transpired he had broken a bone in his knee. He underwent surgery afterwards and the operation went well. Back in work, he will run in handicap hurdles and I would like to think he is on a good mark. Two and a half miles is his trip.

THYME HILL 7 b g Kayf Tara – Rosita Bay
Had a very good season winning the Grade 2 Long Distance Hurdle at Newbury in November and Grade 1 Liverpool Hurdle at Aintree in the spring. Narrowly beaten in the Long Walk Hurdle in between, it was obviously disappointing to miss the Cheltenham Festival due to a muscle problem. It was fantastic to see him win at Aintree though and we were going to take him to Auteuil in France but he had a minor issue with his back. We have sorted that out now though and the plan is for him to remain over hurdles. He has schooled well over fences, but he isn't over big and is one of, if not the best staying hurdlers around in any case. He will reappear in either the West Yorkshire Hurdle at Wetherby (30th October) or Long Distance Hurdle at Newbury (26th November) followed by the Long Walk Hurdle (18th December) once again.

TRUCKIN AWAY (IRE) 8 br g Getaway (GER) – Simons Girl
Produced some good performances last season winning at Doncaster and finishing second at Ludlow on his previous start. The ground at Doncaster was very soft and we were concerned about whether he would handle it, but he won nicely. Not disgraced in the Midlands National, he stays well and we will be aiming him at three miles plus handicap chases.

WILDFIRE WARRIOR (IRE) 6 b g Flemensfirth (USA) – Lady of Fortune (IRE)
Having shaped with plenty of promise in a couple of bumpers the previous campaign, he took well to hurdling last season. A close third at Exeter in November, he overcame greenness to win at Ludlow next time. Unfortunately, he got struck into and missed the rest of the season. A nice young horse, he needs more experience and will stay over hurdles. Handicap hurdles over two and a half miles are the plan.

ZANZA (IRE) 7 b g Arcadio (GER) – What A Bleu (IRE)
Despite winning a decent handicap at Newbury on Ladbrokes Trophy day in November, he didn't have a lot of luck over fences last season. He was travelling strongly when falling at the third last at Cheltenham's December meeting. We then purposely saved him for the Grand Annual Chase at the Festival but he got badly hampered by a faller towards the end of backstraight and was pulled up shortly afterwards. Sixth in the Red Rum Chase at Aintree, he didn't run badly but found the track too sharp. He will follow a similar programme and hopefully win a decent handicap this winter, although he doesn't want extremes of ground.

> **TRAINER'S HORSE TO FOLLOW: LUTTRELL LAD**

Alan KING
Stables: Barbury Castle Stables, Wroughton, Wiltshire.
2020/2021: 54 Winners / 405 Runners 13% Prize-Money £792,351
www.alankingracing.co.uk

CALL OF THE WILD (IRE) 4 b g Fame And Glory – Glory Days (GER)
A horse I have always liked, he was impressive when winning on his debut in a bumper at Huntingdon in May. His work had been good beforehand so his victory wasn't a surprise. From a family we know well, he is a half-brother to Chatez, who did well for us winning seven races. He spent the summer in Ireland with his owner J.P.McManus. We haven't discussed whether he will have another run in a bumper or go hurdling. He has plenty of speed and will start off over two miles once he goes jumping. He is an exciting prospect.

CANELO (IRE) 8 ch g Mahler – Nobody's Darling (IRE)
Enjoyed a good season winning at Aintree in November before taking the Grade 3 Rowland Meyrick Handicap Chase at Wetherby on Boxing Day. A faller in the Grand National last time, I don't know whether he will be aimed at the race again. Like Call of The Wild, he had a summer holiday in Ireland at Martinstown Stud. Rated 147, we will be looking at all the good staying handicap chases. Only eight, I hope he will continue to improve.

CARAMELISED 3 b c Dansili – Caster Sugar (USA)
Raced a few times on the Flat for Richard Hannon before joining us in the summer. He hadn't been here long before winning on his hurdles debut at Stratford in late July. While he hadn't shown much at home, he impressed me on the track and then followed it up with an even more emphatic victory at the same venue less than a month later. His next race will be at Market Rasen (25th September) – Katchit won the same contest in 2006. It was good ground at Stratford, but I don't see why he won't handle some ease underfoot.

COOL STONE 5 b m Kayf Tara – Stoney Path
Half-sister to Stoney's Treasure who we trained, she had a couple of runs in bumpers and I was pleased with her second outing when third behind stablemate Moonamacaroona. Not the biggest, she will go hurdling and, while she will stay further, we might start her off over two miles because she is inclined to be buzzy and needs to learn to settle.

DAL HORRISGLE 5 b g Nathaniel (IRE) – Dalvina
Has been in good form during the summer winning twice at Uttoxeter and Market Rasen. He disappointed at Doncaster in December and we gave him a break and that did him a lot of good. He has got his confidence back now and we have tidied up his wind since his last run. A very good Flat horse, he stays two and a half miles over hurdles and I think he will get further, too. Still a novice, we have plenty of options off his mark of 129 but he doesn't want the ground too soft. He is in good order at home.

DEYRANN DE CARJAC (FR) 8 b g Balko (FR) – Queyrann (FR)
Had surgery after his run at the Cheltenham Festival over a year ago and I was never happy with him last season. I thought he ran well at Warwick in May, but he was sore after he came back from Market Rasen next time. He has always possessed a big engine and I haven't lost faith in him.

EDWARDSTONE 7 b g Kayf Tara – Nothingtoloose (IRE)
Won over hurdles at Market Rasen before running some very good races in defeat. Third in the *Betfair* Hurdle at Newbury, he was a close fifth in the County Hurdle at the Cheltenham Festival before finishing third at Aintree over two and a half miles. He schooled very well over fences last season but, unfortunately, didn't get very far at Doncaster on his chasing debut over Christmas. We then thought it was too late in the season to carry on over fences hence we switched back to hurdles. The plan is to resume his chasing career and, while he has enough speed for two miles, he is settling much better now and stays further. He should make a very useful novice chaser.

ERNEST GRAY (IRE) 4 b g Walk In The Park (IRE) – Emily Gray (IRE)
Out of a Listed and Grade 3 winning mare, he is an interesting horse who we bought at the Cheltenham March Sale at Newmarket. Successful in a point-to-point bumper at Punchestown earlier the same month when trained by Colin Bowe, we gave him a pop over hurdles soon after arriving. Trotting at the moment, we haven't discussed whether he will run in another bumper or go hurdling.

FINEST VIEW 4 b f Passing Glance – Call Me A Legend
The dam won six races for us and this filly has always worked well at home. She looked good when winning on her debut in an all-weather bumper at Lingfield in February. We then ran her in the Grade 2 mares' bumper at Aintree and she travelled well for a long way before tiring. She was still a bit weak last year and has benefited from her summer break. It is tough for four year old fillies against older mares in those Graded/Listed events. She has a lot of speed and we may run her in a Listed bumper in the Autumn and then take a view as to whether to send her hurdling.

GREEN PLANET (IRE) 4 b g Australia – Maleha (IRE)
Bought at the Tattersalls February Sale, he was placed on the Flat at Chelmsford and Lingfield before disappointing at York last time. It was one run too many so we gave him a break afterwards. Fourth in a bumper for his previous connections, he will go novice hurdling over two miles.

HASEEFAH 4 b f Teofilo (IRE) – Halaqa (IRE)
Ex-French, she had three runs on the Flat for us during the summer. Runner-up at Chelmsford and Goodwood, she has had a break since which has done her good. We have schooled her over hurdles and she jumps well. We will give her another run on the Flat, but we are looking forward to sending her jumping.

HAZARD COLLONGES (FR) 4 b g Coastal Path – Prouesse Collonges (FR)
He has a good pedigree and we sent him to Lingfield for a bumper in February expecting him to go close. However, he didn't run his race so perhaps he didn't enjoy the all-weather. He has grown a lot since – it is possible he was still weak when he ran. I like him and he has schooled well over hurdles. I don't know whether he will have another run in a bumper.

HER INDOORS (IRE) 4 b f Raven's Pass (USA) – Superfonic (FR)
She took well to jumping and enjoyed a fine season. Having won a Listed fillies' juvenile hurdle at Doncaster in late January, she rounded off the campaign with victory in a Grade 3 fillies' juvenile handicap hurdle at Cheltenham in April. Given a break since, she may have a run on the Flat before being aimed at the decent mares' hurdles. Two miles suits her, but I think she will improve for a step up to two and a half miles this year.

JAY BEE WHY (IRE) 6 b g Yeats (IRE) – Lady Bernie (IRE)
A lovely big horse who won an Irish point before we bought him. I like him a lot and we are hoping he will develop into a smart novice chaser this season. A dual winner over hurdles at Warwick, he wasn't beaten far in a Grade 2 novice at the same track in between. Still quite leggy last year, he has done well physically during the summer and I think he is a very good horse. Two and a half miles is his trip.

KALMA 3 b f Mukhadram – Peters Spirit (IRE)
Dual winner on the Flat this year, she scored at Nottingham and Wolverhampton. She has schooled well over hurdles and the plan is to send her jumping in the Autumn. I think she will stay the trip and doesn't mind some ease in the ground. The Listed fillies' juvenile hurdle at Aintree (4th December) is likely to be her first target with one run beforehand. It is a race we have won three times in the past.

MAID ON THE MOON 4 b f Pether's Moon (IRE) – Handmaid
By a stallion who is doing OK, she is a likeable filly who was a bit free early on when making her debut at Newbury. She learned plenty though and was unlucky not to be second next time at Fontwell. She has progressed through the summer and will run in mares' novice hurdles this season.

MAJOR DUNDEE (IRE) 6 b g Scorpion (IRE) – Be My Granny
A bit in and out last year, he won over hurdles at Chepstow and finished second a couple of times. He disappointed at Kempton and Ayr but came back with a nasty cut from the former track having suffered an over reach. It is possible he doesn't want to be crowded in his races. Rated 124, he will go over fences and we will start him off in a suitable novices' handicap chase over two miles six plus.

MASACCIO (IRE) 4 gr g Mastercraftsman (IRE) – Ange Bleu (USA)

A horse I have always liked, we purposely didn't over race him last year. He ran two good races in bumpers winning on his debut at Doncaster in November and then we gave him plenty of time because he was still weak. Runner-up under a penalty at Ayr's Scottish National meeting in the spring, he was unlucky not to maintain his unbeaten record, but I was still delighted with the run. We haven't decided whether to give him one more run in a bumper or go hurdling.

MESSIRE DES OBEAUX (FR) 9 b g Saddler Maker (IRE) – Madame Lys (FR)

He is an exciting horse who took well to chasing winning twice at Wincanton, including the rescheduled Grade 2 Dipper Novices' Chase. Pulled up over three miles at Wetherby last time, he was too free during the race and didn't stay the trip. He was fine afterwards and we will drop him back to two and a half miles. A strong traveller in his races, we won't over race him.

MIDNIGHTREFERENDUM 8 b m Midnight Legend – Forget The Ref (IRE)

An easy winner on her chasing debut at Fontwell, she should have won a Listed mares' chase at Exeter in February but was in front too soon. Still lightly raced over fences, I think there is more to come from her in mares' chases.

MIDNIGHTS LEGACY 4 b c Midnight Legend – Giving

Has been running very well on the Flat this summer winning a valuable handicap at Epsom on Derby day before finishing fourth in the Old Newton Cup at Haydock. The plan is for him to go back over hurdles having run twice at Wetherby last season. He wasn't at his best on either occasion because he was struggling with his breathing at the time. That has been sorted out and he has proved he is a very decent horse with his runs on the Flat this year. He is a gorgeous horse who should do well in novice hurdles.

MOONAMACAROONA 5 b m Flemensfirth (USA) – Forever Present (IRE)

A lovely mare who won two of her three races in bumpers last term. Having finished third on her debut at Market Rasen, she produced good performances to win at Warwick and Chepstow. While she could start off over two miles over hurdles, stamina looks to be her strong suit and she will benefit from stepping up to two and a half miles.

NINA THE TERRIER (IRE) 5 b m Milan – Shees A Dante (IRE)

Sweet filly who won first time out in a bumper at Doncaster. She then narrowly missed out on some black type when fourth in a Listed event at Huntingdon before Christmas. Following a couple more runs, we switched her to hurdles and she did it well at Warwick in May. Strong at the finish, she will be even better over two and a half miles. She will continue in mares' novice hurdles.

NOBBY 7 b g Authorized (IRE) – Magic Music (IRE)

A smart bumper horse, he suffered a horrific injury at Newbury and was off the track for nearly two years. He ran well on his hurdles debut at Newbury before having two more runs at Hexham and Southwell. He still retains plenty of ability and will continue in novice hurdles.

NOTACHANCE (IRE) 7 b g Mahler – Ballybrowney Hall (IRE)
Produced two good performances to win the Anne Duchess of Westminster Memorial Handicap Chase at Bangor followed by the Grade 3 Classic Handicap Chase at Warwick. Disappointing on his next two starts, it transpired he had spread a hind shoe and got a nail in his foot when running in the Grand National Trial at Haydock. We then thought he was OK to run in the Scottish National at Ayr but found he had split his hoof in half afterwards. We can therefore put a line through those last two runs. He has had some remedial work done since and is 100% again. Long distance staying handicap chases will once again be on his agenda.

OCEANLINE (IRE) 3 b g Adaay (IRE) – Ocean Bluff (IRE)
A tough and progressive horse on the Flat, he has been bought by Million In Mind with a view to going juvenile hurdling. A winner at Nottingham in June and Sandown in August, he stays well and I have been pleased with his schooling over jumps.

ON TO VICTORY 7 b g Rock of Gibraltar (IRE) – Clouds of Magellan (USA)
Twice a winner over hurdles at Wincanton and Warwick, he ran well at Sandown on the final day of the season. Runner-up in a Listed race at Goodwood in May, he will go back over jumps and we will aim him at some decent handicap hurdles over two miles.

POTTERMAN 8 b g Sulamani (IRE) – Polly Potter
He is a star winning twice last season, including the bet365 Gold Cup at Sandown. Runner-up in the Listed Badger Beers Silver Trophy at Wincanton, too, things didn't happen for him at Perth last time. He has had a good break since though and we will probably give him one run before aiming him at the Ladbrokes Trophy at Newbury (27th November). He doesn't want the ground too soft though.

RAYMOND TUSK (IRE) 6 b h High Chaparral (IRE) – Dancing Shoes (IRE)
A grand horse who joined us earlier in the year and he has run some very good races on the Flat this spring/summer. Third in Listed company at Nottingham in April on fast ground, he appreciates some ease underfoot and I was delighted with his performance at Royal Ascot. Not beaten far in second in the Duke of Edinburgh Stakes, he has had a holiday since and the plan is to send him hurdling. Still an entire, he will have another run on the Flat before going jumping. Rated 105, he is an exciting horse.

SCEAU ROYAL (FR) 9 b g Doctor Dino (FR) – Sandside (FR)
Enjoyed a tremendous season winning the Welsh Champion Hurdle, Grade 2 Elite Hurdle and Grade 2 Game Spirit Chase. It was a great pity what happened in the Queen Mother Champion Chase at Cheltenham because he was beaten less than four lengths having been badly squeezed up on the rail before the home turn. He would have gone very close with a clear run. We haven't made any plans for him yet, but we could switch between hurdles and fences once again. I have been keen for a while to try him over two and a half miles, so that is something we will consider. He doesn't want heavy ground though.

SENIOR CITIZEN 8 b g Tobougg (IRE) – Mothers Help
A winner at Newton Abbot, he ran two very good races over the National fences at Aintree. Two miles six is the limit of his stamina range and he prefers decent ground. His first target is the Grand Sefton Handicap Chase at Aintree (6th November) once again – seventh in it last year on unsuitably soft ground, the race is a month earlier this year.

SON OF RED (IRE) 4 b g French Navy – Tarziyma (IRE)
Successful on his hurdles debut at Newcastle, he incurred a setback after his run in the Grade 2 Adonis Hurdle at Kempton. Back in work, he remains lightly raced and there is more to come from him. Still immature physically last year, he will be aimed at two miles handicap hurdles and is on a workable mark.

SONNING (IRE) 3 gr g The Gurkha (IRE) – Moon Empress (FR)
Placed behind the subsequent Epsom Derby and King George winner Adayar as a two year old, he won over ten furlongs at Beverley in April. He has had a break since his last run at Newbury in July but will have another run on the Flat before going juvenile hurdling. A mile and a quarter appears to be his best trip, having tried a mile and a half a couple of times, but I am hoping he will stay two miles over jumps.

THE GLANCING QUEEN (IRE) 7 b m Jeremy (USA) – Glancing (IRE)
A former winning Irish pointer, she was smart in bumpers and over hurdles winning twice at Warwick and Bangor. Third in the Grade 1 Challow Hurdle at Newbury and fifth at the Cheltenham Festival, we are looking forward to schooling her over fences with a view to her going novice chasing. She could be an exciting chaser and, while we will probably start her off over two miles, she stays two and a half miles very well.

TRITONIC 4 ch g Sea The Moon (GER) – Selenography
Rated 97 on the Flat, he took well to hurdling winning at Ascot before producing a very good performance at Kempton in the Grade 2 Adonis Hurdle. A ten lengths winner, he wasn't right at Cheltenham when finishing fifth in the Triumph Hurdle. We ran him in the Duke of Edinburgh Stakes at Royal Ascot and, although he ran well for a long way, he did too much early on in testing ground and didn't see out his race. Laid back at home, he raced with the choke out. We gave him a break afterwards and he will go back hurdling in the Autumn. The Masterson Holdings Hurdle for four year olds at Cheltenham (23rd October) looks an obvious starting point.

UNIVERSAL DAVE 5 b g Universal (IRE) – Nant Y Myndd
A winning Irish pointer, he was bought for the Noel Fehily Racing Club at the Goffs UK Spring Sale at Doncaster in May. He spent the summer with Noel and he is likely to go straight over hurdles in the Autumn. Having raced in three points, plus a bumper, he has got some experience.

VALLERES (FR) 6 b g Coastal Path – Duchesse Pierji (FR)
A horse I like a lot, he won twice over hurdles at Wetherby and Fontwell and finished runner-up on his three other outings. Despite that, he was still suffering a bit from sore shins, so I think he will improve again this year. We were going to school him over fences in the spring, but the ground dried up. I don't envisage him having any problems though because he is a good jumper and a winning Irish pointer. There is more to come from him and he is one to look forward to over fences.

WYNN HOUSE 6 ch m Presenting – Glorious Twelfth (IRE)
She has done well during the summer and I have always thought she is very good. A winner of her first couple of runs over hurdles at Bangor and Ludlow, she has always worked very well. Fourth in a Grade 2 novice hurdle at Cheltenham in December, she filled the same position in a Listed mares' novice hurdle at Doncaster next time. I was hoping she may have progressed more than she did and I wouldn't rule out trying some headgear at some stage. Rated 123, I think she is better than that mark.

> **TRAINER'S HORSE TO FOLLOW: JAY BEE WHY**

Tom LACEY
Stables: Cottage Field Stables Ltd., Sapness Farm, Woolhope, Herefordshire.
2020/2021: 34 Winners / 240 Runners 14% Prize-Money £323,345
www.cottagefield.co.uk

ADRIMEL (FR) 6 bb g Tirwanako (FR) – Irise De Gene (FR)
Developed into a smart novice hurdler winning three times, including the Grade 2 Leamington Novices' Hurdle at Warwick in January. He had won twice over two miles at Sandown and Haydock and we always felt he would benefit from stepping up in trip. We fitted him with cheekpieces for the first time at Warwick, too, and they helped him because they sharpened him up. Pulled up at both Cheltenham and Aintree, the ground was too quick for him on each occasion. He wants mid winter deep ground and we are looking forward to sending him over fences. We haven't schooled him yet, but he won an Irish point and I don't envisage any problems. Two and a half miles is probably his trip at the moment, but I wouldn't be against dropping back to two miles on testing ground over fences. A race such as the Grade 1 Scilly Isles Novices' Chase at Sandown in February could be an ideal target later on.

ARGONAUTA (IRE) 5 b g Getaway (GER) – Oscar Ladensa (IRE)
He has always been a good work horse and, while it doesn't necessarily translate to the racecourse, we weren't surprised when he won on his debut in a bumper at Newcastle in January. Fifth next time under a penalty at Ayr in the spring, I was disappointed with him because he made life hard for himself by racing keenly and hanging. He has schooled well over hurdles though and I hope he will develop into a nice novice hurdler. We will start him off over hurdles and it is possible he will wear cheekpieces at some stage. He isn't ungenuine but it will help him concentrate.

CRUZ CONTROL (FR) 4 b g Saint Des Saints (FR) – En La Cruz (FR)
A lovely unraced four year old, he joined us last season and we have brought him along slowly. A big rangy type, I like him a lot and he has been schooled over hurdles. I would imagine he will be running in two and a half miles novice hurdles this season.

DIBBLE DECKER (IRE) 5 b g Jet Away – Bella Minna (IRE)
Successful in his only Irish point-to-point in May, I picked him out at the Cheltenham Sale at Newmarket later the same month. Bought on behalf of ValueRacingClub.co.uk, he is by a decent sire and I hope he will prove a good addition to the team. His vendor told us that he will be quick enough for two miles. Novice hurdling will be on his agenda this winter.

GINNY'S DESTINY (IRE) 5 b g Yeats (IRE) – Dantes Term (IRE)
Well related being a half-brother to triple Grade 1 winner God's Own, he hasn't run yet but has done well and I like him. His owners have been very patient and, while his future lies in staying chases, he will go hurdling this season and, all being well, will be in action during the Autumn.

GLORY AND FORTUNE (IRE) 6 b g Fame And Glory – Night Heron (IRE)
Nothing went right for him last year. Following a couple of runs over fences at Carlisle and Ayr, he had a wind operation and we decided to go back over hurdles with him. While he didn't run badly finishing second at Stratford and Ludlow, plus he was fifth in the Scottish Champion Hurdle at Ayr, he rather lost his way. If we can get him right, I feel he is a well handicapped horse. We will run him over fences again later on, but I am keen to win with him over hurdles to boost his confidence.

GLORY AND HONOUR (IRE) 5 b g Elusive Pimpernel (USA) – On Khee
Twice a winner at Huntingdon and Lingfield last season, he is rated 129 and is still on a good mark. The Silver Trophy at Chepstow (9th October) is a possible target because I think a strongly run two and a half miles on decent ground is ideal. We won the race last year with Tea Clipper and he could be tailormade for it. I would put a line through his last run at Newton Abbot because he wasn't right and scoped badly afterwards.

HESQUE DE L'ISLE (FR) 4 b g Saddler Maker (IRE) – Naiade de L'Isle (FR)
Purchased at the Goffs Landrover Sale last year, he is a lovely horse. Yet to run, he needs to learn his trade over hurdles this season and will improve with time. He isn't as fast as he thinks he is at the moment and will be running him over two and a half miles.

HIGHEST SUN (FR) 7 b g Sunday Break (JPN) – Highest Price (FR)
A new arrival during the summer, he is a dual winner over hurdles and has scored over fences, too. The handicapper has given him a chance by dropping him a few pounds and hopefully a change of scenery will benefit him. We are still getting to know him, but he appears to stay well and will continue over fences.

HIGHSTAKESPLAYER (IRE) 5 b g Ocovango – Elivette (FR)
A grand horse who was third on his debut in a bumper at Sandown in November before being narrowly beaten next time at Ayr. We then ran him at Wetherby over Christmas but the race came too soon, plus it was very deep ground and he didn't like it. Like a few of ours, he suffered with a virus during the second half of the season, so we decided to put him away. He is a nice horse for novice hurdles and will begin over two miles.

JOHNBB (IRE) 7 b g Stowaway – Flemins Evening (IRE)
I am looking forward to him because he is capable of winning a nice staying handicap chase. A winner over fences at Wetherby in December, he ran a cracking race at Aintree in the spring finishing runner-up over three miles one. He stayed the trip well and enjoyed the better ground. Good fresh, he could be suited by a race such as the Badger Beers Trophy at Wincanton (6th November). Still lightly raced, he is open to further improvement.

KIMBERLITE CANDY (IRE) 9 b g Flemensfirth (USA) – Mandys Native (IRE)

Runner-up in the Becher Chase at Aintree (4th December) for the second consecutive year, we purposely saved him for the Grand National but the ground dried up and he was hampered early on and never really got involved. We haven't finalised any plans, but I would imagine he will go back to Aintree in December and then we will decide what he is going to do for the rest of the campaign. A very good jumper, soft ground is the key to him.

L'INCORRIGIBLE (FR) 6 b g No Risk At All (FR) – Incorrigible (FR)

He is a talented horse winning two of his three career starts but has had rotten luck with injuries. Having suffered with a pelvic injury earlier in his career, he then split a pastern. Back in action last season winning over hurdles at Doncaster, he then finished runner-up at the same track in January. Unfortunately, he had a recurrence of his pelvic injury and has been off since. A free going sort, he lacks experience and will continue over hurdles for the time being. Indeed, a strongly run two miles will suit him.

LOSSIEMOUTH 6 b g Makfi – First Bloom (USA)

A smart bumper horse a few years ago, he was second a couple of times over hurdles but only raced once last season. He had problems with his feet but hopefully we have sorted that out. Back in work following his summer break, he looks a different horse now. The plan is for him to remain over hurdles.

MARTY TIME (FR) 5 gr g Martaline – Shahwarda (FR)

Twice raced in bumpers at Newcastle and Chepstow, he suffered with a kissing spine which has been operated on. He spent time in the water treadmill and, following his summer break, he looks a million dollars. We have schooled him over hurdles, he jumps well and I am hoping he will develop into a nice novice hurdler because I have always liked him. I am expecting him to stay well.

PIAFF BUBBLES (IRE) 5 bb g Fame And Glory – Liss Na Tintri (IRE)

Bought at the Tattersalls Derby Sales as a three year old, he is a big raw angular gelding who will improve with time. He possesses an engine though running well in bumpers at Plumpton and Warwick. He still needs to mature but is one to look forward to having schooled well over hurdles.

POUNDING POET (IRE) 5 b g Yeats (IRE) – Pestal And Mortar (IRE)

Progressive over hurdles in the spring winning at Southwell and Warwick. Despite an eight pounds rise for his latest win, he remains well treated and has more to offer. Still a novice until the end of October, I am inclined to go chasing sooner rather than later and find a suitable novices' handicap chase. He jumps well and, while he has been winning over two and a half miles, I think he would be effective over most trips. Good to soft or softer ground suits him.

QUICK DRAW (IRE) 5 b g Getaway (GER) – Sept Verites (FR)

Another who is likely to go for a novices' handicap chase with his mark of 118. The cheekpieces made a difference when he won over hurdles at Chepstow in April, but he wasn't at his best next time at Perth. Placed a couple of times at Uttoxeter and Carlisle during the Autumn, he suffered with the virus at the turn of the year. He has been schooled over fences and is more than capable of being competitive off his mark.

ROGER RAREBIT 4 b g Black Sam Bellamy (IRE) – Rebekah Rabbit (IRE)
A nice horse who made his debut in a junior bumper at Hereford in December. He needed the experience on that occasion and has been given plenty of time since. I have been pleased with him during the summer and he will go hurdling.

SCIPION (IRE) 5 b g Shantou (USA) – Morning Calm
He is a very nice horse who finished runner-up in a couple of point-to-points last season. Beaten three lengths on his debut at Larkhill in December, he ran well but found two and a half miles too sharp and was beaten by a five year old. We then sent him to be trained in Ireland by Colin Bowe and he was beaten narrowly at Cork in a three miles point. The pair pulled a dozen lengths clear of the third. Colin liked him and I am expecting him to develop into a useful novice hurdler. I could envisage him starting off over two and a half miles at somewhere like Chepstow on soft ground.

SEBASTOPOL (IRE) 7 b g Fame And Glory – Knockcroghery (IRE)
Ran some very good races in defeat during the spring/summer finishing second on five occasions. Runner-up in the Sussex Champion Hurdle at Plumpton in April, he was beaten less than a length on his next three starts. A winning pointer, he will go novice chasing and, with a rating of 142, I am hoping he will do well over fences. We haven't schooled him over fences since his pointing days, but he is a very good jumper. Top of the ground is ideal and, even though he stays three miles, I wouldn't mind dropping him back in trip.

TEA CLIPPER (IRE) 6 b g Stowaway – A Plus Ma Puce (FR)
A lovely horse who I have always liked a lot. He produced a very good performance to win the Grade 3 Silver Trophy Handicap Hurdle at Chepstow last Autumn. He then finished third in the Coral Cup at the Cheltenham and would have been runner-up had he not been hampered by the faller at the last. We then stepped him up to three miles for the first time under Rules at Aintree in April and he ran another good race in third. A three miles chaser in the making, he will start off over two and a half miles over fences. The Listed Robert Mottram Memorial Trophy Novices' Chase at Chepstow (9th October) over two miles three is an option provided the ground isn't too soft. He likes good or good to soft ground.

TEESCOMPONENTSLASS (IRE) 6 b m Presenting – Northern Native (IRE)
Bought privately having finished second in a bumper at Ayr in November, she also showed promise in another couple of bumpers at Doncaster and Newcastle. Twice raced over hurdles, she needs one more run and will then be qualified for handicaps. She is crying out for a step up in trip and ought to provide her owners ValueRacingClub.co.uk with a lot of fun once going handicapping over two and a half miles plus on good to soft or soft ground.

TRAINER'S HORSE TO FOLLOW: PIAFF BUBBLES

Please see page 195
for details of
Ahead on the Flat 2022

Donald McCAIN

Stables: Bankhouse, Cholmondeley, Cheshire.
2020/2021: 66 Winners / 486 Runners 14% Prize-Money £594,754
www.donaldmccain.co.uk

A DIFFERENT KIND (IRE) 4 b g Doyen (IRE) – Ma Minx (IRE)
Derek O'Connor recommended him having ridden him to finish second in his only point-to-point in Ireland. He finished his race off well and is a grand sort. We might run him in a bumper before going hurdling.

BANNIXTOWN GLORY (IRE) 7 b m Fame And Glory – Me Auld Segosha (IRE)
She is a wonderful mare who had an excellent season over hurdles winning four times, including Listed mares' events at Kempton and Cheltenham. Following her victory at the latter track in April, we decided to school her over fences and she took to it well. She made a winning start to her chasing career when scoring at Cartmel, despite finding the track on the sharp side. She is only a small mare but is honest and will do both jobs this season mixing between hurdles and fences. We have given her a break since her last run and she will be back in action in the Autumn. Two and a half to three miles on good ground are her conditions.

BAREBACK JACK (IRE) 5 b g Getaway (GER) – Dubh Go Leir (IRE)
A winning Irish pointer, he developed into a smart novice hurdler winning three out of four. His only defeat came in the Grade 2 novice at Kelso in March where he got bogged down in the ground – it was like a bog and they were awful conditions. He never looked happy from an early stage. He copes with wet soft ground but is ideally suited by good or good to soft. We were preparing him for the Grade 1 novice hurdle over two miles at Aintree after that, but he had a problem beforehand which ruled him out. That has been dealt with, but we aren't in a rush with him. We have yet to decided whether to continue over hurdles or go chasing. If he remains over timber, we could have a look at something like the Greatwood Hurdle at Cheltenham (14th November). A speedy horse, he jumps well and two miles is his trip.

BARNABAS COLLINS (IRE) 6 b g Shantou (USA) – G Day Sile (IRE)
Won a bumper on his debut at Carlisle in November for Stuart Crawford, we bought him the following month at the Cheltenham Sale hosted at Newmarket. I was keen to buy him because he beat Barrichello, who I like. Yet to run for us, he had a little niggle which meant we gave him some time off, but he is fine now and ready to go hurdling. He comes from a good source and we know he handles slow ground.

BARRICHELLO 5 b g Gentlewave (IRE) – Tambourine Ridge (IRE)
Ran well without winning over hurdles last season, which was frustrating. Runner-up on a handful of occasions, we felt something was stopping him at Wetherby last time. We have therefore operated on his breathing and hopefully that will make a difference. Capable of winning over hurdles, his future lies over fences with trips around two and two and a half miles suiting him.

BARROWDALE (IRE) 6 b g Cloudings (IRE) – Tanya Thyne (IRE)
Mr Hemmings has kindly sent me him having won his only point-to-point by ten lengths for Mick Winters in Ireland. A half-brother to Testify and Wymott, who were both Grade 2 winners for us, he is an exciting prospect and one to look forward to.

BARRULE PARK 5 b g Kayf Tara – Rare Vintage (IRE)
A nice unraced horse, he is a smashing type belonging to Mr Hemmings. He has a very good pedigree being a half-brother to Cheltenham Festival winner Vintage Clouds and he arrived late last year. We could have run him in the spring but the ground dried out, so we decided to give him more time. A big fine chasing type for the future, we might give him a run in a bumper for educational purposes, but it won't be long before he goes hurdling.

CALZA NERA (IRE) 4 b f Milan – Gazzas Dream (IRE)
Ian Ferguson bought her at the Goffs Landrover Sale last year and she has been broken and done a bit of work. We will start off in a bumper to teach her before we look to send her jumping.

CHASE OUTLAW 5 b g Gentlewave (IRE) – Asola Blue (FR)
A fine big horse by the same sire as Barrichello, he ran in two Irish points for Denis Murphy winning on the second occasion. I watched the video and, having looked beaten, he rallied well and led close home. Bought at the Goffs UK Spring Sale at Doncaster in May, he will go hurdling over two or two and a half miles.

DEDANSER (IRE) 5 b g Frammassone (IRE) – Courtown Bowe VII
Raced in two Irish points falling on his debut. He stayed on well last time though to finish third and looks a tough horse. He will probably go straight over hurdles.

DREAMS OF HOME (IRE) 5 b g Jet Away – Knocktartan (IRE)
We are looking forward to sending him chasing. A point winner in Ireland for Donnchadh Doyle, he won three out of three over hurdles for us last season, but I still don't think he knows what he is doing. He has done well during the summer and, despite winning over two miles last season, he is bred to want much further being a half-brother to Minellacelebration (Listed chase winner over 3m 2f). His jumping in his point-to-point was exceptional and I think he is a really nice horse who we have got nowhere near to the bottom of yet. A winner at Wetherby, Carlisle and Newcastle, he will probably start off over two and a half miles over fences.

FALANGHINA 4 gr f Ocovango – Whisky Rose (IRE)
Unraced, we bought her at the Goffs UK Summer Sale at Doncaster last year and is a well bred filly. A half-sister to Grumpy Charley and One For Rosie, she will make her debut in a mares' bumper and is a lovely filly.

FIVEANDTWENTY 4 br f Farhh – Fen Guest
Like a lot of Middleham Park's horses, she spent the summer with Ann Duffield. She took well to jumping winning three times at Musselburgh, including the Listed Scottish Triumph Hurdle in February. She wasn't disgraced at Aintree finishing third behind the best juvenile hurdler (Monmiral) we saw last season in Grade 1 company and then I shouldn't have run her at Cheltenham later the same month. She had had enough by that stage, plus I think she will always be at her best on flat tracks. Her first target is the Listed mares' hurdle at Wetherby (30th October) and then we will aim her at the other Pattern races for mares at tracks such as Doncaster.

FRUIT N NUT (IRE) 5 b g Carlotamix (FR) – Perilously (USA)
Grand horse who we bought privately at the Goffs UK November Sale at Yorton Farm having finished runner-up in his point-to-point. He won his first couple of bumpers at Musselburgh and Catterick before taking his chance in the Grade 2 event at Aintree in April. A bit free and forward going, he is a likeable horse who has done well through the summer. Not slow, he will start off in a two miles novice hurdle.

GAELIK COAST (FR) 7 br g Coastal Path – Gaelika (IRE)
One of my favourites, he is a bit nervy and timid but is a smashing horse. Twice a winner over fences at Fakenham and Musselburgh, we ran him in the Red Rum Chase at Aintree last time. We elected to drop him in and he travelled well and was getting into contention when making a mistake at the third last. He ran better than his finishing positions suggests. He is not really a two miler and wants further. Two and a half miles handicap chases will be his target and I have already got my eye on the Topham Chase in April. A very neat and precise jumper, he should be competitive off his mark of 134.

GOOBINATOR (USA) 5 ch g Noble Mission – Lilac Lilly (USA)
Has been running well on the Flat during the summer winning at York over two miles in July. Quite a free going type, we held him up that day and it suited him. The plan is to go back over hurdles though in the Autumn. He won the Scottish Champion Hurdle Trial at Ayr in October, but got wiped out when upsides Tommy's Oscar at the last at Musselburgh in January. I think he lost his confidence as a result because he was disappointing on his next two starts over hurdles at Aintree. With his confidence restored, I think he is well handicapped off 126.

GREDIN (FR) 5 ch g Masked Marvel – Valbrune (FR)
By a sire I like, he ran in two Irish points for Donnchadh Doyle finishing runner-up on his second outing. A fine big horse, he was an expensive store and we bought him at the Cheltenham April Sale shortly after his latest start. He will go novice hurdling.

HEARTBREAK KID (IRE) 6 b g Getaway (GER) – Bella's Bury
Had a couple of niggles last season and I am hoping he is going to be more straightforward to train this season because he has the ability to win a nice race. Having won over hurdles at Sedgefield in November, he chased home Cheddleton at Carlisle on his chasing debut, which is good form. However, he hated the ground at Kelso next time and wasn't at his best at Sedgefield either. Only six, he is rated 123 over fences and will be aimed at novices' handicap chases over two and a half miles.

HIDALGO DE L'ISLE (FR) 4 b g Coastal Path – Agence de L'Isle (FR)
Bought at the Goffs Landrover Sale last year, he is by a good sire and we have done some work with him. It is too early to say what ability he possesses though and is a real unknown quantity.

JUNGLE JACK 5 ch g Doyen (IRE) – Skew
Full-brother to eight times winner Valdez, he won his only Irish point for Colin Bowe in October. A fine big horse, he appreciates soft ground and will go novice hurdling.

LARGY REACH 5 b g Phoenix Reach (IRE) – Kallithea (IRE)
He is by an unfashionable stallion, but I am a fan of Phoenix Reach. Third in his only point-to-point for Stuart Crawford, he finished nicely and the form is OK. We acquired him at the Goffs UK Spring Sale in May and he will go novice hurdling over two miles to begin with.

MACKENBERG (GER) 6 b g Jukebox Jury (IRE) – Mountain Melody (GER)
Had a good season winning three times, twice over hurdles at Carlisle and Kempton, plus a 'jumpers' bumper' at Newcastle. Fourth in the Grade 2 Dovecote Novices' Hurdle at Kempton, we stepped him up in trip at the same track last time and he won well. Unexposed over trips around two and a half miles, he is learning to settle better now and is therefore staying further. Still quite raw though, we haven't decided whether to stay over hurdles or go chasing. He wasn't the best of jumpers in his two Irish points failing to complete on both occasions – he is quite straight backed. He doesn't want the ground too soft either.

MILANS EDGE (IRE) 6 b m Milan – The Keane Edge (IRE)
She won her only point for Colin Bowe before being bought by James and Jean Potter. They kindly sent her to us and I was pleased with her win in a bumper at Wetherby in February. We then ran her in the Grade 2 mares' bumper at Aintree in the spring, but she was too free. A fine big mare, we decided to run her over hurdles at Hexham in May and she should have won but greenness caught her out. She propped at the final hurdle and got beaten (winner has won again). We might ride her in behind horses in future because it will suit her getting a lead. Mares' novice hurdles over two and two and a half miles are the plan.

MINELLA DRAMA (IRE) 6 b g Flemensfirth (USA) – Midsummer Drama (IRE)
I am hoping he will be our best novice chaser this season. Back in work, he has done well through the summer and looks a racehorse. Runner-up in both his point-to-points in Ireland, I have always thought he was very good and he proved it throughout last season. A dual winner at Sedgefield and Bangor, he was unlucky not to win the Grade 2 Rossington Main Novices' Hurdle at Haydock in January getting caught close home on the long run-in. Back to winning ways in the rescheduled Listed Sidney Banks Novices' Hurdle at Market Rasen, he won well. He rounded off his season with an excellent second in Grade 1 company at Aintree behind a very smart horse (My Drogo). The step up to two and a half miles on his last couple of runs has suited him. Still raw, he was doing a few things wrong last year but is growing up and the hood has helped him. We may start him off over two miles at somewhere like Carlisle, but his first main target is the Grade 2 Altcar Novices' Chase at Haydock in January. A two and a half miles event, we have won it three times in the past.

MINELLA TRUMP (IRE) 7 b g Shantou (USA) – One Theatre (IRE)
Ran well on his chasing bow at Carlisle but then disappointed next time at Doncaster and I think he lost his bottle. We switched him back over hurdles in the spring and, having been placed at Carlisle and Sedgefield, he won at Perth in May. He is going the right way again now hence we reverted to fences and he won twice at Perth in August and September, including over three miles last time.

MISTER WHITAKER (IRE) 9 b g Court Cave (IRE) – Benbradagh Vard (IRE)

A high-class horse over fences and a former Cheltenham Festival winner, we bought him on behalf of Tim Leslie with the Grand National in mind. Purchased at the Goffs UK Spring Sale at Doncaster, he isn't guaranteed to stay but he jumps and travels well and is the sort to be going well crossing the Melling Road before they turn for home. Still a novice over hurdles, that is something we are going to try and exploit, although we need to make sure he is qualified for the National by being placed at least once over three miles over fences beforehand. I have been pleased with him since he arrived.

NAVAJO PASS 5 b g Nathaniel (IRE) – Navajo Charm

Like Bareback Jack, he was due to run at Aintree in the spring but a minor niggle ruled him out, which was annoying. Having done well as a juvenile hurdler winning a Grade 2 and finishing fourth in the Triumph Hurdle, I thought he was going to have a difficult second season over hurdles. However, he did well winning at Musselburgh on New Year's Day and then beating Buveur D'Air in the Grade 2 Champion Hurdle Trial at Haydock. Third in the Grade 2 Kingwell Hurdle at Wincanton next time, it was strange ground and he lost his action. We tidied up his wind afterwards and, while we haven't made any plans, he will hopefully have another good season over hurdles. He stays two and a half miles but would need very slow ground over two miles, which it was when he won at Haydock in January.

PRESENTANDCOUNTING (IRE) 7 b g Presenting – Count On Me (IRE)

We couldn't win a race over hurdles with him, but he has thrived since sent chasing. Brian (Hughes) has done a very good job with him and he has been a different horse this spring/ summer winning five times. A very slick jumper, he is lightning over his fences and I haven't seen many better jumpers as a novice. Even though he won by a wide margin at Cartmel in July, the track didn't play to his strengths because there is a run-in of nearly half a mile. He will be better on a bigger track when the emphasis is on jumping. He doesn't want winter ground, so we may aim him at Chepstow or Cheltenham in October before giving him a break. The Topham Chase over the National fences is certainly a possibility one day.

RAMBLE WEST (IRE) 5 b m Leading Light (IRE) – Lady Moon (FR)

A half-sister to staying chaser Sheneededtherun (fourth in the Midlands National), she was trained in Ireland by Colin Bowe who liked her. Runner-up in two of her three starts in points, she is a grand mare with a good attitude. She could run in a mares' bumper before going hurdling.

SINCE DAY ONE (IRE) 5 b g Fame And Glory – Collou (IRE)

Bought at the Cheltenham April Sale, he was previously owned by Rob James and trained in Ireland by Sean Doyle. Not over big, he is a good size and was runner-up in a couple of point-to-points. A forward going type, he will spend this season in novice hurdles.

SOMEWHAT CLOUDY (IRE) 5 b m Presenting – Clara Mc Cloud (IRE)

Purchased at the Cheltenham March sale staged at Newmarket, she was runner-up in a point-to-point bumper at Tipperary for Aidan Fitzgerald. We ran her over hurdles at Cartmel in May and she finished third. She will have learned plenty from that and has benefited from a summer break since. She will be suited by a step up in trip.

SULLIVAN'S BROW (IRE) 6 b g Flemensfirth (USA) – Beths Bell (IRE)
An older pointer, he is by a top sire and, having finished third on his debut, he bolted up next time. Previously trained by Colin Bowe, we bought him at the Cheltenham May Sale at Newmarket a few days later. He is one for northern novice hurdles on winter ground.

THE CON MAN (IRE) 8 b g Oscar (IRE) – Phillis Hill
Back in work having missed the whole of last season, we could have run him in the spring but decided to give him more time. A three times winner over hurdles and rated 138, he is a bit fragile but is a useful horse. Effective on soft ground, he stays two and a half miles well and I think he will get three miles this season. We are keen to go chasing with him.

WORD HAS IT (IRE) 7 b g Jeremy (USA) – Rathfeigh (IRE)
A tough hardy sort, he has had a few problems but he came good over hurdles last season winning twice at Carlisle and Kelso and the form has worked out well. Rated 130, he has schooled nicely over fences and we will look at a novices' handicap chase over two miles, although he will stay further.

Unnamed 4 b f Walk In The Park (IRE) – Lakil Princess (IRE)
A half-sister to Lastbutnotleast, who won five times for us including a Listed hurdle, she is a lovely filly who we did plenty of work with last year. She is nearly as big as her sister, too, and we will run her in a mares' bumper in the Autumn.

> **TRAINER'S HORSE TO FOLLOW: MINELLA DRAMA**

Gary MOORE
Stables: Cisswood Racing Stables, Sandygate Lane, Lower Beeding, Horsham, West Sussex
2020/2021: 61 Winners / 435 Runners 14% Prize-Money £595,878
www.garymooreracing.com

ALBERT VAN ORNUM (FR) 4 b g Authorized (IRE) – Diena (FR)
A winner on the Flat in France, we bought him at the Tattersalls Autumn Horses in Training Sale last year. He raced three times for us last season, including twice over hurdles. Fourth in a 'jumpers' bumper' at Lingfield on his penultimate start, he was runner-up over hurdles at Fontwell last time. We decided to put cheekpieces on him because I wasn't happy with the way he travelled in his race on his hurdles debut at Newbury, but I don't think they made a lot of difference. He is a big horse who has done well during the summer and is open to improvement. We will keep him to two miles for the time being, but I am expecting him to stay further.

AUTHORISED SPEED (FR) 4 b g Authorized (IRE) – Tangaspeed (FR)
Bought at the Goffs Landrover Sale last year, I love him. I thought he would win on his debut in a bumper at Market Rasen in May, but he was unlucky meeting trouble in running before staying on strongly. I have no doubts it cost him the race. He is a decent horse who will run in another bumper in the Autumn, possibly at somewhere like Fontwell over two miles two, before going hurdling. We have schooled him and he jumps well. There is a lot of speed on the dam's side of his pedigree, but I am expecting him to stay well, too.

BENEVOLENTDICTATOR 7 ch g Schiaparelli (GER) – Kim Fontenail (FR)
An improving horse who has taken time to come to himself, similar to a lot of the Schiaparelli's. He took well to chasing winning twice at Lingfield and Plumpton before finishing third in the Sussex National at the latter venue early in the New Year. We were going to run him again, but the ground dried out and we have purposely looked after him and not over raced him. He enjoys soft ground and will be aimed at the regional Nationals this winter. Still lightly raced, he is on a workable mark and I am expecting him to continue to progress.

BLACK GERRY (IRE) 6 b g Westerner – Triptoshan (IRE)
Runner-up in his only Irish point for Donnchadh Doyle, he won over hurdles for us the previous season but missed the whole of last term due to injury. We have given him plenty of time and he remains a horse with good potential. I would think he will have another run over hurdles, but it won't be long before he goes chasing.

BOTOX HAS (FR) 5 b g Dream Well (FR) – Bournie (FR)
We schooled him over fences at the end of last season and, while he isn't over big (16hh), he jumped nicely and is well balanced. I don't think we have seen the best of him. A useful juvenile hurdler a couple of seasons ago, he won at Cheltenham on his reappearance in October but then lost his way. Two and a half miles is his trip at the moment, but it wouldn't surprise me if he stayed three miles. I think he will make a good chaser.

CASA LOUPI 4 ch g Casamento (IRE) – Kameruka
A bit of a freak, he is only rated 69 on the Flat but improved over hurdles winning twice and is rated 131. Narrowly beaten on his jumping debut at Ascot behind Tritonic, he finished runner-up behind the same rival in the Grade 2 Adonis Juvenile Hurdle at Kempton next time. An easy winner at Plumpton and Wincanton in April, he remains a novice until the end of October. We will then aim him at the decent two miles handicap hurdles, but I am keen to exploit his mark on the Flat, too, because he is well handicapped.

DORKING LAD 6 b g Sholokhov (IRE) – Brookville (IRE)
Consistent, he won over hurdles at Newton Abbot during the spring but was unlucky not to win before then. We are going to send him over fences and he's one to look forward to. Rated 115 over hurdles, I am expecting him to make a better chaser and feel he is well treated. We will start him off in a suitable novices' handicap chase over two or two and a half miles.

EDITEUR DU GITE (FR) 7 b g Saddex – Malaga De St Sulpice (FR)
A very good jumper, he finished second a couple of times at Ascot but improved in the spring winning twice at Newbury and Aintree. I was delighted with his victory in the Red Rum Chase at the latter venue in April. The drying ground suited him and, while it won't be easy for him this season off a mark of 140, he is capable of being competitive and is still lightly raced. The plan is to run him in the Autumn before the ground gets soft.

FIFTY BALL (FR) 6 b g Cokoriko (FR) – Voix De Montot (FR)
Dual bumper winner in France, he developed into a decent horse over hurdles last season. Twice successful at Ascot and Sandown, he ran a very good race in the *Betfair* Hurdle at Newbury finishing second. We have schooled him over fences and I am very pleased with him. Two miles suits him but he will stay further in due course. He should make a very nice chaser.

FULL BACK (FR) 6 b g Sinndar (IRE) – Quatre Bleue (FR)
A bit of an enigma, he won twice over fences at Plumpton and Exeter before pulling up in the Grade 2 Reyonoldstown Novices' Chase at Ascot. His jumping was poor and let him down. We can't do enough schooling with him and, while it won't be easy this season with a rating of 140, he is a capable horse who stays three miles well and I think he will benefit from racing on better ground.

FURLOUGH ME (IRE) 5 b g Doyen (IRE) – Nohabodder (IRE)
He is a nice horse who ran in a couple of bumpers last season winning at Fontwell in late March. A big weak horse last year, he has needed time but has done well during the summer and his schooling has been good. He is one to look forward to in novice hurdles.

GIVEGA (FR) 5 b g Authorized (IRE) – Sivega (FR)
A very athletic horse who we are still learning about. From the family of Quevaga, he won his only Irish point-to-point for Colin Bowe and they tell me he is pretty good. Owned by Ashley Head, he is a brilliant jumper so he is likely to go straight over hurdles.

GOLDEN BOY GREY (FR) 5 b g Diamond Boy (FR) – Betwixt (IRE)
A big improver last season winning two of his four starts over hurdles, gaining victories at Sandown and Fontwell. Rated 123, we are going to send him chasing and he could be anything. Two and a half miles is his trip and we will aim him at novices' handicap chases to begin with.

GOSHEN (FR) 5 b g Authorized (IRE) – Hyde (FR)
He's been walking and trotting during the summer and is in great form at home. We are going to give him a run on the Flat before aiming him at a Listed hurdle at Kempton (17th October), provided the ground is suitable. The key to him is the ground and, the only time he got his conditions last season, was in the Grade 2 Kingwell Hurdle at Wincanton in February and he won by 22 lengths. The ground was too quick for him at Punchestown last time. I am also keen to keep him to right-handed tracks. Admittedly, he would have won the Triumph Hurdle a couple of seasons ago, but he has run poorly twice at Cheltenham since and doesn't like the place. He didn't even want to go into the paddock before the Champion Hurdle last season. He has a slight kink in him, but I think that is the Montjeu in him (the sire of Authorized). We haven't run him beyond two miles, but he will stay further and something like the Grade 2 Ascot Hurdle (20th November) would be tailormade for him.

HADDEX DES OBEAUX (FR) 4 b g Saddex – Shifra (FR)
A new arrival, he is a lovely horse who won an AQPS Flat race in France before winning over hurdles at Auteuil in April. He arrived in the spring and we turned him away to give him plenty of time to acclimatise during the summer. He is novice until the end of October and will therefore be forced to run in conditions/handicap hurdles thereafter. Long-term, his future lies over fences and he is a horse I like a lot.

HIGH UP IN THE AIR (FR) 7 ch g Famous Name – You Got The Love
A revelation over fences last season, he won five times with his rating climbing from 100 to 132. Bad ground brings the best out of him and his first main target is the Grand Sefton Chase over the National fences at Aintree (4th December). Provided that goes well, we will then aim him at the Topham Chase over the same course and distance in April.

HOUKA D'OUDAIRIES (FR) 4 gr f Gris De Gris (IRE) – Quinine (FR)

She is a gorgeous filly who we were advised to buy having won both her bumpers in France during the spring. We gave her a break after she arrived to give her the chance to acclimatise and I have watched a few videos of her jumping. It is no good if they show a lot of ability on the Flat but can't jump. She is from a good family and I love her. She will be running in mares' novice hurdles and is an exciting prospect.

HUDSON DE GRUGY (FR) 4 b g Falco (USA) – Queen De Grugy (FR)

A gorgeous horse, I love him. A French bumper winner, he was still a big baby last year but won over hurdles at Sandown twice. Third at Newbury last time, he has done well during the summer and I like him a lot. A born chaser, he will spend another season over hurdles and his first aim is the Masterson Holdings Hurdle for four year olds at Cheltenham (23rd October), a race we won last year with Botox Has.

LAVORANTE (IRE) 5 br g Milan – Pinkeen Lady (IRE)

Runner-up in an Irish point-to-point, he is a nice horse who shaped with promise in a couple of bumpers before going hurdling at Fontwell last time. Third on that occasion, he has needed time and I would expect him to improve this year. He will continue in novice hurdles over two and two and a half miles.

MAKE MY DAY (IRE) 5 b g Galileo (IRE) – Posset

Lightly raced, he was bought at the Tattersalls Autumn Horses in Training Sale in October last year. However, he has yet to run for us having had a few niggles. He was declared to run over hurdles at Plumpton in January but the ground was too soft. Rated 94 on the Flat for John Gosden and Ralph Beckett, he has plenty of ability and remains lightly raced. He will be going hurdling in the Autumn.

MOULINS CLERMONT (FR) 3 b g Free Port Lux – Ania De Clermont (FR)

A lovely horse who finished third on his only run over hurdles in France in April. We are still getting to know him, but he reminds me of Hudson De Grugy. He arrived during the summer and will go novice hurdling. I like him a lot.

NASSALAM (FR) 4 ch g Dream Well (FR) – Ramina (GER)

He is a good horse who will go chasing this season. I don't usually send my horses over fences as four year olds but he is a very good jumper and his schooling has been excellent. Runner-up over hurdles in France, he won easily twice at Fontwell before finishing second in both the Grade 1 Finale Hurdle at Chepstow and at Haydock behind subsequent Grade 1 winner Monmiral. We made the mistake of running him in the Boodles Juvenile Hurdle rather than the Triumph Hurdle at Cheltenham. To win the former event, the horse needs to have been laid out for it. I think he will make a better chaser and we will run him in two miles novice chases, although he will stay further.

NATURAL HISTORY 6 b g Nathaniel (IRE) – Film Script

A three times winner on the Flat for Andrew Balding, he is another who was acquired at the Horses in Training Sale at Newmarket last Autumn. Successful over hurdles at Plumpton in March, he was sixth in the Imperial Cup at Sandown before finishing second at Newton Abbot last time. He has benefited from a break since and his owners are keen to aim him at the big handicap hurdles.

OZZIE MAN (IRE) 5 b g Ask – Parkdota (IRE)
A winning Irish pointer, he was a relatively cheap buy and is a horse with plenty of ability. Runner-up in a bumper at Fontwell, he was then third over hurdles at the same track. He likes soft ground and is capable of winning over hurdles this season.

PORTICELLO (FR) 3 b g Sholokhov (IRE) – Chinawood (FR)
An exciting horse who joined us earlier this year having won his only start over hurdles at Auteuil in April. He is a great big horse and I can't believe he even ran, let alone won. The form looks OK, too, with the third winning next time. His new owner Olly Harris paid good money for him and he is a lovely horse who I really like. We have given him time since arriving only doing a bit of trotting and I love him. He will spend this season in juvenile hurdles but will jump fences in time.

ROBIN'S DREAM 5 b g Kayf Tara – Sudden Light (IRE)
A lovely horse who was unlucky finishing a close second at Newbury and Wincanton and falling at Sandown in between. He deservedly got his head in front at Huntingdon in May but came back jarred up on the quick ground. Still a novice for this season, he could be decent and will stay further than two miles. I like him.

ROYAUME UNI (IRE) 4 bb g Galileo (IRE) – Night Lagoon (GER)
A winner on the Flat for Andre Fabre in France, he is still a maiden over hurdles but ran some good races in defeat. Runner-up at Ascot in March, he was then fourth in a decent novices' handicap hurdle on the final day of the season at Sandown. He won a 'jumpers' bumper' and on the Flat at Lingfield during the winter and is a lovely horse for the future. We will run him again on the Flat, but I think he is on a good mark over hurdles. He will get two and a half miles later on.

SHALLWEHAVEONEMORE (FR) 4 b g Authorized (IRE) – Princess Roseburg (USA)
I am excited by him. He jumps for fun and I love him. He possesses so much speed and could be anything. We started him off in a bumper at Kempton in March and I thought he would take a lot of beating. However, when we arrived at the track, we were told Nicky Henderson's (Walking On Air) was an aeroplane and also Richard Spencer's runner (Roll With It) was fancied, too. He won in good style though and the track really suited him. While he isn't as big as Authorised Speed, he is sharper mentally. I think he is a very good horse who will run in another bumper before going hurdling.

SOPRAN THOR (FR) 6 b g Authorized (IRE) – Sopran Slam (IRE)
Great big horse who came good at the end of the season winning over hurdles at Warwick. Runner-up a couple of times at Sandown prior to that, he will go novice handicap chasing and could be well handicapped off 120. Two and a half miles suits him.

ZHIGULI (IRE) 6 b g Flemensfirth (USA) – Grangeclare Flight (IRE)
Did nothing wrong over hurdles last season winning at Huntingdon and Plumpton. Anything he achieved over hurdles was always going to be a bonus though because he is a born chaser. He is another who will start off in a novices' handicap chase. I love him.

TRAINER'S HORSE TO FOLLOW: SHALLWEHAVEONEMORE

Olly MURPHY

Stables: Warren Chase Stables, Wilmcote, Stratford Upon Avon.
2020/2021: 80 Winners / 567 Runners 14% Prize-Money £634,998
www.ollymurphyracing.com

AFRICAN DANCE (IRE) 6 br g Shirocco (GER) – Dani California
Twice a winner over hurdles at Sedgefield and Plumpton, he was struggling with his breathing last season. We have therefore operated on his wind and he should benefit from it and improve this year. He will go over fences and I think he will develop into a nice handicapper over two and a half miles. Rated 122, we will start him off in a novices' handicap chase.

ALLAVINA (IRE) 6 b m Getaway (GER) – One Cool Kate (IRE)
A smart mare who enjoyed a good season over hurdles winning three times. Her only blemish came in the Grade 2 mares' novice hurdle at the Cheltenham Festival. I thought she would run well beforehand but something was amiss. Thankfully, she bounced back with an easy win at Perth next time. Fourth in a Listed bumper at Cheltenham in November, she travelled strongly that day but didn't quite finish off her race. She will go chasing this season and I will be disappointed if she doesn't earn some black type. Trips around two or two and a half miles are ideal because she isn't slow.

ALPHA CARINAE (IRE) 6 ch m Robin Des Champs (FR) – Annas Present (IRE)
She is another who will switch to fences this season. A winning Irish pointer, she jumps very well and was successful over hurdles at Perth in the Autumn. Third in a Listed mares' novice hurdle at Doncaster in March, it would be nice to think she could win some more black type over fences. She is tough and tries hard and is another who has had a wind operation since her last run.

ARMAND DE BRIGNAC (IRE) 5 b g Fame And Glory – Bolly (IRE)
A chaser in the making, he ran well on his debut in a decent bumper at Sandown finishing fifth. He was then very unlucky not to win at Wetherby having been squeezed out at the wing of what would normally be the final hurdle. Beaten narrowly, he is a staying type who will probably start off over either a stiff two miles or two and a half miles. I think he is a dark horse to keep an eye on because I like him a lot.

AUDITORIA 4 b f Gleneagles (IRE) – Authora (IRE)
Placed twice on the Flat in France, she was bought at the Arqana Sale in November. Runner-up on both her runs over hurdles for us at Hereford and Perth, she has improved enormously during the summer. Rated 107, we have plenty of options for her. She could go for a mares' maiden hurdle or we could go down the handicap route because I think she is on a lovely mark. I am expecting her to improve a lot this season.

BARONY LEGENDS (IRE) 5 b g Yeats (IRE) – Monty's Sister (IRE)
I think a lot of him and we are hoping he will develop into a nice novice hurdler. Runner-up in his only point-to-point in Ireland in December, he was third in a bumper at Southwell during the spring. A strong galloper, he will be suited by two and a half miles on soft ground.

BELIEVE JACK (FR) 4 b g Make Believe – Sandslide
Bought at the Cheltenham May Sale at Newmarket, he was placed a couple of times on the Flat before finishing second on his hurdles debut at Tipperary in May. He handles soft ground and is still unexposed and I hope he will pay his way over hurdles this winter.

BOMBS AWAY (IRE) 5 b g Westerner – Miss Greinton (GER)
I love him and, even though he did plenty of things wrong on his debut at Southwell, he still ran well in second and wasn't beaten far. Too keen during the early stages, he will have learned a lot from that and I have been delighted with him during the summer. A full-brother to Ribble Valley, he jumps fantastically well and has enough speed for two miles. I think he will be right up there with our best novice hurdlers this season.

BREWIN'UPASTORM (IRE) 8 b g Milan – Daraheen Diamond (IRE)
He is in good form at home and was much happier back over hurdles last season. Having won a handicap at Taunton off top weight in January, he produced an excellent performance to win the Grade 2 National Spirit Hurdle at Fontwell. Considering he didn't jump well and was caught wide for much of the race, I thought he ran well to finish fifth in the Grade 1 Aintree Hurdle. Two and a half miles appears to be his trip, although I wouldn't mind trying him over three miles at some stage. The plan is for him to reappear in a two and a half miles conditions hurdle at Aintree (6th November). I don't think he will be going back over fences because he frightened himself.

CALIPSO COLLONGES (FR) 9 b g Crossharbour – Ivresse Collonges (FR)
Ran some good races in defeat last season, including when finishing third at Sandown in February and fourth in a Grade 3 handicap chase at Aintree on Grand National day. We have tinkered with his wind since then and, while he could be aimed at the Becher Chase (4th December) once again, having finished fourth last season, we are looking to run him in some of the valuable veterans' chases in the New Year. They will give us a few more options.

CAPTAIN BIGGLES (IRE) 6 gr g Milan – Timon's Present
Runner-up in all three of his runs over hurdles last season, I can't believe he didn't manage to win one. He ran well behind Third Time Lucki at Wetherby in October and Stoner's Choice at Market Rasen (both rated in the 140s), but wasn't suited by the track at Plumpton last time. I am keen to win a maiden hurdle with him before switching to fences. He has plenty of ability and should win his share of races.

CHAMPAGNESUPEROVER (IRE) 6 b g Jeremy (USA) – Meldrum Hall (IRE)
We have always liked him and viewed him as a chaser in the making. I think there will be plenty of improvement forthcoming now he switches to fences. Indeed, we could start him off in a novices' handicap chase because I don't think he is on a bad mark off 134. He won over hurdles at Ayr and ran well in the Grade 1 Albert Bartlett Novices' Hurdle at the Cheltenham Festival. He endured a hard race though and was over the top by the time he ran at Aintree. Given a long break since, he will start off over two and a half miles.

CHOSEN PORT (IRE) 5 b m Well Chosen – Despute (IRE)
Half-sister to Burton Port, I was disappointed that she didn't win a bumper last season. Runner-up at Wetherby and placed at Southwell last time, she is a winning Irish pointer who jumps very well. She is a nice mare who will go hurdling starting off over two miles.

CONTEMPLATEMYFAITH (IRE) 5 b g Califet (FR) – Liss A Chroi (IRE)
Purchased at the Cheltenham March Sale, we haven't had him long but he is a lovely big horse. Third in a point-to-point and bumper for Sam Curling in Ireland, he belongs to the Owners Group and is a nice prospect for novice hurdles this season. His future lies over fences though.

COPPERLESS 6 b g Kayf Tara – Presenting Copper (IRE)
I think he is a very good horse. We are in two minds whether to aim him at the Greatwood Hurdle at Cheltenham (14th November) because he doesn't want the ground too soft. Alternatively, we could run him in the Welsh Champion Hurdle at Ffos Las (16th October) and then, all being well, the Grade 1 Fighting Fifth Hurdle at Newcastle (27th November). He was very impressive in the Swinton Hurdle at Haydock barely coming off the bridle to win by over eight lengths. He needs to improve again but I don't think its unrealistic to think he could develop into a Champion Hurdle contender. If things don't work out over hurdles, we have the option of going chasing.

COREY'S COURAGE 5 b m Dunaden (FR) – Valdas Queen (GER)
Surprised us when winning on her debut in a mares' bumper at Uttoxeter during the spring. Not the easiest to train, she did it well though and the form is good (the runner-up finished second at Cheltenham next time and the third has won subsequently). We have schooled her and she jumps well and will be aimed at mares' novice hurdles. I think she will keep improving.

DOCTOR KEN (FR) 5 b g Doctor Dino (FR) – Kendoretta (FR)
Half-brother to Grade 2 winning chaser Salsaretta, he is a gorgeous horse who I really like. Anything he achieves this season over hurdles will be a bonus because he is very much a chaser in the making. He showed a good level of form in bumpers last season finishing second on his debut at Ludlow – that race has worked out very well. He bolted up at Market Rasen last time even though the track didn't suit him. We will start him off over a stiff two miles over hurdles. I love him.

DOMINIC FAULT 4 b g Camelot – Midnight Angel (GER)
A very nice unraced four year old, he is a half-brother to Listed hurdle winner Midnight Game. An expensive store at the Goffs UK Summer Sale last year, we have given him plenty of time and he is a lovely horse for the future.

DUKE OF ROCKINGHAM 5 b g Kayf Tara – Our Jess (IRE)
He is my dark horse for the season because he worked as well as any of our four year olds last term. Things didn't go to plan on his debut in a bumper at Newbury and then he had a few issues which sidelined him for the rest of the campaign. I have been pleased with him during the summer and I would like to win a bumper with him before going hurdling. He lacks experience at the moment but is potentially a very nice horse.

EAGLEHILL (FR) 7 gr g Blue Bresil (FR) – Ratina De Vaige (FR)
Took well to chasing winning at Taunton and Plumpton before finding the ground too quick at Cheltenham last time. Still lightly raced, he should continue to be competitive off his mark in two and a half to three miles chases.

EAVESDROPPING 5 b m Kayf Tara – Leading On
Second on her debut in a bumper at Southwell, the winner franked the form by scoring again. She confirmed that promise by winning next time at Fontwell and will go hurdling now. Her schooling has pleased me and, while she has only raced on good ground, I don't think an easier surface will be a problem.

FABRIQUE EN FRANCE (FR) 6 b g Yeats (IRE) – Knar Mardy
Placed in two of his three Irish points, he benefited from a wind operation after his first run for us at Leicester when winning over hurdles at Wincanton. Third at Perth last time, we have tinkered with his wind once again and he will go chasing in the Autumn. Rated 119, he is on a good mark and will reappear in a novices' handicap chase.

FINAWN BAWN (IRE) 8 b g Robin Des Champs (FR) – Kayanti (IRE)
Has been off the track for nearly two years but is back in work and ready to resume his chasing career. Indeed, he was ready to run last spring, but the ground dried out. Twice a winner over hurdles, he finished third behind Truckers Lodge on his chasing debut at Chepstow in October 2019. If we can keep him sound, he is a horse with a lot of ability.

FOXINTHEBOX (IRE) 5 b g Presenting – Forces of Destiny (IRE)
A nice horse who was second in his only point-to-point for Francesca Nimmo in December. He was unlucky not to win on his first run for us in a point-to-point bumper at Aintree in May. A straightforward horse, he jumps well and will be suited by stepping up to two and a half miles over hurdles.

GETAWAY LILY BEAR (IRE) 5 b m Getaway (GER) – Jemima Jones (IRE)
A grand mare who finished runner-up in her point-to-point in Ireland (winner was subsequently sold for £330,000 to J.P.McManus) before being bought at the Goffs UK Sale in December. She doesn't show a lot at home but I am expecting her to stay well and we will run her in mares' novice hurdles.

GETAWAY LUV (IRE) 6 b g Getaway (GER) – Ut Love (FR)
Dual winner over hurdles at Huntingdon and Ludlow, he is much better than he showed at Market Rasen last time. Good ground is important to him and it won't be long before he goes chasing.

GO DANTE 5 b g Kayf Tara – Whoops A Daisy
I think an awful lot of him and feel he could be the best of our novice hurdlers this season. An impressive winner on his debut at Wincanton, it may not have been the strongest of bumpers but I was very taken by the manner of his victory. He was declared to run in the Grade 2 championship bumper at Aintree in April but he pulled some muscles, which ruled him out. It might prove a blessing in disguise because he has done well during the summer and we are looking forward to sending him hurdling. He isn't slow, so we will start him off over two miles at a track such as Uttoxeter. Long-term, he will stay further.

GUNSIGHT RIDGE 6 b g Midnight Legend – Grandma Griffiths
Despite winning at Doncaster and being placed on his four other starts, he didn't achieve as much as we expected over hurdles last season. He produced a good performance when second at Newbury in January but didn't build on it on his next two outings. He jumps very well and I think he will improve once switched to fences. A winning pointer in Ireland, we haven't seen the best of him and he could be well handicapped off 127. I am keen to drop him back to two miles.

HARDI DU MESNIL (FR) 4 b g Masterstroke (USA) – Athena Du Mesnil (FR)
A half-brother to Grade 1 winning novice hurdler Gaillard Du Mesnil, he is an exciting prospect owned by Robert Waley-Cohen who kindly sent him to me in September. Bought at the Arqana Sale in February, he won an AQPS Flat race and over hurdles in France. The form of his win at Pau in January has worked out well and we are delighted to be training him. We haven't made any plans yet because we are still getting to know him but he has a good profile.

HERE COMES MCCOY (IRE) 6 br g Dylan Thomas (IRE) – Is It Here (IRE)
Still a big weak baby last year, he won a couple of times over hurdles at Uttoxeter and Market Rasen. Sixth at Cheltenham in April on his final outing, he ran better than his position suggests. We will probably give him another run over hurdles before deciding whether to send him chasing. He is open to further improvement off his mark, especially over fences.

HUNTERS CALL (IRE) 11 b g Medaaly – Accordiontogelica (IRE)
A winner at Southwell in the summer last year, he ran some very good races in defeat finishing fourth in the Galway Hurdle and Greatwood Hurdle. Placed in the Lanzarote Hurdle at Kempton, too, he isn't getting any younger but will continue to be competitive in the good handicap hurdles. We have operated on his wind since his last run at Kelso.

ITALIAN SPIRIT (IRE) 5 b g Fame And Glory – Coco Milan (IRE)
A sharp sort, I like him. Runner-up on his debut at Ascot, he won a bumper next time at Market Rasen. We then sent him hurdling in the spring because we were keen to get some more experience into him and he ran creditably in fourth. A straightforward horse, he will hopefully develop into a nice novice hurdler.

ITCHY FEET (FR) 7 b g Cima De Triomphe (IRE) – Maeva Candas (FR)
A Grade 1 winning novice chaser the previous season, it was never going to be easy last term but he ran some very good races. Third in the Old Roan Chase and the Grade 1 Melling Chase both at Aintree, I was delighted with his run in the latter. His only disappointing run came back over hurdles at Haydock in February. He has spent a lot of time schooling at Henrietta Knight's and, while it will be tough off his mark, he will continue in the good two and a half miles chases. The Grade 2 Old Roan Chase (24th October) is his most likely starting point once again.

JETAWAY JOEY (IRE) 6 b g Getaway (GER) – Present Your Own (IRE)
I have always thought a lot of him but it took him a while to get off the mark over hurdles. He did it well at Perth and hopefully he will continue to progress. Still a novice until the end of October, he will probably go chasing later in the season. Two and a half miles is his trip and he isn't short of ability.

LET'S HAVE ANOTHER (IRE) 5 b g Fame And Glory – Rocella Lady (IRE)
Still babyish when making his debut at Ffos Las in May, he did nothing wrong finishing third and will improve for the experience. His work since has been good and he jumps well. He is now owned by Harry Redknapp and will go hurdling.

LINELEE KING (FR) 6 gr g Martaline – Queen Lee (FR)
Didn't achieve as much as we were expecting over hurdles last season. A winner on his reappearance at Kelso, he was second a couple of times but I thought he would win a few more. He jumps fences very well though so I think he will improve once switched to chasing. A former winning Irish pointer, he stays well and will contest a novices' handicap chase over two and a half miles plus off his mark of 125.

LORD OF KERAK 6 b g Martaline – Mille Et Une (FR)
A lovely horse with a good pedigree, he ran very well first time out over hurdles finishing second at Uttoxeter. He filled the same position at Sandown and was unlucky not to win having made a bad mistake at the third last. He won nicely next time at Uttoxeter but his run in the Grade 2 Leamington Novices' Hurdle at Warwick was a disaster. Runner-up at Newcastle, he struggled with his wind last time at Perth. He has therefore had a breathing operation since and will go over fences. Slow ground suits him and he is capable of developing into a useful chaser.

LUPUS REGEM 5 b g Iffraaj – Miss Villefranche
A new arrival, he is a nice scopey horse who won a bumper on his debut at Wetherby in March when trained by Henry Daly. Bought privately, he will start in a maiden hurdle in the Autumn and is a lovely addition to the team.

MACKELDUFF (FR) 5 gr g Martaline – Evitta (FR)
I like him and feel he is open to plenty of improvement. Fourth and third at Uttoxeter and Haydock respectively on his first couple of runs, he won nicely last time at Southwell. Still a novice for this season, we have plenty of options because he is on a lenient mark. Long-term, he will jump fences.

MEXICAN BOY (IRE) 5 gr g Kayf Tara – J'y Viens (FR)
Ran well on his debut finishing runner-up in a bumper at Warwick in March. He was over the top by the time he ran again at Market Rasen. Given a break since, he is straightforward and should pay his way in novice hurdles. He jumps well.

MOORE MARGAUX (IRE) 6 b g Flemensfirth (USA) – Omas Glen (IRE)
He is a very smart horse who was too free at Newbury on his first run. However, he ran much better less than a month later at Warwick finishing second behind a useful winner (Calico). We purposely didn't run him again because we wanted to keep him as a novice for this season. He will appreciate stepping up to two and a half miles and is suited by soft ground.

NICKOLSON (FR) 7 b g No Risk At All (FR) – Incorrigible (FR)
Having run well on his reappearance behind Ribble Valley in an intermediate hurdle at Carlisle, his form went downhill thereafter. He failed to handle heavy ground at Sandown and wasn't at his best on his next two starts either. He had a few issues last season and is much better than he showed. We are hoping a switch to fences will see him return to his best because he has always shown plenty at home.

NO RISK DES FLOS (FR) 6 gr g No Risk At All (FR) – Marie Royale (FR)
A very nice horse who we kept to two miles last season because he wasn't ready mentally to step up in distance. He won over hurdles at Uttoxeter and Southwell but had had enough for the season by the time he ran at Perth in April. He hasn't done a lot wrong and enjoys soft ground. His rating of 128 looks fair and he will benefit from stepping up to two and a half miles this time around.

NOTRE PARI (IRE) 7 br g Jeremy (USA) – Glynn Approach (IRE)
Not the easiest to train, he has been treated for a kissing spine since his last run. Back in work, he was never right last season even though he didn't run badly at Uttoxeter in April. I have always thought a lot of him and feel he will progress this year. Still a maiden over fences, we have got a few options.

OVERTHETOP (IRE) 7 br g Flemensfirth (USA) – Dawn Bid (IRE)
A dual winner over hurdles a couple of seasons ago, he missed the whole of last term due to a leg injury. However, he is back in work and will hopefully be running around Christmas time. He won a point-to-point before joining us and will go straight over fences.

PORT OF MARS (IRE) 7 b g Westerner – Sarahall (IRE)
He won nicely over fences at Hereford in January but we don't know what went wrong next time at Kelso. Pulled up, we have operated on his wind since and hopefully he will get back on track in staying handicap chases. Still lightly raced, he should improve.

RAMBO T (IRE) 4 b g Ocovango – Biddy's Boru (IRE)
A lovely forward going type, he ran in two Irish points finishing fourth and second before we bought him in May. Still for sale, he will have a run in a bumper before going hurdling.

RESTANDBETHANKFUL 5 br g Califet (FR) – Persian Forest
A bumper winner at Perth, he took well to hurdling winning two out of three and is rated 126. Both victories at Market Rasen and Stratford were in May so he remains a novice for this season. We might consider the Grade 2 Persian War Novices' Hurdle (8th October) or the Grade 3 Silver Trophy (9th October) both at Chepstow because he won't have a problem stepping up to two and a half miles. He is a nice horse who has had a wind operation since his last run.

STORM OF LIGHT (IRE) 5 b g Fame And Glory – Blazing Moon (IRE)
Fourth on his only start in a bumper at Huntingdon during the spring, he is better than he showed that day. He will be suited by soft ground and stepping up in trip over hurdles.

SURE TOUCH 5 b g Yeats (IRE) – Liberthine (FR)
A horse I like a lot, he was an impressive winner on his debut at Wincanton in January. We then ran him in the Grade 2 bumper at Aintree but he got behind early on. He is much better than that run suggests and is one to look forward to in novice hurdles this season. He has a very good pedigree and, while he will probably start over two miles, he will stay further. I think he is very good.

TAMAR BRIDGE (IRE) 6 b g Jeremy (USA) – Mise En Place
He is a lovely horse who has done nothing wrong in his short career. A bumper winner at Haydock, the form of his victory over hurdles at Ayr has been given a boost since. A proper staying type, he likes soft ground and will be aimed at a decent two and a half miles handicap in the Autumn. I like him a lot.

THOMAS DARBY (IRE) 8 b g Beneficial – Silaoce (FR)
I have always thought he was a very good horse and he ran a tremendous race at Aintree finishing third in the Grade 1 Liverpool Hurdle. Beaten less than five lengths, I had been keen to step him up to three miles for a while. He should continue to be competitive in the top staying hurdles and the Grade 2 West Yorkshire Hurdle at Wetherby (30th October) is the obvious starting point.

THUNDER ROCK (IRE) 5 b g Shirocco (GER) – La Belle Sauvage
A nice horse who was runner-up in an Irish point before joining us last season. Placed in a bumper at Newcastle in December, he won next time at Exeter and has done very well during the summer. He jumps nicely and will run in a maiden hurdle in mid October.

TIGERBYTHETAIL (IRE) 5 b g Yeats (IRE) – Talktothetail (IRE)
Half-brother to Roksana, he has a good pedigree and is a lovely horse. Narrowly beaten on his debut at Market Rasen during the spring, he would have preferred a more galloping track. I know the winner (Sauce of Life) is well regarded and we have the option of running in another bumper or going straight over hurdles. Two and a half miles is likely to be his trip over jumps.

TINNAHALLA (IRE) 4 b g Starspangledbanner (AUS) – Bright Bank (IRE)
A tough horse who took well to jumping winning at Catterick and Ludlow. Fourth at Ascot in between, he ran a good race but Aidan (Coleman) wishes he had made more use of him. I hope he will progress again this year and we will start him off in the four year old handicap hurdle at Chepstow (8ᵗʰ October).

URBAN GRIT (IRE) 4 b g Cityscape – Lady Azamour (IRE)
Has a good attitude and, despite showing signs of greenness, he ran well in a bumper at Huntingdon finishing second. That experience won't have been lost on him and I expect him to improve a lot. He is capable of winning a bumper in the Autumn.

VOKOLOHS (IRE) 5 ch g Sholokhov (IRE) – Quarry Thyne (IRE)
Purchased at the Cheltenham May Sale at Newmarket, he is still for sale. Runner-up in an English point for Tom Ellis, he looked green that day and should improve. A straightforward type, I like him and we will probably run him in a bumper before going hurdling.

WASHINGTON 5 br g Westerner – Present Leader
A sharp type, he did nothing wrong last season winning both his bumpers at Fakenham and Huntingdon. He has a lot of ability and I think he will be at his best over hurdles rather than fences because he isn't the tallest or most robust of horses. I am expecting him to develop into a very nice hurdler starting off over two miles because he was quite keen at Huntingdon last time.

WOLFSPEAR (IRE) 5 b g Fame And Glory – Espresso Lady (IRE)
Half-brother to Listed chase winner Sensulano, he took time to come to himself but impressed me when winning first time out in a bumper at Huntingdon in May. The runner-up has won over hurdles since. He jumps very well at home and is ready to go hurdling in the Autumn. I think he will appreciate softer ground and is one to look forward to.

> **TRAINER'S HORSE TO FOLLOW: GO DANTE**

Please see page 195
for details of
Ahead on the Flat 2022

Champion Trainer 2005/2006, 2006/2007, 2007/2008, 2008/2009, 2009/2010, 2010/11, 2011/12, 2013/2014, 2014/2015, 2015/2016, 2018/2019 & 2020/2021

Paul NICHOLLS

Stables: Manor Farm Stables, Ditcheat, Somerset.
2020/2021: 176 Winners / 705 Runners 25% Prize-Money £2,470,877
www.paulnichollsracing.com

ASK FOR GLORY (IRE) 7 b g Fame And Glory – Ask Helen (IRE)
Picked up an injury soon after running over hurdles at Cheltenham in October and missed the remainder of the season. All being well, he will be back in action around Christmas and the plan is to send him chasing. A winning Irish pointer, he is still lightly raced and very much a chasing type.

ATHOLL STREET (IRE) 6 b g Jeremy (USA) – Allthewhile (IRE)
Won nicely on his first two starts over hurdles at Taunton. He pulled up next time in the Grade 2 Dovecote Novices' Hurdle at Kempton and we found he had a tiny hairline fracture, which kept him off for the rest of the campaign. He is fine now and will go over fences. I think he will develop into a nice novice chaser over two miles.

BARBADOS BUCK'S (IRE) 6 b g Getaway (GER) – Buck's Blue (FR)
From the family of Big Buck's, he looked good when winning novice hurdles at Southwell twice and Kempton. A bit disappointing in the Albert Bartlett Novices' Hurdle at Cheltenham in March, he has had a good break since and is ready to go chasing. Runner-up in his only point-to-point in Ireland, he jumps well and should develop into a very nice staying novice chaser.

BOB AND CO (FR) 10 b g Dom Alco (FR) – Outre Mer (FR)
Enjoyed a good season in hunter chases winning three times, including the Champion hunters chase at the Punchestown Festival. It was a great result for David (Maxwell) and he is keen for him to continue in hunter chases once again this season and hopefully ride him in the Foxhunters' at the Cheltenham Festival in March, which he was unable to do last season due to the covid restrictions.

BRAVE KINGDOM (FR) 5 b g Brave Mansonnien (FR) – New Foundation (IRE)
We are delighted to be training for Andrew and Kate Brooks, who kindly sent their horses to us during the summer. We are still getting to know the horses, but he won nicely in a bumper at Fontwell in late February and looks a nice horse to go novice hurdling in the Autumn.

BRAVEMANSGAME (FR) 6 b g Brave Mansonnien (FR) – Genifique (FR)
Developed into a high-class novice hurdler winning three times, including the Grade 1 Challow Novices' Hurdle at Newbury over Christmas. Third in the Ballymore Novices' Hurdle at Cheltenham, he had a hard race and that probably cost him at Aintree because he was a bit flat. He is another winning Irish pointer and is ready to go chasing. We will start him off over two and a half or two miles six but he stays three miles and it wouldn't surprise me if he was contesting something like the Grade 1 Kauto Star Novices' Chase at Kempton on Boxing Day. There are plenty of good two and a half miles novice chases before then though, including at Newbury (Grade 2 on Friday 26th November).

BREWERS PROJECT (IRE) 7 b g Aizavoski (IRE) – Shaylee Wilde (IRE)
Won a couple of times over hurdles at Wincanton and Chepstow and also finished runner-up behind a decent horse (Grumpy Charley) at the latter track in between. He will go over fences and, with his rating of 126, we will look for a suitable novices' handicap chase over two miles.

BROKEN HALO 6 b g Kayf Tara – Miss Invincible
Lightly raced, he is a horse with plenty of potential. He won over hurdles at Wincanton in March but then found the ground too quick at Chepstow last time. We always felt he was struggling a bit with his breathing so we have operated on his wind and hopefully that will make a difference. His future lies over fences, but he remains a novice over hurdles until the end of October and he will have another run or two before going chasing. I think three miles will be his trip.

CAP DU MATHAN (FR) 6 b g Kapgarde (FR) – Nounjya Du Mathan (FR)
Missed last season due to having a few issues, he is a decent horse if we can get him right. He won over hurdles at Plumpton the previous season and will go chasing.

CAPTAIN DESTINY 4 b g Kapgarde (FR) – New Destiny (FR)
We have a very nice team of bumper horses for this season including this Kapgarde gelding. A half-brother to dual Listed winner Papagana, I like him a lot.

CAT TIGER (FR) 7 b g Diamond Boy (FR) – Miss Canon (FR)
Like Bob And Co, he did well in hunter chases last season winning at Leicester before finishing third in the Foxhunters' at Aintree. He will continue in such events and follow a similar campaign.

CHAVEZ (IRE) 5 b g Yeats (IRE) – Rock The Baby (IRE)
A lovely big horse who won a bumper at Chepstow on his debut in November. It was desperate ground next time at Exeter and he didn't like it. We have given him plenty of time since and he will go novice hurdling over two and a half miles. Long-term, he is a staying chaser in the making.

CLAN DES OBEAUX (FR) 9 b g Kapgarde (FR) – Nausicaa Des Obeaux (FR)
He was in fantastic form during the spring winning the Grade 1 Bowl at Aintree and then followed it up by winning the Grade 1 Punchestown Gold Cup. We decided to put the cheekpieces on at Aintree and they made a big difference. The plan is for him to go straight to Kempton for the King George on Boxing Day because we know he is very good fresh. Then we will aim him at the Denman Chase at Newbury in February followed by Aintree and Punchestown once again.

COMPLETE UNKNOWN (IRE) 5 b g Dylan Thomas (IRE) – Silver Stream (IRE)
Bought at the Cheltenham March Sale which was held at Newmarket, he won a bumper at Thurles a couple of weeks beforehand. He is a nice big strong horse who I like. He will go novice hurdling and will jump fences in time.

CONFIRMATION BIAS (IRE) 6 b g Presenting – Bonnie Parker (IRE)
Consistent, he won over hurdles at Wincanton in late March and therefore is still a novice until the end of October. Rated 117, I think he is well treated and we will try and exploit that before he goes chasing.

CYRNAME (FR) 9 b g Nickname (FR) – Narquille (FR)

Looks tremendous following his summer holiday. Indeed, I don't think he has ever looked better. We have tweaked his wind again since his last run and the intention is to start him off in the Charlie Hall Chase at Wetherby (30th October), which he won impressively last season. As regards the rest of the season, we will make a plan after Wetherby, but it is unlikely he will go for the King George at Kempton.

DANNY KIRWAN (IRE) 8 b g Scorpion (IRE) – Sainte Baronne (FR)

Twice a winner over hurdles at Ascot and Wincanton, he has been fragile but is a useful horse on his day. He will go chasing over two and a half miles.

DARGIANNINI (IRE) 6 b g Fame And Glory – You Take Care (IRE)

We are still learning about him having arrived in the summer. He has shown a decent level of form winning a bumper and twice over hurdles. Still a novice until the end of October, his mark looks fair and we will keep him over hurdles for the time being. He will be jumping fences one day though.

ENRILO (FR) 7 bl g Buck's Boum (FR) – Rock Treasure (FR)

A seriously nice horse who took well to chasing winning at Exeter and Newbury and was unlucky not to win the Bet365 Gold Cup at Sandown. He has a few quirks but is an immense talent. He travelled so well during the race and ended up in front too soon and started wandering about. We nearly put a pair of cheekpieces on. However, he did well to run such a big race because it was touch and go whether he was ready in time for it. He had been held up earlier in the season with a few issues. The original plan was to aim him at the Scottish National, but he knocked his shin a few days beforehand and everything was a bit of a rush to get him to Sandown. Still lightly raced over fences, his target is the Ladbrokes Trophy at Newbury (27th November) and he will go there first time out. I think it will really suit him because they will go a strong gallop.

FIDELIO VALLIS (FR) 6 b g Saint Des Saints (FR) – Quora Vallis (FR)

Had a productive spell over fences during the spring winning four times, including handicap chases at Kempton and Warwick. He is still a novice until the end of October, so the plan is for him to run in the two miles three novices' chase at Chepstow (9th October) followed by a trip to Cheltenham (23rd October) for a similar event and then he will be forced to run in open company. Rated 149, he is effective over two or two and a half miles and appreciates decent ground.

FLASH COLLONGES (FR) 6 b g Saddler Maker (IRE) – Prouesse Collonges (FR)

From the family of Neptune Collonges, he is a lovely big strong horse who surprised us when winning on his debut over hurdles at Exeter. He won another couple, including a handicap hurdle at Kelso last time. He will go novice chasing and, while he will start off over two and a half miles, he will stay three miles.

FLEMENSTIDE (IRE) 6 b g Flemensfirth (USA) – Keep Face (FR)

A very nice horse who I like a lot. Still backward last year, he ran well on his debut at Sandown in a decent bumper before winning at Exeter in January. We took a team of eight horses to Ayr's Scottish National meeting, including him, and they all ran terribly. I would therefore put a line through that run and he is one to look forward to over hurdles. Two and a half miles will suit him.

FLIC OU VOYOU (FR) 7 b g Kapgarde (FR) – Hillflower (FR)

Another lovely big horse who won three times early on last season racking up victories at Chepstow, Newton Abbot and Wincanton. He likes decent ground and ended the campaign with a very good run at Sandown finishing second in a valuable novices' handicap hurdle on the final day of the season. He will go novice chasing.

FRIEND OR FOE (FR) 6 b g Walk In The Park (IRE) – Mandchou (FR)

A winner over hurdles at Wincanton in December, he also won on his chasing debut at Uttoxeter in early May and could be an interesting two mile novice this season. He jumps well and is a sharp horse who likes good ground. There is a two miles novice chase at Newton Abbot (10th October) which could suit him. I think he will be a fun horse over fences.

FRODON (FR) 9 b g Nickname (FR) – Miss Country (FR)

We were thrilled with him last season winning three times, including the King George at Kempton on Boxing Day. Bryony (Frost) gave him a very good ride on the final day of the season, too, when winning the Grade 2 at Sandown. The plan is for him to start off in the Grade 1 Champion Chase at Down Royal (30th October). I think the track will suit him and then he will go back to Kempton for the King George once again. I don't think we will be aiming him at the Gold Cup this season but we might consider the Irish Hennessy at Leopardstown because he should be suited by the track.

GAULOIS (FR) 5 b g Samum (GER) – Pail Mel (FR)

Half-brother to Alcala, he was placed in his two runs over hurdles at Gowran and Fairyhouse when trained by Shark Hanlon in Ireland. He arrived in the summer and will continue in novice hurdles.

GELINO BELLO (FR) 5 b g Saint Des Saints (FR) – Parade (FR)

I really like him, he is a lovely big horse who won a bumper at Plumpton on his debut. He then ran a very good race finishing third in a Listed event at Newbury in February. He will go novice hurdling over two and a half miles and is very much one for the future.

GOLD BULLION (FR) 5 b g Fame And Glory – Tornade D'Ainay (FR)

Another lovely bumper horse from last season, he won first time out at Warwick in January. A bit disappointing next time under a penalty at Chepstow when finishing fourth, he has schooled well and is ready to go novice hurdling.

GRACE A VOUS ENKI (FR) 5 b g Dream Well (FR) – Cadiane (FR)

An interesting horse who arrived from France last season but has yet to run for us. He is a half-brother to Yala Enki and won twice over fences at Auteuil. His future is over fences but he is a maiden over hurdles, so we are going to aim him at staying novice hurdles with some cut in the ground.

GREANETEEN (FR) 7 b g Great Pretender (IRE) – Manson Teene (FR)

I love him, he improved a lot last season winning the Haldon Gold Cup at Exeter, running a blinder in the Champion Chase at Cheltenham and then winning a Grade 1 at Sandown at the end of the season. Only seven, he is learning to relax and there is more improvement to come from him. I thought Bryony (Frost) rode a great race on him at Sandown and he was very impressive. The Tingle Creek Chase at Sandown (4th December) is his first big target, although he could run in the Haldon Gold Cup (2nd November) beforehand. Then, he may go to Ascot for the Clarence House Chase in January before the Queen Mother Champion Chase in March.

HACKER DES PLACES (FR) 4 b g Great Pretender (IRE) – Plaisance (FR)
A very nice horse who was a bit disappointing on his first run for us at Wincanton but he won by a wide margin at Wetherby over Christmas. Unfortunately, he struck into himself and missed the rest of the season, which means he isn't the easiest horse to place. However, he loves soft ground and will contest handicap hurdles off his mark of 136.

HALO DES OBEAUX (FR) 4 gr g Al Namix (FR) – Almeria Des Obeaux (FR)
He is a nice big chasing type who was placed in a couple of French bumpers before winning on his hurdles debut at Auteuil in March. We have done plenty of schooling with him and he remains eligible for novice hurdles until the end of October. With that in mind, he is a possible for the Grade 2 Persian War Novices' Hurdle at Chepstow (8th October). There is every chance he will go chasing after that.

HELL RED (FR) 4 gr g Martaline – Queen Margot (FR)
Runner-up behind Monmiral at Auteuil before we bought him, he won on his first run for us at Chepstow but then had an issue with his breathing at Cheltenham in November. I thought he ran well in the Boodles Juvenile Hurdle at Cheltenham before winning nicely at Newton Abbot in April. He likes decent ground and he could run in the four year old handicap hurdle at Chepstow (8th October).

HENRI THE SECOND (FR) 4 b g Saddler Maker (IRE) – Rock Treasure (FR)
An unraced half-brother to Enrilo, he is a lovely horse who has been given time and will start off in a bumper in the Autumn.

HERMES BELLEVUE (FR) 4 gr g Jeu St Eloi (FR) – Venise Bellevue (FR)
Another new arrival from France, we haven't done much with him yet. He raced twice over hurdles at Pau for Arnaud Chaille-Chaille in January finishing third last time. Given a break, he will go novice hurdling.

HIGHLAND HUNTER (IRE) 8 gr g Subtle Power (IRE) – Loughine Sparkle (IRE)
A real stayer, he ran well in the Midlands National finishing fifth, but everything was a bit of a rush. He needed to run three times over fences to qualify so he had a couple of quick runs at Carlisle and Exeter and the Uttoxeter race came a bit soon. His first main target is the Welsh National at Chepstow (27th December) because he loves soft ground and stays well.

HITMAN (FR) 5 b g Falco (USA) – Tercah Girl (FR)
A big strong horse who is only five, he has so much ability and I love him. Twice a winner over fences at Ffos Las and Newbury, he travelled like the best horse in the race in the Grade 1 at Aintree, but I am not sure he got the trip over two and a half miles. There are plenty of options for him in the Autumn, including the Haldon Gold Cup at Exeter (2nd November). We could consider the Old Roan Chase at Aintree (24th October) or the Grade 2 intermediate chase at Down Royal (30th October), which we have won seven times. He is a very nice horse who I think will continue to improve.

HOLETOWN HERO (FR) 4 br g Buck's Boum (FR) – Voix du Coeur (FR)
Bought at the Goffs Landrover Sale as a three year old, I like him and we will aim him at a bumper in the Autumn.

HUFLOWER (FR) 4 b g Saddex – Send Me Flower (FR)
He is a lovely horse I like who we bought in the spring. He ran in four bumpers in France winning twice. We have schooled him over hurdles and he jumps well.

HUGOS NEW HORSE (FR) 4 b g Coastal Path – Pour Le Meilleur (FR)
Another one for bumpers in the Autumn, he is a half-brother to Black Corton and is a lovely horse.

IL RIDOTO (FR) 4 b g Kapgarde (FR) – L'Exploratrice (FR)
Ex-French, he won twice over hurdles at Pau before switching to fences. Having fallen on his chasing debut, he was runner-up next time and is therefore still a novice. Only four, he will go novice chasing and is a nice horse.

INDIVIDUALISTE (FR) 3 ro g Cima De Triomphe (IRE) – Intellingencia (FR)
Bought at the Arqana summer sale in July, he will go juvenile hurdling. He raced three times on the Flat in France being placed on a couple of occasions. We gave him a holiday after he arrived and he looks well.

IRISH HILL (GER) 3 gr c Kingston Hill – Irresistable (GER)
We bought him in August having won two of his four races on the Flat in France. Previously trained by Peter Schiergen, he won over a mile and six at Longchamp in July. He will go juvenile hurdling.

JEREMY PASS (IRE) 6 b g Jeremy (USA) – Toulon Pass (IRE)
A winner on his hurdles bow at Wincanton, he was placed at Doncaster and Kempton. We have operated on his wind and, while he will probably have another run over hurdles, it won't be long before he goes chasing. He is a big horse who ran in an Irish point and is a staying chaser in the making.

KANDOO KID (FR) 5 gr g Kapgarde (FR) – Scarlett Du Mesnil (IRE)
From the family of Politologue, he took a bit of time to win his bumper. but I like him. Having run well at Ascot and Wincanton, he appreciated the better ground when winning at Taunton in the spring. He will go straight over hurdles.

KAYF TAOI 5 b g Kayf Tara – Patsie Magern
Fourth on his debut at Taunton in early March, he is not really a bumper horse. Having been outpaced, he stayed on well and will be suited by running over two and a half miles over hurdles. I think he is a very nice horse.

KNAPPERS HILL (IRE) 5 b g Valirann (FR) – Brogella (IRE)
A lovely horse who kept improving last season winning all three of his starts in bumpers. A Listed winner at Ascot before Christmas, he then produced a very good performance to win the Grade 2 championship event at Aintree on Grand National day. The plan is to start him off in the same two miles novice hurdle at Chepstow (8th October) which Bravemansgame contested last season. He handles decent ground and has the speed for two miles.

KNOWSLEY ROAD (IRE) 4 b g Flemensfirth (USA) – Rowanville Lady (IRE)
Only four, he is a nice big horse who was narrowly beaten in his only Irish point-to-point for Colin Bowe in May. We bought him a few days later at the Cheltenham Sale held at Newmarket. It is possible he will have a run in a bumper before going hurdling.

LALLYGAG (GER) 4 b g It's Gino (GER) – Laviola (GER)
A full-brother to Grade 1 winner Lalor, who has also joined us, he finished fifth behind Kandoo Kid in a bumper at Taunton last spring. He has settled in well since arriving and we will probably give him another run in a bumper in the Autumn.

LALOR (GER) 9 b g It's Gino (GER) – Laviola (GER)
His owner kindly sent him to us during the summer and we have operated on his wind since arriving. He obviously has some very good form winning a Grade 1 novice hurdle and Grade 2 bumper and novice chase. However, he has had his share of issues, too, including a fibrillating heart. We will take our time with him and see what he is capable of. I think he wants three miles and it is possible we will aim him at the Grade 3 handicap chase at Ascot (30th October).

LARGY TRAIN 4 b g Yorgunnabelucky (USA) – Snow Train
A bumper winner at Ayr during the spring when trained by Stuart Crawford, he was bought privately afterwards by Anthony Bromley on behalf of Million In Mind. We haven't discussed plans but we might give him another run in a bumper before going hurdling.

LE CHIFFRE D'OR (FR) 5 gr g No Risk At All (FR) – Miss Vitoria (FR)
Third behind the aforementioned Brave Kingdom on his debut at Fontwell, he won nicely next time at Wincanton in another bumper. He is ready to go hurdling now and is likely to start off over two miles.

LIME AVENUE (IRE) 4 b f Walk In The Park (IRE) – Carrigeen Kohleria (IRE)
Owned by Highclere Thoroughbreds, she is a half-sister to the Irish National winner Rogue Angel. Bought as a three year old at the Tattersalls Derby Sale, she will start off in a mares' bumper.

MAGIC SAINT (FR) 7 b g Saint Des Saints (FR) – Magic Poline (FR)
Won a decent two miles handicap chase at Cheltenham's November meeting and I thought he ran very well in a Grade 2 handicap chase over two and a half miles at the same track in April on his final start. I have always thought he wanted two and a half miles and, while he won't be easy to place off a mark of 155, he could be ideal for the Grand Sefton Chase over the National fences at Aintree (6th November) because he is such a good jumper.

MAGISTRATO (FR) 3 b g Kapgarde (FR) – Franche Alliance (FR)
A big strong gelding by Kapgarde, he is a lovely horse who finished runner-up at Auteuil in April. He has done very well physically since arriving and we are thinking of starting him off in the juvenile hurdle at Chepstow (9th October), which we won last year with Hell Red. NB. The stable have won the race six times in the last eleven years.

MAKIN'YOURMINDUP 4 b g Kayf Tara – Subtilty
Bought at the Goffs UK Spring Sale at Doncaster, he finished third in his only point-to-point in Ireland earlier the same month. In all likelihood, he will go straight over hurdles.

MASTER TOMMYTUCKER 10 b g Kayf Tara – No Need For Alarm
A horse with a lot of ability, he had another good season winning three times. An easy winner of the Grade 2 Silviniaco Conti Chase at Kempton in January, he wasn't beaten far in the Grade 1 Ascot Chase next time. Suited by small fields, we will probably enter him in the King George. If we place him right, he is capable of winning a big prize this year.

MATTERHORN (FR) 3 b g Martaline – Sacarine (FR)

He is a beautiful horse who was trained in France by Gabriel Leenders. Third on his debut at Auteuil in April, he was unlucky because he was travelling strongly when making a mistake at the second last. The form is very good because the winner (Paradiso) is the best juvenile hurdler in France winning twice since, including a Grade 3 at the same track in June. We are going to campaign him similar to Monmiral and start him off low key and then perhaps aim him at the Grade 2 Summit Juvenile Hurdle at Doncaster (11th December). He is a lovely horse and one I am excited about.

McFABULOUS (IRE) 7 b g Milan – Rossavon (IRE)

A dual Grade 2 winner last season, he won the Persian War Novices' Hurdle at Chepstow in the Autumn and the rescheduled Relkeel Hurdle at Kempton early in the New Year. Despite those victories, we felt he was struggling a bit with his breathing – he stopped very quickly in the Aintree Hurdle last time. We have therefore operated on his wind and that will hopefully help him. He will go novice chasing starting off over two and a half miles. I think he is a better horse going right handed and, while we will go quietly with him to begin with, a race such as the Grade 1 Kauto Star Novices' Chase at Kempton (26th December) could be a target.

MILAN BRIDGE (IRE) 5 b g Milan – Ice Princess (IRE)

Raced twice in Ireland during the spring, including when third in a point-to-point. A chaser for the future, he looks the sort who will stay all day and will be campaigned in two and a half miles plus novice hurdles this season.

MIRANDA (IRE) 6 b m Camelot – Great Artist (FR)

Rated 146, she did very well over hurdles winning twice, including a Grade 2 mares' hurdle at Doncaster in late January. We might give her a run on the Flat in the Autumn before she goes back jumping. She will follow a similar programme in mares' events and is capable of gaining some more black type.

MONMIRAL (FR) 4 bl g Saint Des Saints (FR) – Achere (FR)

Unbeaten in juvenile hurdles last season, including the Grade 1 Anniversary 4-Y-O Juvenile Hurdle at Aintree in April, we haven't decided whether he stays over hurdles or goes chasing. I think he will be even better in twelve months time and is very much one for the future. There isn't the same incentive to send four year olds over fences anymore but that is where his future lies. He might prove me wrong, but I don't consider him either a Champion Hurdle or Arkle horse because I think he wants two and a half miles. He is a galloper who stays very well. Having said that, he improved a lot last year and, being only a four year old, he should continue to do so. Whichever route he takes, he is an exciting prospect.

MR GLASS (IRE) 5 b g Sholokhov (IRE) – Maryota (FR)

A very nice horse who won two of his three races in bumpers last season. Third on his debut at Newbury, he won by a wide margin at Wetherby over Christmas before following up under a penalty at Haydock. He jumps well and is ready to go novice hurdling. Even though he may start off over two miles, he is a stayer and will benefit from stepping up to two and a half miles.

NEXT DESTINATION (IRE) 9 b g Dubai Destination (USA) – Liss Alainn (IRE)
He possesses a lot of ability and I am very proud of what we achieved with him last season because he was off the track for two and a half years. Runner-up in the Grade 2 West Yorkshire Hurdle at Wetherby in October, he then won Grade 2 novice chases at Newbury and Warwick. I thought he ran very well in the National Hunt Chase at the Cheltenham Festival finishing second. We nearly ran him in the Grade 1 Brown Advisory Novices' Chase but thought it looked a strong race beforehand. He handles soft ground and, if conditions are suitable, he could run in the Grade 1 *Betfair* Chase at Haydock (20th November), which is invariably a small field.

ONETHREEFIVENOTOUT (IRE) 5 b g Milan – Back To Loughadera (IRE)
He has needed time having bought him as a three year old at the Goffs Landrover Sale. He is a lovely horse though who will run in a bumper.

OUTLAW PETER (IRE) 5 b g Mustameet (USA) – My Katie (IRE)
Runner-up in a bumper at Navan in January, he was bought privately and joined us last spring. He will go novice hurdling.

PASO DOBLE (IRE) 4 br g Dawn Approach (IRE) – Baila Me (GER)
I like him a lot. Twice a winner on the Flat in Ireland when trained by Jim Bolger, we bought him in November and gelded him soon afterwards. He ran well in the Grade 2 Adonis Hurdle at Kempton in February finishing third. We then purposely waited until May before winning at the same track. Still a novice for the whole season, he is one to look forward to.

PETROSSIAN (IRE) 5 br g Sageburg (IRE) – Innisfree Dawn (IRE)
Looked a smart horse when winning on his debut in a bumper at Newbury in November. We then had a few issues with him and he wasn't at his best when returning to the same track in the spring. He will go novice hurdling and is a nice horse.

PIC D'ORHY (FR) 6 b g Turgeon (USA) – Rose Candy (FR)
Only five, he will go back over fences and is capable of doing well in two miles novice chases. He was still going well when falling at Ascot on his second run. We switched him back to hurdles at Taunton in February and he ran very well considering we thought he would need the run. Narrowly touched off by our other horse Rockadenn, he didn't stay two and a half miles at Sandown on the final day of the season.

POLITOLOGUE (FR) 10 gr g Poliglote – Scarlet Row (FR)
An amazing horse who won the Grade 1 Tingle Creek Chase at Sandown for a second time. Runner-up in the Clarence House Chase at Ascot, he was due to contest the Queen Mother Champion at Cheltenham but we found a trickle of blood in the paddock, which was frustrating. He is in great shape following his summer holiday and the Tingle Creek (4th December) is once again his first target. Very good fresh, he will go straight there.

POZO EMERY (FR) 6 b g Le Havre (IRE) – Chic Et Zen (FR)
Runner-up in his only Irish point-to-point, he is a lovely horse who won over hurdles at Chepstow in January. Runner-up on his next two outings at Wincanton and Chepstow, he will go novice chasing. I like him.

RAINYDAY WOMAN 6 b m Kayf Tara – Wistow
A smashing mare who joined us last season and developed into a smart bumper performer. She won at Stratford before producing a very good effort when winning a Listed mares' bumper at Huntingdon before Christmas. Beaten in a similar event at Sandown last time, she struggled with her breathing in the bad ground. We have operated on her wind since and she is likely to start off in a mares' novice hurdle at Chepstow (8th October). NB. The stable have won the race three times in the last four years with If You Say Run (2017), Posh Trish (2018) & Silver Forever (2019).

ROUGE VIF (FR) 7 b g Sageburg (IRE) – Rouge Amour (FR)
Rated 161 over fences, he won at Cheltenham last Autumn but we are still getting to know him and haven't made any definite plans. The Grade 2 Shloer Chase at Cheltenham (14th November) is an option.

SAINT CALVADOS (FR) 8 b g Saint Des Saints (FR) – Lamorrese (FR)
Similar to Rouge Vif, he is obviously a very talented horse with a rating of 167. Runner-up in the Ryanair Chase at Cheltenham in 2020, he ran well for a long way in the King George last season before finishing fourth. Trips around two and a half or two miles six appear ideal and we could aim him at something like the Grade 2 Chanelle Pharma 1965 Chase at Ascot (20th November) over two miles five.

SAMARRIVE (FR) 4 b g Coastal Path – Sambirane (FR)
Won over hurdles in France in December before we bought him, he surprised us when winning so easily at Kempton in the spring. His first target is likely to be the four year old handicap hurdle at Chepstow (8th October). Long-term, he will make a lovely chaser.

SANDALWOOD (FR) 4 ch g Martaline – Balli Flight (FR)
Another one to look out for in bumpers this season, he is a very nice horse who I like a lot.

SCARAMANGA (IRE) 6 b g Mastercraftsman (IRE) – Herboriste
Given a break during the winter, he has shown an amazing amount of improvement this spring/ summer. Twice a winner over hurdles at Newbury and Sandown, he then won a good staying handicap on the Flat at the former track in July. Rated 151 over jumps, he likes decent ground and we are thinking of stepping him up to three miles this season. The Grade 2 West Yorkshire Hurdle at Wetherby (30th October) is a definite possibility.

Don't forget to read my Diary @
www.mhpublications.couk

SECRET INVESTOR 9 b g Kayf Tara – Silver Charmer
He won two of his three races last season, including the Grade 2 Denman Chase at Newbury. Unfortunately, he sustained an injury which meant he missed the rest of the season and won't be back until the New Year. The Denman Chase in February will be his target once again.

SECRET SCRIPTURE 5 b g Mount Nelson – Kauto Shiny (FR)
Purchased at the Goffs UK August Sale at Doncaster, he ran in two Irish point-to-points for Donnchadh Doyle winning on the second occasion. We haven't done much with him yet but he will go novice hurdling.

SHEARER (IRE) 5 b g Flemensfirth (USA) – The Crown Jewel (IRE)
A lovely five year old, who was narrowly beaten on his debut in a bumper at Hereford. An easy winner next time at Warwick on New Year's Eve, he took his chance in the Festival bumper at Cheltenham last time. Ready to go hurdling, I think he will stay well.

SILENT REVOLUTION (IRE) 5 b g Sholokhov (IRE) – Watson River (IRE)
Consistent in bumpers, he ran well at Wincanton finishing second before winning next time at Huntingdon. Third under a penalty at Newbury, he will go novice hurdling and is capable of winning more races.

SILVER FOREVER (IRE) 7 gr m Jeremy (USA) – Silver Prayer (IRE)
Listed winner over hurdles, she missed the whole of last season due to a pelvic injury. Given lots of time, she is back in work and we are looking forward to sending her over fences. A winning Irish pointer, she jumps very well and will be campaigned in mares' novice chases.

SIMPLY THE BETTS (IRE) 8 b g Arcadio (GER) – Crimson Flower (IRE)
A previous Cheltenham Festival winner, he only raced once last season and joined us during the summer. It is early days in terms of making plans and we are still learning about him. He is rated 157 with two and a half miles appearing to be his trip.

SKATMAN (IRE) 6 br g Mustameet (USA) – Maid For Action (IRE)
He beat Barbados Buck's in his only Irish point-to-point before we bought the pair of them. Having missed the whole of the previous season, he won well on his first run over hurdles at Musselburgh. The runner-up has won five times over fences since. Still a novice until the end of October, he is another possible for the Grade 2 Persian War Novices' Hurdle at Chepstow (8th October). He is a nice horse.

SOLO (FR) 5 b g Kapgarde (FR) – Flameche (FR)
Having won the Grade 2 Adonis Hurdle at Kempton on his first run for us a couple of seasons ago, it was never going to be an easy year for him last time around. Chasing was always going to be his game though and he will go over fences in the Autumn. He is another who has had a wind operation since his last run.

SONIGINO (FR) 4 b g It's Gino (GER) – Soniador (FR)
By the same sire as Lalor, he is an exciting prospect who joined us during the summer. Successful in two of his three starts over hurdles in France, he won at Auteuil in June and is still a novice for this season. Only four, he is one for the future.

SONNY CROCKETT (IRE) 6 b g Robin Des Champs (FR) – Onewayortheother (IRE)
A beautiful looking horse, he is a big chasing type who will go over fences eventually. He came good at Newbury last time winning nicely and is still a novice until the end of October. Another under consideration for the Persian War Novices' Hurdle (8th October), he is rated 132 and open to further improvement.

STAGE STAR (IRE) 5 b g Fame And Glory – Sparky May
Another very nice prospect for novice hurdles, he did nothing wrong in bumpers last season. Having won first time out at Chepstow, he was placed twice behind Knappers Hill in a Listed event at Ascot and the Grade 2 championship bumper at Aintree. He is more of a staying type compared to Knappers Hill and will have no problem getting two and a half miles.

STORM ARISING (IRE) 7 b g Yeats (IRE) – Ceol Rua (IRE)
Third in an Irish point, he showed a good level of form over hurdles winning twice last season. He won handicaps at Lingfield and Chepstow before running in the Pertemps Final at the Cheltenham Festival. Rated 140, he will go novice chasing.

STRATAGEM (FR) 5 gr g Sunday Break (JPN) – Our Ziga (FR)
Rated 143 over fences having won at Doncaster, he is owned by David Maxwell, who is keen to ride him in hunter chases this season.

SWITCH HITTER (IRE) 6 b g Scorpion (IRE) – Country Time (IRE)
Won an English point before we bought him, he did well over hurdles last season winning at Kempton twice. His future is over fences and he will go novice chasing over two and a half miles.

TAHMURAS (FR) 4 b g Falco (USA) – Alinga's Lass (IRE)
Owned by the Noel Fehily Racing Club, he spent the summer with him having been bought at the Cheltenham May Sale. He won a point-to-point in Ireland for Donnchadh Doyle and, being a four year old, he could run in a bumper to begin with.

TAKE YOUR TIME (IRE) 6 b g Dubai Destination (USA) – Don't Be Bleu (IRE)
Another winning English pointer, he was consistent over hurdles last winter winning at Lingfield and placed on four occasions. With his rating of 122, he will go over fences and contest a novices' handicap chase over two and a half miles.

TAMAROC DU MATHAN (FR) 6 b g Poliglote – Thisbee Du Mathan (FR)
A nice horse who developed into a high-class novice chaser winning the Grade 2 Pendil Novices' Chase at Kempton. Very good fresh, he likes good ground and there are plenty of options for him during the Autumn. There is an intermediate chase at Newton Abbot (10th October), the Old Roan Chase at Aintree (24th October), Grade 2 at Down Royal (30th October) and the Haldon Gold Cup at Exeter (2nd November) – they will all come under consideration.

TANGO TARA 5 b g Kayf Tara – Bling Noir (FR)
Joined us last winter having been bought at the Goffs UK December PTP Sale at Yorton Farm. He won his only Irish point-to-point for James Doyle the previous month and will go novice hurdling.

THREEUNDERTHRUFIVE (IRE) 6 b g Shantou (USA) – Didinas (FR)
Enjoyed a good season over hurdles winning four of his five races. A Listed winner at Perth on his latest start, his only defeat came in the Albert Bartlett Novices' Hurdle at Cheltenham and he wasn't disgraced in sixth. He has done very well during the summer and, while the plan is to send him chasing, we might consider the Grade 2 West Yorkshire Hurdle at Wetherby (30th October) beforehand. He stays well.

THYME WHITE (FR) 5 b g Anodin (IRE) – Jane (GER)
Won the four year old handicap hurdle at Chepstow last Autumn but never showed his best thereafter. We have operated on his wind since his run in the Scottish Champion Hurdle and he will go novice chasing.

TIMEFORATUNE 5 b g Yorgunnabelucky (USA) – Timeforagin
Another purchase at the Cheltenham May Sale, he won a bumper by eleven lengths at Ffos Las earlier the same month. We haven't schooled him over hurdles yet and we might aim him at the bumper at Chepstow (9th October), which we won last year with Knappers Hill.

TRUCKERS LODGE (IRE) 9 b g Westerner – Galeacord (IRE)
The Welsh National at Chepstow (27th December) is his main target. He has run in the race a couple of times and, while he ran well enough it in last year, plus the Midlands National, he was probably a few pounds too high. He stays well and copes with testing ground.

TULIN 4 b g Gleneagles (IRE) – Talawat
A winner on the Flat in France, he won twice over hurdles for us at Taunton in the spring and is still a novice until the end of October. Over the top by the time he ran at Newton Abbot in May, he has had a good break since and will stay over hurdles this season.

WORTHY FARM (IRE) 8 b g Beneficial – Muckle Flugga (IRE)
Only raced once last season finishing last of three at Wincanton during the Autumn. He had a few issues and therefore missed the rest of the campaign. His target is the three miles one handicap chase at Wincanton (26th December), which he won a couple of years ago. Soft ground is ideal.

ZABEEL CHAMPION 4 b c Poet's Voice – Stars In Your Eyes
Has only just arrived having been bought at the Tattersalls August Sale. Rated 103 on the Flat for Mark Johnston, he has a good pedigree and is a six times winner. A three times winner this year, he was third in the Duke of Edinburgh Stakes at Royal Ascot in June and has some high-class form. We are looking forward to sending him jumping.

TRAINER'S HORSE TO FOLLOW: HITMAN
TRAINER'S ASSISTANT (HARRY DERHAM) HORSE TO FOLLOW: HUFLOWER

Jonjo O'NEILL

Stables: Jackdaws Castle, Temple Guiting, Cheltenham, Gloucestershire.
2020/2021: 71 Winners / 479 Runners 15% Prize-Money £903,194
www.jonjooneillracing.com

ADICCI (IRE) 6 b g Shirocco (GER) – Lughnasa (IRE)
A horse we have always liked, he has been consistent throughout his career and won at Fontwell on his reappearance last season. Runner-up a couple of times at Wincanton and Sandown, he is the sort of horse who should improve with time. He is likely to go chasing and, having jumped hurdles well, we are hoping he will develop into a nice horse over fences. With his rating of 129, we will start him off in a novices' handicap chase over two and a half miles. From the family of Black Jack Ketchum, it wouldn't be a surprise if he ends up staying three miles.

ALL THE GLORY 4 b f Fame And Glory – Glorybe (GER)
She is a grand filly who finished third on her debut in a bumper at Ludlow in May. There is every chance she will have another run in a mares' bumper before going hurdling.

ANNIE MC (IRE) 7 b m Mahler – Classic Mari (IRE)
She is a lovely mare who has provided us with a lot of fun and I think she will continue to do so. Successful in Listed mares' chases at Doncaster and Warwick, we were aiming her at the mares' chase at the Cheltenham Festival before she met with a minor setback. With the ground drying up, it may have been a blessing in disguise because she does prefer some cut in the ground. She will follow a similar programme and we will be delighted if she can win more mares' chases. Two and a half miles is her trip.

ANYHARMINASKING (IRE) 4 b g Getaway (GER) – Colleen Beag (IRE)
A new arrival who was bought at the Goffs Punchestown NH Sale in late April, he won his only point-to-point for Donnchadh Doyle a few days beforehand. We are still learning about him and haven't decided whether he will run in a bumper or go straight over hurdles. Cantering at the moment, he looks a nice horse.

ARRIVEDERCI (FR) 6 gr g Martaline – Etoile D'Ainay (FR)
Rated 140 over hurdles, he is one to look forward to over fences this season. He won at Wetherby on his first run of the season and was still travelling well when falling at the third last in a decent handicap hurdle at Haydock's *Betfair* Chase meeting. Placed twice at Ascot, including when second in a Grade 3 handicap in January, he jumped hurdles like a chaser and I think he will be open to more improvement over fences. He stays two and a half miles and is likely to get further.

BETTY'S BANJO (IRE) 4 b f Fame And Glory – Betty's The Best (IRE)
Half-sister to Listed bumper winner Irish Roe, she won her only Irish point in May and we purchased her later that month at the Cheltenham Sale, which was staged at Newmarket. It is early days because we haven't done a lot with her, but she looks a nice filly at home. Only four, she may have a run in a bumper.

CARRIGDOUN BOY (IRE) 4 b g Valirann (FR) – Coosan Belle (IRE)
Bought at the same sale as Betty's Banjo, he raced in two point-to-points in Ireland for Shark Hanlon winning on the second occasion. We are still getting to know him, but he has settled in well.

CLOTH CAP (IRE) 9 b g Beneficial – Cloth Fair (IRE)
It was fantastic to win the Ladbrokes Trophy at Newbury, especially for Trevor Hemmings who has been such a great supporter to us over the years. He then followed it up with another victory in a Listed chase at Kelso in March. Unfortunately, things didn't go to plan in the Grand National but we have tweaked a few things since, including his wind. With his rating of 157, it is going to be much tougher this season. We will see if he can mix it in Graded races, otherwise he will be forced to carry big weights in handicaps. We haven't made any plans yet.

COEUR SEREIN (IRE) 7 b g Fame And Glory – Balvenie (IRE)
Having had some time off, he came good in the spring winning three times over hurdles. I was impressed with his performance at Huntingdon last time because he put the race to bed quickly. He is rated 136 and the intention is to school him over fences with a view to sending him chasing. He stays well and appears to be versatile in terms of ground.

FAME AND CONCRETE (IRE) 5 b g Fame And Glory – Masiana (IRE)
A nice horse who did it well on his debut in a bumper at Southwell in December. It may not have been the strongest of races, but he impressed me. Disappointing at Warwick next time, he wasn't right afterwards so I would put a line through that run. A three miles chaser in the making, he has filled his frame during the summer and will spend this season over hurdles. I would expect him to start off over two and a half miles. I like him.

FLIGHT DECK (IRE) 7 b g Getaway (GER) – Rate of Knots (IRE)
We trained his mother who stayed well and won three races for us. Sent chasing at Huntingdon last Autumn, he frightened himself and fell at the second last. Back over hurdles, he won well at Bangor in January and wasn't disgraced last time at Ascot finishing fourth. The form of that race has worked out well with the winner (J'Ai Froid) scoring again before finishing runner-up at Aintree. In all likelihood, he will go back over fences this season and will be suited by a galloping track. He is a capable horse but needs everything to go right for him.

GARRY CLERMONT (FR) 6 b g Maresca Sorrento (FR)
We have always liked him and, having won a couple of times over hurdles the previous campaign, we sent him chasing last season. Still in contention when making a mistake at the second last at Carlisle, he then finished fifth at Chepstow. We decided to switch him back to hurdles in the spring and, having finished third at Newbury, he won next time at Warwick. The step up to two and a half miles appeared to suit him and it gives us a few more options in the future. A good jumper, there is every chance he will go back over fences this season. He seems to handle any ground.

HEAD LAW (FR) 4 b g Network (GER) – Law (FR)
A half-brother to Grade 2 winning novice chaser GA Law, he won a bumper in France in November before being bought at the Arqana Sale later the same month. We schooled him last season and have given him plenty of time. He is a good looking horse who will go novice hurdling.

HENRY GONDOFF 6 b g Great Pretender (IRE) – Mi Money
A former Irish pointer, he didn't show a lot in his first couple of runs before winning over hurdles in bad ground at Wetherby in January. I think it was a case of him handling the ground better than the favourite (Rockstar Ronnie). Runner-up at Carlisle a couple of months later, he wasn't suited by the inner track but still ran well and was mugged late on. He is likely to go chasing and will be aimed at novice handicaps over two and a half and three miles. I hope he will progress as the season goes on.

HOLLY (FR) 4 b f Voiladenuo (FR) – Righty Malta
She only arrived during the summer and we are still getting to know her. A winner of three of her four bumpers in France, including a couple of Grade 3 AQPS Flat races, she will be aimed at mares' novice hurdles.

IRON BRIDGE (IRE) 5 b g Milan – Chit Chat
A fine big horse who Trevor (Hemmings) kindly sent to us during the summer. We trained the dam and we like what we see so far and he is hopefully one to look forward to. He won a point-to-point bumper at Tipperary in March and will spend this season in novice hurdles. Long-term, he is a proper chaser in the making.

ITSO FURY (IRE) 4 b g Fame And Glory – Qui Plus Est (FR)
Another purchase from the Goffs Punchestown NH Sale in late April, he shaped with promise when keeping on in second in the George Mernagh Memorial Sales bumper at the Fairyhouse Easter Festival earlier that month. It is usually a decent race and he has settled in well since arriving. We haven't made any plans, but he has the option of running in another bumper before going hurdling.

JUDICIAL LAW (IRE) 4 b g Fame And Glory – Miss Overdrive
From the family of Diamant Noir who we trained to win six races, including the Grade 2 River Don Novices' Hurdle, he was bought at the Cheltenham May Sale. Fourth in a Listed bumper at Limerick on his debut in March, he won next time at Killarney despite meeting trouble in running. Derek (O'Connor) recommended him and he is bound to be well schooled. He will go novice hurdling.

LA DOMANIALE (FR) 5 b m No Risk At All (FR) – La Pinede
A hurdles winner in France, we were disappointed with her last season because she works nicely at home. Third in an introductory hurdle at Ludlow, she was beaten by a couple of decent horses, but she was disappointing next time at Exeter. Hopefully she will improve as she gains in experience. I suspect she will stay over hurdles for the time being but ought to jump fences later on.

MERCUTIO ROCK (FR) 5 b g Maresca Sorrento (FR) – Mondovi (FR)
Related to Saint Calvados, we have always liked him and he ran well on his debut in a bumper at Chepstow last Autumn in fourth. Switched to hurdles, he was runner-up at the same track before finishing fourth at Uttoxeter. Still weak last year, we have purposely given him time and kept him to two miles. Once he strengthens up, he should stay further and we have the option of running him in a handicap off his mark of 112.

MONBEG GENIUS (IRE) 5 b g Shantou (USA) – Ella Watson (IRE)
Runner-up in his only Irish point-to-point for Sean Doyle last Autumn, we acquired him at the Goffs UK November Sale at Yorton Farm. He was due to have his first run for us in a bumper at Chepstow during the spring but the ground dried out, so we put him away. We like him though and, while he may have a run in a bumper beforehand, the plan is to send him hurdling.

MORNING SPIRIT (IRE) 6 b g Milan – Morning Legend (IRE)
Consistent last season, he won nicely at Ascot in December and was narrowly beaten at Ffos Las on his latest start in the spring. Even though he won on testing ground at Ascot, I don't think he needs it and feel he is versatile in terms of underfoot conditions. Rated 129, he will go chasing and we are expecting him to improve for the switch to fences. He stays well.

PALMERS HILL (IRE) 8 b g Gold Well – Tosca Shine (IRE)
He is a talented horse but has had his issues and is a difficult horse to keep sound. Disappointing last season, we tried him over fences at Taunton but then reverted back to hurdles. Ninth in the Coral Cup at the Cheltenham Festival last time, he won a point-to-point at the beginning of his career and we might try him over fences once again.

PAPA TANGO CHARLY (FR) 6 ch g No Risk At All (FR) – Chere Elenn (FR)
Another winning pointer, he hasn't had a lot of racing, but it was good to see him get his head in front at Worcester during the summer. Placed a couple of times at Wetherby and Warwick prior to that, he will go chasing. Hopefully, his win last time will have done his confidence good and he will improve for the switch to fences. He jumps well.

PRINCE ESCALUS (IRE) 6 b g Jeremy (USA) – So You Said (IRE)
Twice a winner over hurdles at Huntingdon and Market Rasen, he likes to front run and will go over fences. In and out on occasions, he has enough speed for two miles but also stays two and a half miles. We will start him off in a novices' handicap chase in the Autumn and he is capable of winning more races.

RED MAPLE (IRE) 5 b g Sholokhov (IRE) – Champagne Ruby (IRE)
Bought at the Goffs Landrover Sale in Ireland as a three year old, we weren't sure what to expect on his debut in a bumper at Bangor last Autumn. He did it nicely though and then we sent him hurdling in the New Year. It has taken him a while to get the hang of it and then he rather fell apart as the season went on. We have given him a break since his last run at Stratford and hopefully he will improve this year. Stepping up trip should help him.

ROCKED UP (IRE) 5 b m Westerner – Rock Gossip (IRE)
She gained plenty of experience in point-to-points and bumpers in Ireland. Third in a bumper at Down Royal in March, she was beaten less than three lengths by Me Too Please, who subsequently won the Grade 2 mares' bumper at Aintree. That is the reason why we bought her at the Goffs UK Spring Sale at Doncaster. She will be aimed at mares' novice hurdles.

SHANTOU'S MELODY (IRE) 5 b g Shantou (USA) – Glens Melody (IRE)
Out of a Grade 1 winning mare, he is a nice horse with a touch of class. He hasn't been the easiest horse to keep sound but he showed last season what he is capable of. Runner-up on his debut at Fontwell, he wasn't disgraced at Cheltenham next time before winning well at Huntingdon in the spring. He showed a good turn of foot there and I think he is above average. The ground that day was good, but we are expecting him to handle slower ground, too, especially as he strengthens up. He jumps well and, while we will start him off over two miles over hurdles, he will be suited by further. We like him.

SKY PIRATE 8 b g Midnight Legend – Dancingwithbubbles (IRE)
He was a completely different horse last season enjoying a tremendous campaign winning three times, including the Grand Annual Chase at the Cheltenham Festival. We dropped him back in trip and, while that helped, I don't think that was the only reason. If you watched him work at home, he looks more like a four miler than a two miler, but everything clicked and he never stopped improving. With his rating of 159, life will be much tougher this season and it is a case of seeing whether he can match it in Graded company. His programme will be governed by the ground though – he wants decent ground and we will be avoiding testing conditions. Something like the Haldon Gold Cup at Exeter (2nd November) could be an option but it will depend on the ground.

SOARING GLORY (IRE) 6 b g Fame And Glory – Hapeney (IRE)
Had a very good season over hurdles and it was great to see him win the *Betfair* Hurdle at Newbury, which had been the plan for sometime. He wasn't himself when running in the *Sky Bet* Supreme Novices' Hurdle at Cheltenham and came back with some pulled muscles. A horse with a turn of foot, he is another who enjoys good ground. Still a young horse, he is in good form at home, but we haven't decided whether to stay over hurdles or go chasing.

SPRINGWELL BAY 4 b g Kayf Tara – Winning Counsel (IRE)
Half-brother to the 140 rated hurdler Mint Condition, he was purchased at the Punchestown Sale in April. Beaten less than a length in the Goffs Land Rover Bumper at the Festival a couple of days earlier when trained by Mags Mullins, it is always a good race and the form is likely to be strong. The experience he gained there should stand him in good stead and he is one to look forward to. We haven't decided whether he runs in another bumper or goes hurdling.

STEADY THE SHIP (IRE) 5 ch g Ocovango – Vinnie's Princess (IRE)
Placed in bumpers at Ascot and Southwell, he was then runner-up on his hurdles debut at Wincanton. A bit disappointing thereafter, he was still quite weak last year and we are hoping he will improve having strengthened up during the summer. We might send him chasing sooner rather than later.

THEME TUNE (IRE) 6 b g Fame And Glory – Supreme Melody (IRE)
A horse who only does enough, he won over hurdles at Ludlow and Carlisle. Workmanlike in victory on the latter occasion, he was fourth at Uttoxeter last time. He is a strong stayer and, while he is not a bad horse, we are hoping he will improve once switched to fences. He didn't jump particularly well over hurdles, so we are going to do a lot of intensive schooling. Still a shell of a horse last year, he has grown a lot during the summer and looks very well. He is one to look forward to over fences.

TIME TO GET UP (IRE) 8 ch g Presenting – Gales Return (IRE)
Surprised us last season but we were delighted with his win in the Midlands National at Uttoxeter. We thought he wanted better ground having disappointed at Wetherby on Boxing Day. However, he produced a good performance to win on heavy ground at Wincanton. He then won at Uttoxeter on only his fourth start over fences, which was an excellent effort. The ground that day wasn't too bad at all and he appears versatile. The Grand National is his main target but, with his rating of 144, he will need a rise in the weights. We haven't made any plans on where he will start but we are hoping he will be high enough to get a run at Aintree in the spring. He doesn't show a lot at home but has been progressive on the track.

UPTOWN LADY (IRE) 6 b m Milan – Lady Zephyr (IRE)
A nice mare who wants plenty of cut in the ground, she had a wind operation and then got her act together winning at Warwick in February. Third on her final run at Haydock, the ground probably wasn't soft enough, plus the track didn't really suit her. She will go chasing and could be an interesting prospect in mares' novice chases.

WALK IN MY SHOES (IRE) 5 b m Milan – Bonnies Island (IRE)
She finished second behind the subsequent Grade 2 Dawn Run Mares' Novices' Hurdle runner-up Magic Daze in her only point-to-point in Ireland last Autumn. Previously trained by Sean Doyle, we gave her some time off having bought her and we quite like her. She has done some nice pieces of work at home and will be running in mares' novice hurdles.

WHEN YOU'RE READY (IRE) 7 gr g Malinas (GER) – Royale Wheeler (FR)
Dual winner over hurdles at Stratford and Leicester, we always thought he wanted better ground, but it was heavy on the latter occasion. He jumps hurdles like a future chaser and will go over fences. With his mark of 125, he will reappear in a novices' handicap chase.

YES INDEED (FR) 4 b g Martaline – She Hates Me (IRE)
Another interesting recruit from France, he has a good level of form winning over hurdles and fences at Auteuil. A Listed chase winner at the end of April, he wasn't disgraced in a Grade 1 chase last time finishing fifth. We haven't done much with him yet, but he is a fine big horse and looks more like a seven year old than a four year old. He will continue over fences with his four year old allowance and seems to like plenty of cut in the ground. He is a nice type.

> **TRAINER'S HORSE TO FOLLOW: SHANTOU'S MELODY**

Don't forget to read my Diary @
www.mhpublications.couk

David PIPE

Stables: Pond House, Nicholashayne, Wellington, Somerset.
2020/2021: 52 Winners / 346 Runners 15% Prize-Money £633,913
www.davidpipe.com

ADAGIO (GER) 4 b g Wiener Walzer (GER) – Aspidistra (GER)
Proved to be a fantastic claim having won on the Flat at Clairefontaine in August last year. He improved with each start over hurdles winning three of his six starts. Having won the Grade 1 Finale Hurdle at Chepstow in January, he justified his place in the line up in the Triumph Hurdle. Considering he didn't have the best of preparations having suffered with colic, he ran very well in second at Cheltenham. He then produced another good effort at Aintree chasing home Monmiral, who was arguably the best juvenile hurdler last season. He made a mistake at the last, but I don't think it cost him victory – the winner looks a very good horse. It is never easy for four year olds during their second season but he has had a good summer and we will be aiming him at the leading two miles handicap hurdles. The Greatwood Hurdle at Cheltenham (14th November) looks an obvious target.

ANGLERS CRAG 6 bl g Multiplex - Overyou
A winning Irish point-to-pointer, he had some very good form in bumpers last season, notably when third in a Listed contest at Navan behind subsequent Cheltenham Festival Bumper winner, Sir Gerhard. He will go novice hurdling this season and I am looking forward to him arriving at Pond House. We enjoyed great success for owner Derrick Mossop with popular staying chaser Soll and I am sure he will be another exciting addition to the team.

ASTIGAR (FR) 5 gr g No Risk At All (FR) – Sissi De Teille (FR)
A horse I have always liked, he was unlucky not to win in first two races at Uttoxeter and Exeter. Disappointing at the latter venue next time, he was runner-up at Plumpton on his latest start. We have operated on his wind since and he has summered well. Only five, he hasn't reached his full potential yet and we still have high hopes for him. Despite the fact he remains a novice, I would imagine he will reappear in a handicap.

BARRIER PEAKS (FR) 5 b g Blue Bresil (FR) – La Balzane (FR)
Runner-up on his debut in a bumper at Chepstow in February, he ran no sort of race next time at Uttoxeter looking a weak finisher in the process. Fifth at Ayr last time, he has had a wind operation during the summer and we will start him off low key over hurdles. We liked him prior to his debut and I am hoping he will improve this season. We will probably start him off over two miles but he won't have any problems staying further.

Please see page 195
for details of
Ahead on the Flat 2022

BELGUARDO (FR) 4 b g Kapgarde (FR) – Bella Giaconda (GER)
Unraced, he was in training last season but was still on the weak side, so we decided to give him more time. He has a bit of spirit about him and has shown ability. He has strengthened up during the summer and will start off in a bumper.

BRINKLEY (FR) 6 gr g Martaline – Royale Majesty (FR)
Had a good season over hurdles winning twice at Wincanton and Exeter. He disappointed on his reappearance at Exeter in December and we don't know why. Thankfully, he bounced back on his next two starts. We ran him in the Pertemps Final at the Cheltenham Festival, but the drying ground was against him. He copes very well with soft ground and stays well, too. Still only six, he could have another run over hurdles before turning his attentions to chasing. We haven't schooled him over fences yet, but he is a very good jumper of hurdles. The Betfair Exchange Stayers' Handicap Hurdle at Haydock (20th November) is a possible target (stable have won the race four times since 2010). Two and a half miles plus on soft ground are his optimum conditions.

BUMPY JOHNSON (IRE) 5 ch g Imperial Monarch (IRE) – Country Flora
A former Irish pointer, he won a bumper at Fontwell last Autumn and, while the form hasn't worked out particularly well, he was an easy winner. He jumps well at home but hasn't put it together over hurdles so far. Third at Exeter last time, that form looks solid and there is no doubt he has ability. Two miles on soft ground is probably ideal at the moment, although he does stay further. He isn't slow.

CROSSING LINES (IRE) 7 b g Jeremy (USA) – Coco Opera (IRE)
A dual winning pointer, he has yet to run for us having suffered a tendon injury, which has kept him off the track for nearly two years. A big chasing type, he wants the mud and will be suited by two and a half miles plus. He won't be in action until the second half of the season and, while his future is over fences, he will go novice hurdling.

DOYEN LA LUTTE (IRE) 5 b m Doyen (IRE) – Castletown Girl
She won an Irish point in December and we bought her at the Cheltenham Sale at Newmarket a few days later. We acquired her for a new syndicate and were keen to give her a run in a bumper before her summer break. She ran OK but the good ground didn't really suit her. I have been very pleased with her during the summer because she has grown and filled her frame. She is a big mare who will be at her best in two and a half miles mares' novice hurdles this season.

DUC DE BEAUCHENE (FR) 8 b g Saddler Maker (IRE) – Quatia D'Angron (FR)
Not an easy horse to predict, or get right, but he has ability and loves soft ground. Indeed, we feared the ground had dried out too much at Chepstow in March, but he stayed on well to lead close home. We always thought he wanted three miles but when we tried him over it, he didn't seem to stay. Two and a half miles handicap chases on soft ground will be his target.

FIRST LORD DE CUET (FR) 7 gr g Lord Du Sud (FR) – Alyce (FR)
Consistent throughout his career, he won over hurdles at Wincanton in February. We then ran him in my father's race (Martin Pipe Conditional Jockeys' Handicap Hurdle) at Cheltenham but it proved to be a step too far. We gave him a couple of runs over fences in the spring finishing second on both occasions. He doesn't have a lot in hand in terms of his rating, but he will win races over fences when things go his way. Two and a half to three miles is his trip.

GERICAULT ROQUE (FR) 5 b g Montmartre (FR) – Nijinska Delaroque (FR)

Fourth in his only Irish point, he ran well on his first start for us finishing runner-up in a bumper at Newton Abbot in October. However, he made a noise that day, so we subsequently cauterized his palate. He hasn't looked back since winning two of his three starts over hurdles at Plumpton and Sandown. His only defeat over hurdles came at Fakenham where he didn't appear to handle the track or enjoy wearing a tongue tie hence we left it off at Sandown. He is quite a nervy horse and very much a long-term prospect. He wasn't the greatest of eaters last year, so we were pleased to get four runs into him. A big horse, he should be more of the finished article this year and I am hoping he will progress through the ranks. There is every chance he will go over fences and we will start him off in a suitable novices' handicap chase. Both his wins last season came over two miles, but I am expecting him to stay three miles one day.

GRANGECLARE GLORY (IRE) 6 b g Fame And Glory – Annies Joy (IRE)

Ran well on his first two runs over hurdles at Plumpton and Doncaster and we thought he was favourably treated when stepping up in trip at Fontwell last time. He wasn't at his best that day though. Given a break since, he has summered well and we have the option of staying over hurdles or going chasing. Another ex-pointer, we have always thought he would stay further.

HEURE DE GLORIE (FR) 4 b f Kapgarde (FR) – Lounoas (FR)

She won her only start over hurdles in France in December and we bought her soon afterwards. Quite a keen, free going filly, she was very light when she first arrived, but we wanted to give her a run before her summer break. She ran at Huntingdon during the spring and performed well in second conceding weight to the winner. The form has worked out OK, too, and she will be much more at home on a galloping track – Huntingdon was too sharp for her. Not over big, she has undergone wind surgery and we are looking forward to having a proper season with her. Two miles handicap hurdles will be the plan to start with. I like her.

INDUNO (IRE) 7 b g Flemensfirth (USA) – Vast Consumption (IRE)

Won twice as a novice hurdler the previous season and we thought he had a good chance on his reappearance at Cheltenham's November meeting. Having finished fourth, he incurred an injury and missed the remainder of the season. Back in work now, he has a lot of potential and we are hoping he starts to fulfil it this year. I need to speak to his owner Ronnie Bartlett as to whether he remains over hurdles for the time being or goes chasing.

ISRAEL CHAMP (IRE) 6 b g Milan – La Dariska (FR)

A high-class bumper horse a couple of seasons ago, he won two Listed events at Cheltenham and Ascot and has some strong form. It was therefore very disappointing when he was forced to miss last term due to a tendon injury. A big bull of a horse, he is back now and should be in action around November/December time. He remains a horse with huge potential and we have always liked him. A winning Irish pointer, we haven't ruled out the possibility of going straight over fences with him. At the moment, we are undecided whether to stay hurdling or go chasing. Either way, he is one to look forward to.

ITACARE (FR) 4 gr g Silver Frost (IRE) – Steadfast (FR)

Only a four year old, he has gained plenty of experience over hurdles and fences in France winning under both codes. We claimed him for €23,000 having won over fences at Auteuil in April. He has some nice form to his name and we have operated on his wind since arriving. There is every chance he will be campaigned over fences as a four year old starting off over two miles before stepping up in trip later on.

KEPAGGE (IRE) 7 b g Getaway (GER) – Miracle Lady
Unbeaten in three starts during the 2019/2020 season, he was disappointing last term and I am inclined to put a line through it. Fourth on his reappearance at Cheltenham in November, he didn't run badly that day. We then stepped him up in trip in a Pertemps qualifier at Warwick but he got cut up on the hometurn. His final run came at Ascot and, having jumped and travelled well, he cut out quickly and didn't finish his race off. He is another we have yet to decide whether to stay hurdling or go chasing. Two and a half miles on soft ground are probably his conditions.

KINGOFTHEWEST (IRE) 5 b g Westerner – Other Salsa (FR)
Bought at the Goffs UK Spring Sale at Doncaster in May, he finished runner-up on his only start in an Irish point for Donnchadh Doyle. He would have been third but one of his rivals fell at the last. Tipperary is a sharp track and it wouldn't have suited him. Still not the finished article, he will probably have a run in a bumper before hopefully developing into a nice hurdler.

LADYKILLER (GER) 5 ch g Kamsin (GER) – Lady Jacamira (GER)
Highly rated on the Flat in Germany, where he won a couple of Pattern races, he had one run over hurdles for us at Southwell last Autumn. He incurred an injury afterwards and hasn't run since. Back in training, he has strengthened up and, while he is quirky, he is talented, too. A free going sort, he will resume over two miles but will get further later on. We might give him a run on the Flat before going back over jumps.

LAST QUARTER (IRE) 4 b g Walk In The Park (IRE) – Lunar Path (IRE)
He is the first horse I have trained by Walk In The Park and we bought him privately on behalf of Brocade Racing having won a point-to-point bumper at Punchestown in March. Previously trained by Colin Bowe, he battled on well and is a fine individual and a very good mover. We have had a lot of luck from the same source in the past and he is very much one to look forward to. He has enjoyed a good summer and, in all likelihood, we will send him straight over hurdles.

LEONCAVALLO (IRE) 9 br g Cape Cross (IRE) – Nafura
A cracking horse we train for ValueRacingClub.co.uk, he did us proud last year winning over fences at Stratford before winning on the Flat at Haydock and finishing sixth in the Cesarewitch. Sixth in my father's race at Cheltenham (Martin Pipe Conditional Jockeys' Handicap Hurdle), he didn't quite see out his race as well next time at Aintree but still finished fourth. Back in action on the Flat at Sandown in June, he came back jarred up on the fast ground so we have given him a break since. Rated 139 over hurdles, he will be going jumping again in the Autumn.

LITTLE RED LION (IRE) 7 b g Sans Frontieres (IRE) – Rever Up (IRE)
He is a thorough stayer and, even though he won three times over fences last season, I think he remains fairly handicapped. A bit lazy during his races, he was in the process of running well in the Eider Chase at Newcastle last time. He was creeping into contention when falling. Very much ground dependent, he enjoys testing conditions and is one for those regional Nationals.

MARTINHAL (IRE) 6 b g Westerner – Gweedara (IRE)
A horse I have always liked, he was disappointing on his first couple of runs over hurdles at Wetherby and Ffos Las and wasn't finishing off his races. We decided to operate on his breathing and he has done well since. A dual winner at Exeter, he beat a couple of useful opponents and his form is sound. The Cheltenham Festival proved a step too far for him at that stage in his career but the experience will have done him good. He has a good engine and, while he is still a bit keen at times, he will settle better as he gets older. I think he will gallop all day and will be suited by three miles eventually. No decision has been made as to whether he continues over hurdles or goes over fences.

NEON MOON (IRE) 5 b g No Risk At All (FR) – Hidden Horizons (IRE)
Colin Bowe trained him to win an Irish point before we bought him last Autumn. A weak finisher on his first couple of starts at Southwell and Chepstow, we cauterized his palate afterwards. He then won over hurdles at Wincanton in March despite running in snatches. Idling once in front, he did it nicely and I hope he will continue to progress. Only a five year old, he stays two and a half miles but isn't slow at home and could drop back to two miles at some stage. He doesn't want it too soft though.

NEW AGE DAWNING (IRE) 7 ch g Stowaway – Captain Supreme (IRE)
He was ready to run last season but picked up a different injury, which means he hasn't raced since the spring of 2019. An out and out galloper who loves the mud, he has some decent form winning a bumper and over hurdles. If we can keep him in one piece, he will develop into a lovely three mile chaser.

OCEAN HEIGHTS 4 ch g Dubawi (IRE) – Ethereal Sky (IRE)
Bought at the Goffs UK August Sale at Doncaster, he was progressive in bumpers for Lucy Wadham winning at Southwell in June. We haven't done a lot with him yet but the plan is for him to go hurdling and he appears to like decent ground.

PANIC ATTACK (IRE) 5 b m Canford Cliffs (IRE) – Toto Corde Meo (IRE)
A lovely mare who can be in and out but is very capable. Twice a winner over hurdles at Uttoxeter and Newbury, she was runner-up at Aintree in May. We gave her a wind operation prior to that run and she also benefited from stepping up in trip. She doesn't want it too soft and I feel she has more to offer.

RAMSES DE TEILLEE (FR) 9 gr g Martaline – Princess D'Orton (FR)
A horse who has been very good for us and he battled on well to win a valuable staying handicap chase at Cheltenham's November meeting. We then ran him in the Becher Chase at Aintree but he never jumped a fence and left his season behind there. He made a mistake at the first fence in the Welsh National and was on the backfoot thereafter. I thought he ran OK in the Midlands National but the ground wasn't soft enough for him. There is every chance we will take him back to Auteuil in the Autumn but otherwise he will be following a similar programme. He won't be going back to Aintree though.

RED LION LAD (IRE) 5 b g Flemensfirth (USA) – Hotline (FR)
A big strong three mile chaser in the making, he won his only Irish point for Colin Bowe before we bought him. We gave him three runs over hurdles last season finishing third a couple of times at Exeter and Chepstow. A bit disappointing at Ffos Las in between, he wants soft ground and we might go straight over fences with him. He ought to be competitive in a novices' handicap chase off his mark of 116. We have operated on his wind and I think he will stay all day.

REMASTERED 8 ch g Network (GER) - Cathodine Cayras (FR)
Had a very good season over fences winning three of his four races, including the Grade 2 Reynoldstown Novices' Chase at Ascot in February. We then ran him in the National Hunt Chase at the Cheltenham Festival and, while he performed creditably in fifth, I am not convinced he stayed the trip, plus the ground had dried out. Trips around three miles on soft ground are ideal. He held his form much better last season, which was pleasing. He could be one for the same staying handicap chase at Cheltenham (13th November), which Ramses De Teillee won last season. There is also every chance we will enter him in the Ladbrokes Trophy at Newbury (27th November).

ROMAIN DE SENAM (FR) 9 b g Saint Des Saints (FR) - Salvatrixe (FR)
Judith Wilson bought him at the Doncaster May Sales with the Grand National being his main target. He is a talented horse who has done well for Paul Nicholls and Dan Skelton and is a Saturday horse. A winner at Musselburgh on New Year's day, he will be running in good staying handicap chases prior to Aintree.

SEVENTEEN O FOUR (IRE) 4 ro g Gutaifan (IRE) - Bali Breeze (IRE)
Twice a winner on the Flat at Catterick and Carlisle in May when trained by Grant Tuer, we bought him at the Goffs UK Spring Sale at Doncaster later the same month. We have schooled him over hurdles and he jumps well. Given a break since, he may have another run on the Flat before making his hurdles debut. He appears to like the mud.

SEXY LOT (GER) 5 b m Camelot - Saldennahe (GER)
Well placed to win four times over hurdles last season, she did very well and picked up plenty of prize-money. Despite having such a good year, I still don't think she is badly handicapped and remains unexposed over two and a half miles. She was suited by being held up in her races and loves heavy ground. Having said that, she handled much better ground at Haydock last time and I don't see why she won't stay further, if necessary. At the moment, two and a half miles on soft ground are probably her optimum conditions.

SIDI ISMAEL (FR) 7 b g Great Pretender (IRE) - Tetouane (FR)
Bought at the Goffs UK Spring Sale in May, I don't think he was bad value having shown some OK form for Keith Dalgleish. A bumper and hurdles winner, he was placed in an Irish point, too, and I hope he will develop into a fun horse. A big strong horse, he will go novice handicap chasing and his new owners are a group of lads who are keen to have runners at Aintree and Haydock.

SIRUH DU LAC (FR) 8 b g Turgeon (USA) - Margerie (FR)
Unfortunately, things didn't go to plan with him last season. Having unseated his rider at the first in the Paddy Power Gold Cup at Cheltenham, we schooled him a week later and he jumped beautifully. However, we then found he had incurred an injury behind and was forced to miss the rest of the campaign. Still a relatively young horse with few miles on the clock, we will hopefully have a full season with him this time around. I think he is worth a try over three miles at some stage and he remains a novice over hurdles.

THANKSFORTHEHELP (FR) 4 gr g Martaline - Agathe Du Berlais (FR)
Arrived halfway through last season and we were keen to give him a run in a bumper last spring. Fourth on his debut at Southwell, he is a lovely big horse and I don't think the track played to his strengths. He has strengthened up since and is a well bred horse who will go novice hurdling. He has got the pedigree and looks to develop into a nice horse.

UMBRIGADO (IRE) 7 br g Stowaway – Dame O'Neill (IRE)
Took well to chasing winning on three occasions, including the Grade 3 Greatwood Gold Cup at Newbury. He picked up well on the run-in handling good ground in the process. We then aimed him in the Grade 1 novice chase at Aintree, but he wasn't at his best that day and came back with a nasty cut and it took a while to heal. Not an easy horse to get right, he has improved over fences and we will be looking at races such as the Haldon Gold Cup at Exeter (2nd November) or the Paddy Power Gold Cup at Cheltenham (13th November). He won't have any trouble dropping back in trip because he possesses plenty of speed.

> **TRAINER'S HORSE TO FOLLOW: ASTIGAR**

Nicky RICHARDS
Stables: Rectory Farm, Greystoke, Penrith, Cumbria.
2020/2021: 33 Winners / 252 Runners 13% Prize-Money £320,536
www.nickyrichardsracing.com

CASTLE RUSHEN (IRE) 6 b g Fame And Glory – Rosie Suspect (IRE)
Has returned from his summer break looking well and we are looking forward to sending him novice chasing. Progressive over hurdles last season, he got better as the year went on. A dual winner at Ayr, he was runner-up in a Listed event at Perth over three miles on his final start. We haven't schooled him over fences yet, but he is a lovely jumper and I don't envisage any problems. We will probably start him off over two and a half miles, but he is a three mile chaser in the making.

CHAPEL STILE (IRE) 9 b g Scorpion (IRE) – Peggy Cullen (IRE)
A winner at Carlisle in February, he is a nice staying chaser who could be ideal for something like the Eider Chase at Newcastle in February. Still lightly raced over fences, he stays well and handles soft ground and is capable of winning a nice handicap.

CRYSTAL GLORY 5 b g Fame And Glory – Nile Cristale (FR)
A lovely looking horse, he won both his Irish point-to-points for Donnchadh Doyle last Autumn. He was recommended to us and we did some homework on him and managed to strike a deal. His form looks OK and I think we will have plenty of fun with him. A chasing type, his future lies over fences, but he will spend this season in novice hurdles.

EVERYDAY CHAMPAGNE (IRE) 5 gr g Doyen (IRE) – Magie De Toulouse (FR)
We ran two in the same bumper at Ayr in January and I was expecting the pair to run well but neither handled the ground, which was bottomless. Thankfully, he performed much better next time at Perth in the spring, but our horses weren't at their best during the last few months of the season. He is a big strong horse and anything he achieves over hurdles this year will be a bonus. We will start him off over two or two and a half miles and he is capable of winning races over hurdles. His long-term future is over fences though and I am expecting him to end up being a three miler.

FINDTHETIME (IRE) 5 b g Shantou (USA) – Bisoguet (IRE)

Similar to Crystal Glory, he is an interesting horse who has joined us having run in a point-to-point in Ireland. Previously trained by Colin Bowe, he was unlucky when falling at the last when looking like the winner. We made a few enquiries and bought him and he is a nice type of horse who will make a lovely chaser one day. The horse who won his point has won a bumper and finished second over hurdles since for Oliver Sherwood. He will go novice hurdling and hopefully has a bright future.

FLY BY MILAN (IRE) 6 b g Milan – So Proper (IRE)

Another chaser in the making, he finished runner-up in three of his four bumpers and was very consistent. He stayed on well in his races and will benefit from stepping up to two and a half miles plus over hurdles this winter. He is a nice horse who handles soft ground and is suited by a big galloping track. Despite finishing second at Market Rasen on his penultimate start, the track wasn't ideal because he found it a bit sharp.

GEGE VILLE (FR) 5 b g Protektor (GER) – Auvloo Ville (FR)

A nice big unraced horse we bought at the Goffs Landrover Sale as a three year old. He did some decent pieces of work last season and was nearly ready to run but had a minor setback. It is possible he will have a run in a bumper, otherwise we will send him straight over hurdles. He is a proper chasing type for the future though. His owner Mrs Starkie formerly had horses with my father.

GLENDUFF (IRE) 7 b g Gold Well – Last of The Bunch

Still a maiden over fences, Raymond Anderson Green bought him at the Goffs UK Spring Sales in May and kindly sent him back to us. He looked a useful horse when winning over hurdles at Carlisle the previous season before we sent him chasing last year. Third a couple of times at Doncaster and Haydock, we are still not sure what his optimum trip is because he tended to travel well in his races but not finish them off last winter. He is a good jumper who appreciates better ground. We also feel he wants time between his races.

HOME FIRE 5 b g Frankel – Hot Snap

He ran well on his debut in a bumper at Ayr's Scottish National meeting finishing fourth. We then decided to keep him going during the summer and ran him twice over hurdles at Perth in July. On the first occasion, he looked ill at ease on the track being such a big horse. However, I thought he performed much better next time. His jumping was sharper and he handled the bends. We have given him a break since and he will continue over hurdles in the Autumn. He will be more at home on galloping tracks over two or two and a half miles.

MAROWN (IRE) 7 b g Milan – Rosie Suspect (IRE)

Lightly raced hurdles, we were keen to get as much experience into him over fences last season, which will hopefully stand him in good stead later on. A dual winner at Ayr and Wetherby, he ran very well when finishing second in a Grade 2 novices' chase at Haydock in January. He had a few hard races on bad ground though and I think that caught up with him by the time he ran at Ayr in April. He looks well following his summer holiday and we are looking forward to running him some nice staying handicaps. It would be nice to think he will end up in some of the major handicap chases at some stage. More immediately, the Listed Colin Parker Memorial Chase over two and a half miles at Carlisle (31st October) could be a good starting point. Then, we may consider something like the Rehearsal Chase at Newcastle (27th November), which we won with Takingrisks a couple of years ago.

MURVAGH BEACH (IRE) 6 ch g Doyen (IRE) – Magic Park (IRE)

I was disappointed with him to begin with because I thought he would run well in his bumper at Newcastle. Still green and backward, he is starting to get the hang of things and ran a lot better over hurdles at Newcastle last time. Rated 98, we have the option of running him in a handicap over hurdles, but it wouldn't surprise me if he was chasing by Christmas.

NELLS SON 6 b g Trans Island – Miss Nellie (IRE)

From a family we know well being a half-brother to the recently retired Amberose and Rubytwo, he has won two of his three bumpers and could be anything. Beaten a nose on his debut at Doncaster the previous season, he won both his starts at Ayr last term. He has done nothing wrong during his career and we are hoping he will develop into a high-class horse. His schooling over hurdles has gone well and he enjoys soft ground. More than likely, he will start over two miles but will have no trouble staying two and a half miles.

PADDOCK COTTAGE (IRE) 5 b g Pour Moi (IRE) – Blend

Bought as a three year old at the Goffs UK Spring Sale, he has yet to run but everyone who has ridden him at home likes him. He is a nice young horse who will run in a bumper in the Autumn.

PARISENCORE (FR) 5 b g Walk In The Park (IRE) – Folk Dancing (FR)

Made his debut in the same bumper at Ayr as Everyday Champagne in January but got bogged down in the ground. We thought he would run well beforehand but didn't handle the conditions. He ran much better next time though finishing second at Bangor in the spring. It was an encouraging performance because he kept galloping. We may give him another run in a bumper in the Autumn before going hurdling. While he is likely to end up being a three miler, he will run in two or two and a half miles novice hurdles to begin with.

RELEASE THE KRAKEN (IRE) 5 b g Shantou (USA) – Guydus (IRE)

Long-term, he is a chaser in the making but ran two nice races in bumpers last season. Fourth on his debut at Kelso in February, he was subsequently disqualified and placed last having gone the wrong side of a wing at what is normally the final hurdle. He then stayed on well in second at Hexham last time. Staying is going to be his game and he appreciates soft ground. He jumps well and I think he will develop into a nice horse over hurdles this winter.

RIBBLE VALLEY (IRE) 8 b g Westerner – Miss Greinton (GER)

A grand horse who won impressively in a small field intermediate hurdle at Carlisle in October. We then ran him in the Grade 1 Fighting Fifth Hurdle at Newcastle and, while he finished third, he made a couple of uncharacteristic mistakes and wasn't at his best. Unfortunately, he picked up an injury during the race and missed the remainder of the season. He underwent surgery but is fine now and back in work. His owner David Wesley Yates has been very patient and we are looking forward to sending him chasing. Provided he stays in one piece, he could be anything over fences. We have yet to school him, but he is a good jumper and I will be surprised if he doesn't take to fences. All being well, he will be in action in November.

ROSE OF SIENA (IRE) 4 b m Califet (FR) – The Tabster (IRE)

A lovely unraced filly owned by Mrs Pat Sloan who kindly sent her to us last year. We gave her plenty of time during the winter. She goes nicely at home and has had a racecourse gallop, too. We will start her in a mares' bumper in the Autumn and we are looking forward to seeing her run.

ROYAL ARCADE (IRE) 6 bb g Arcadio (GER) – Miss Excitable (IRE)
Ran three times over hurdles at Carlisle and performed well on each occasion. An easy winner on his second outing, he finished third last time having got racing too far out and paid for it late on. Rated 122, we will probably give him one more run over hurdles before going chasing. There is every chance we will drop him back to two miles on his reappearance. He jumps well and is a promising young horse.

SAUCE OF LIFE (IRE) 6 b g Califet (FR) – Salsaparilla (FR)
A lovely horse who won both his starts in bumpers last term. He won well first out at Musselburgh and Brian (Hughes) was very pleased with him. He then defied a penalty at Market Rasen having hit the front soon enough. It takes an above average horse to win two bumpers and he ought to make a very nice novice hurdler. Better ground seems to suit him and we will run him over two miles to begin with.

SNOWY CLOUDS (IRE) 5 gr g Cloudings (IRE) – Wednesday Girl (IRE)
A big strong chasing type, he was trained last season by Brian Harding and dead-heated in a point-to-point bumper at Sandon on Easter Saturday. We knew a bit about him because he had worked here before he ran and we liked him. The other horse who dead-heated (Another Brown Bear) has joined Nicky Henderson. I am delighted to be training for Highclere Thoroughbred Racing and he will go hurdling this season.

SOFT RISK (FR) 5 b g My Risk (FR) – Douce Ambiance (FR)
A smashing horse we bought at the Goffs UK Spring Sale as a three year old. He looked good when he won on his debut in a bumper at Ayr in May. His victory wasn't a surprise because he has always done his work well at home and had had a racecourse gallop beforehand. The decision to run him at Ayr was a bit of an afterthought because we thought it was getting too late, but they produced lovely ground and he couldn't have won any easier. Brian (Hughes) loved him and we will get him educated over hurdles this season. A great big horse who will jump fences later on, he is owned by James Westoll and we will start him off at a nice track such as Ayr, Carlisle or Newcastle. Two miles will be his trip because he has got bags of speed.

SUMMERGROUNDS 5 b g Phoenix Reach (IRE) – Hannah Jacques (IRE)
Out of a mare we trained to win twice, I bred him and he ran a lovely race on his debut. Runner-up in a bumper at Kelso in the spring, he wasn't beaten far but would have been even closer with a clearer run. It can get quite tight on some of those bends at Kelso and he was still green. We will probably give him another run in a bumper before going hurdling. He is a grand horse.

TAKINGRISKS (IRE) 12 b g Golden Tornado (IRE) – Downtown Rosie (IRE)
He's been a great horse for us winning the Scottish National, Rehearsal Chase and then the Listed *Skybet* Chase at Doncaster last season. I thought he was unlucky not to win the Rehearsal Chase at Newcastle for a second time in December because he was badly hampered by a faller before staying on well. He spent the summer in Northumberland doing some roadwork before he came back to us. We will probably run him in the same three miles handicap hurdle at Ayr (30th October), which he has contested for the last three years before following a similar programme.

TFOU (FR) 5 b g Authorized (IRE) – Fire Moon Julie (FR)

A grand horse we have given him plenty of time having purchased him as a three year old at the Goffs Landrover Sale. We sent him down to Henrietta Knight's last year and she loved him. She told me to train him like my father would have done and that's what we are doing. Jerry McGrath rode him whilst he was with Henrietta and he loved him, too. We took him to work at Carlisle during the spring. There were eight horses in the gallop, including Soft Risk, and it has already produced two winners. It was a proper piece of work and he went nicely. He jumps brilliantly but will have a run in a bumper in the Autumn before going hurdling.

TRAINER'S HORSE TO FOLLOW: NELLS SON

Value Racing Club

"Winning Together"

Our aim at Value Racing Club is to introduce new people into the world of horse racing. We provide a cost effective and simple way of becoming a racehorse owner. There are never any hidden costs or extras. Once the initial purchase has been paid, no further monies are required during the entire racing season.

What we offer and benefits:

- An opportunity to become involved in racehorse ownership.
- What we pay for a horse is what you pay, there are no added fees of any kind.
- A one-off cost covers the entire racing season.
- Stable visits arranged to watch your horse work on the gallops.
- Free owners badge every time your horse runs guaranteed.
- Each syndicate keeps 100% of all prize money won.
- 68% overall strike rate of our runners finishing in the first three places.
- Horses in training with David Pipe, Mick Appleby, Jamie Snowden, Tom Lacey & Tristan Davidson.
- Racing TV pundit Mark Howard is our Club Ambassador.
- We are members of the ROA "Racehorse Owners Association" & RSA "Racehorse Syndicates Association" to ensure good practice.

Big race wins include the £70,000 Imperial Cup, £30,000 Betfred Summer Hurdle, £30,000 Durham National, £20,000 Lincolnshire National. Valuable flat winners at York, Newmarket & Haydock.

Over £700,000 of prize money won for owners.

Website: www.valueracingclub.co.uk email: contact@valueracingclub.co.uk Twitter: @valueracingclub

Call James for more information: 07939800769

128

BROMLEY'S BEST BUYS

Anthony Bromley heads up the buying team at Highflyer Bloodstock, which also includes David Minton and Tessie Greatrex. They have been responsible for many household names over the last 25 years or so. In the latest season, they had a memorable Aintree Festival with four Grade 1 winners, namely Clan Des Obeaux, Monmiral, Protektorat and Shishkin, the latter adding to his Arkle Chase victory at the Cheltenham Festival. Frodon taking the Grade 1 King George VI Chase at Kempton over Christmas meant that Anthony has now been responsible for purchasing the winner of the three miles event in 13 of the last 15 runnings. Here are details of some of the Highflyer purchases bought this year at both public sales and privately.

ALL IN LOVE (FR) 5 b g No Risk At All (FR) – Ot Love (FR)
Trainer: Nigel TWISTON-DAVIES
A big, good-looking maiden five year old by a top sire, he showed gradual progressive form in four jumps starts in France, finishing off his career there with decent second places behind the useful pair of Saint Turgeon (over hurdles at Compiegne) and Geskille (over fences at Dieppe). He had a minor setback last winter at Nigel's (Twiston-Davies), but has been given plenty of time to recover and looks an interesting prospect who may even start straight off in a novice handicap chase.

ANOTHER MYSTERY 4 b g Norse Dancer – Misstree Pitcher
Trainer: Lucy WADHAM
A huge four-year-old whom Lucy (Wadham) and I could not believe was ready to run, let alone win, a fourteen runner English point-to-point in early April. However, he did so with the front two pulling a distance clear of the field. By the same sire as Yanworth, we felt that he had to have a good margin of improvement in him just through natural maturity and it will be interesting to watch him develop, particularly as he is English-bred and was produced through our pointing system.

ART OF ILLUSION (IRE) 4 b g Malinas (GER) – Zara (IRE)
Trainer: Warren GREATREX
Tessie Greatrex has been an integral part of the Highflyer buying team for many years now and has a canny knack of unearthing some really good value buys at the sales. This young Irish pointer is a prime example, having run a highly-promising second on his career debut on the 1st May, he split Phantom Getaway (£90,000 to Kim Bailey) and Storming Crossgales (£60,000 to Noel Fehily). Tessie picked him up for what appears a bargain price of £38,000 from the same nursery that produced Monkfish, and he should have enough pace to start in bumpers.

BALKEO (FR) 4 b g Galiway – Hukba (IRE)
Trainer: Nicky HENDERSON
This rangy good-looking French-bred four year old was bought for his owner Marie Donnelly to join Nicky (Henderson) after two very promising efforts to finish second in big field novice hurdles at Auteuil in soft/heavy ground in April and May. He ticks all the boxes you would like to see in a smart jumps prospect and, as a maiden, he can start off quietly and hopefully build up from there.

BALLYCOOSE (IRE) 4 ch g Mahler – Highly Presentable (IRE)
Trainer: Stuart CRAWFORD
We bought this big raw son of Mahler off Stuart's brother Steven (Crawford) a couple of weeks before he debuted in a Down Royal bumper in early May. Thankfully for us all, he made it a winning start in the process beating another promising youngster owned by Simon Munir and Isaac Souede called Champ De Gane. I think both horses have good futures in front of them over jumps.

BLUE STELLO (FR) 5 b g Spider Flight (FR) – Benina (FR)
Trainer: Nicky HENDERSON
The Owners Group have brought racehorse ownership to thousands of people and are doing a fantastic job in portraying racing in a great light. I have certainly had plenty of luck buying for them over the years, most notably Pentland Hills winning the Triumph Hurdle and I have bought a few more new ones this time, including this good-looking chasing type, Blue Stello, who showed plenty of pace before getting collared close home in his only Irish point before Christmas. The winner Connies Choice was subsequently bought privately by Barry Connell and I would say this fellow will be better at shorter than three miles.

CARLO DU BERLAIS (IRE) 4 b g Carlotamix (FR) – Dark Ebony (IRE)
Trainer: Fergal O'BRIEN
This attractive ex-Irish pointer showed plenty of promise in both his four year old points in April at Tipperary on yielding ground. He was still very much in contention on his debut when falling late on, but showed no ill effects thirteen days later when a close second of eleven. He is Fergal O'Brien's first horse for Owners Group and I think he will do well with him.

CITY CHIEF (IRE) 4 b g Soldier of Fortune (IRE) – Galant Ferns (IRE)
Trainer: Nicky HENDERSON
David Minton and Nicky Henderson bought this athletic son of Soldier Of Fortune at the last point-to-point sale of the season at the end of May at Tattersalls in Newmarket. He beat a well-touted debutant Knowsley Road into second and that horse was sold to Paul Nicholls for £135,000 at the same sale, overhauling him up the run-in with a bit in hand at the end. He looked a horse who will progress as he matures and is another exciting prospect for owner Marie Donnelly.

DANCING WITH DECO (IRE) 5 br g Milan – Miss Toulon (IRE)
Trainer: Alastair RALPH
A grand looking dark five year old by top jumps sire Milan, Alastair (Ralph) particularly liked this horse at the Doncaster Sales and he has shown enough in both his points to date (third to Bareback Jack last year and a close second this May) to suggest that he should do well in soft ground jumps races this winter and in the seasons to come.

DARK RAVEN (IRE) 4 br g Malinas (GER) – Mary Wilkie (IRE)
Trainer: Willie MULLINS
Purchased privately in between his two starts this spring, this is one of the most exciting young prospects in the Munir/Souede team for the coming season. Despite racing greenly in each of his bumpers, the last half mile in both races has been impressive and none more so than when taking the very valuable George Mernagh Sales Bumper at Fairyhouse at Easter by eleven lengths. He certainly shapes like a two and a half miles sort for hurdles and it will be interesting to see how Willie campaigns him in novice hurdles this winter, given all the young stars at Closutton.

ERNEST GRAY (IRE) 4 b g Walk In The Park (IRE) – Emily Gray (IRE)
Trainer: Alan KING

They did well to get some action for Irish point-to-point-trained horses earlier this spring, managing it initially by putting on some all-bumper meetings at proper racecourses during March for qualified pointers. These races were restricted to four and five-year-olds, but they were a lifeline for the pointing community who needed to showcase their young stock. This gelded son of Walk In The Park won the four year old bumper at the Punchestown meeting in testing conditions beating How Will I Know, who went on to make £75,000 at the sales, and has joined Harry Fry. Ernest Gray is in training with Alan King and I'm hoping he can do as well for him as another former Colin Bowe-trained inmate we bought, The Glancing Queen.

GALUDON (FR) 5 b g Saddler Maker (IRE) – Nobless D'Aron (FR)
Trainer: Harry WHITTINGTON

Time will probably tell that he has run into some pretty good horses in both his starts. He was fourth to Tango Tara (£120,000 to Paul Nicholls) on his points debut in late November before finishing a very creditable second to the smart and unbeaten Journey With Me (Robcour/De Bromhead) in his point-to-point bumper at Gowran in March, again in testing conditions. He had some decent horses along way behind him at Gowran and he looked a late-maturing type who should progress as he gains more experience. Harry Whittington trains his half-brother Franigane, who is definitely improving with age and their useful elder brother Verni did not win until he was seven years old and was runner-up at the Cheltenham Festival as an eight year old, so there are plenty of grounds for being hopeful with this gelded son of Saddler Maker.

GEORGE BANCROFT 3 ch g Australia – Extensive
Trainer: Charlie LONGSDON

I am a big fan of this lad's sire, Australia, and I was taken by this gelding at the Newmarket July Sales. He had only won his latest start at Chepstow off a mark of 57, but he did it all through stamina, which I feel is a massive factor when it comes to three year old hurdling. He then followed it up with a three lengths victory at Ripon in August on his first start for his new connections. As we don't know whether he will handle soft ground, I think Charlie's plan is to get going with him fairly soon over hurdles.

GREAT OCEAN (FR) 5 b g Great Pretender (IRE) – Diamond of Diana (FR)
Trainer: Philip HOBBS

This elegant son of Great Pretender is out of a Kapgarde mare and looks a promising recruit for Philip Hobbs. He showed talent in both his autumn points, splitting a couple of future bumper winners on his debut in September before finishing third to the smart Percy Warner on his second outing. He had to wait for Irish pointing to resume but was then a very decisive winner at Fairyhouse in mid-April.

HARRY'S HOTTIE (IRE) 4 b f Cloudings (IRE) – Really Royale (FR)
Trainer: Harry WHITTINGTON

It's rare to see progeny of Cloudings doing much of any note before the age of five and, whilst this filly was unable to land a telling blow in either of her four year old points this spring, despite finishing runner up each time, she showed more than enough to interest me. Indeed, time will no doubt tell that she was taking on a couple of stars in both races, finishing second to the Robcour-owned Jenny Flex on debut and then proving no match for Happy D'Ex (£195,000 to Gordon Elliott) at Dromahane on her only other start. I think she represented value at £23,000 at the Doncaster May Sale and I am confident Harry will do well with her (despite her rather corny name!).

HOLLY HARTINGO (IRE) 5 b m Well Chosen – Hazel Toi (IRE)
Trainer: Alastair RALPH
This big five year old mare came from a smaller Irish pointing yard and showed a bit of promise on her debut in April when sixth to First Glance (already placed for Ollie Greenall) and, more importantly, progressed nicely on from that on her second start. That came at Dromahane in early May and she pushed Sharp Shadow (£55,000 to Philip Hobbs) all the way to the line, finishing a close second. This £27,000 purchase is by an under-rated sire in Well Chosen, who has had the likes of Jury Duty, Carefully Selected and Chosen Mate in Ireland from fairly limited opportunities.

HUNTERS YARN (IRE) 4 b g Fame And Glory – Full of Birds (FR)
Trainer: Willie MULLINS
This impressive Thurles bumper winner has joined Willie Mullins for Simon Munir and Isaac Souede after being purchased privately in April. He did not have much luck in running on his debut when a keeping-on third at Naas but made a giant step forward on his second outing when winning by seventeen lengths. He is a full-brother to Michael Scudamore's Grade 1 placed novice hurdler, Do Your Job, and we are obviously harbouring good hopes for this fellow over hurdles.

ICEBURGH BAY (IRE) 5 b g Sageburg (IRE) – Aspelenie (IRE)
Trainer: Philip HOBBS
A big horse, it is no surprise that he took time to find his feet in point-to-points. He showed some ability when fourth on his career debut in early May to a stablemate, House Of Stories, who was bought by Rebecca Curtis afterwards. However, he improved markedly on that first effort (going through the third horse (Goleirihem) in both races, he turned the tables on him by over twenty lengths) by winning easily a fortnight later. The runner-up that day, Tommy Tracey, has joined Paul Webber and the aforementioned third is now with Olly Murphy. I view this laid-back horse as more of a 2m4f/3m novice hurdler rather than a bumper sort for this season.

IN THIS WORLD (FR) 3 b c Saint Des Saints (FR) – Maia Royale (FR)
Trainer: Dan SKELTON
This very attractive three year old colt by France's Champion sire Saint Des Saints is a really exciting recruit. He has a great female pedigree, as his grandam was the Champion French jumps mare, Maia Eria, who beat Kauto Star a number of times in her career, including when easily taking the Champion three year old hurdle at Auteuil. This youngster was a good winner of his only Flat race over a mile and six in early June in the French provinces. It was run at Guillaume Macaire's home track of Royan and I know that team were shocked that their debutant Fil Dor (belongs to UK owner Andrew Brown) was beaten into second that day. In This World's French owner/breeder has kept a quarter of this horse as he has a lot of faith in him, so I am hoping he is right and that he could make up into a Triumph Hurdle contender.

KYNTARA 5 b g Kayf Tara – Speed Bonnie Boat
Trainer: Kim BAILEY
The two most visually impressive UK maiden pointing winners I saw last season were the subsequent Grade 1 scorer Ahoy Senor at Kimble and this son of Kayf Tara, Kyntara, in Devon. Purchased by David Minton for Lady Dulverton, he did exactly the same thing in his sole bumper at Warwick in February after he had joined Kim Bailey - pulverising the opposition. He is certainly a Graded novice hurdler for the coming season and I am excited to see how high he can go.

LARGY TRAIN (IRE) 4 b g Yorgunnabelucky (USA) – Snow Train
Trainer: Paul NICHOLLS
I bought this huge four year old for the Million In Mind Partnership soon after he had won his Ayr bumper in soft ground in May for Stuart Crawford. A big raw baby, he raced greenly but won it in decent style and he surely must improve further as he strengthens into his immense frame. His sire is starting to pop up with a few eye-catching winners from a really small number of foals and I am very hopeful that he will take well to hurdling this winter with Paul (Nicholls).

MAKIN'YOURMINDUP 4 b g Kayf Tara – Subtilty
Trainer: Paul NICHOLLS
This grand big son of Kayf Tara ran in a smart-looking four year old point at Tattersalls Farm in early May. Showing up well in front for a long way, he had no answer at the business end behind useful sorts of Denis Murphy and Colin Bowe's but was only seven lengths off the winner in third at the line and showed lots of promise for the future. Kayf Tara's produce are not recognised for early precocity and I think Owners Group have got a nice "slow-burner" here who may not come into his own until he goes chasing in a year or two, but should be up to winning a middle-distance novice hurdle this time around.

MESSAGE PERSONNEL (FR) 3 b g Saint Des Saints (FR) – Victoria Princess (FR)
Trainer: Dan SKELTON
John and Lisa Hales and Highflyer have teamed up very successfully with progeny of Saint Des Saints over the years with the likes of Monmiral, Protektorat, Aux Ptits Soins and Fidelio Vallis all being by this great French sire. This easy-moving three year old needed the experience of his first hurdle race at Chateaubriant when fourth in mid-May but really stepped up on that next time when a decisive winner of his juvenile hurdle at Dieppe on the 1st July, beating a couple of previous winners in the process. In a slowly-run event, I was impressed with how he came from last to first from the second last jump to power away from his rivals on the run-in. His dam was a good Auteuil jumper herself and more importantly she is a half-sister to three smart jumpers, including a couple of decent staying chasers I bought from France from the same connections, namely Wonderful Charm and Royal Charm. He should acquit himself well over hurdles this time, but I am more excited about him over fences in years to come.

OCEANLINE (IRE) 3 b g Adaay (IRE) – Ocean Bluff (IRE)
Trainer: Alan KING
Despite being by the speedy Adaay, this youngster seems to have picked up lots of stamina from his female side, which is full of decent Flat stayers and he has been bought over the summer to stay at Alan's for the Million In Mind Partnership to run over hurdles. He relished the step up to a mile and six on the Flat when winning at Nottingham in June and Sandown in August and has been schooling well at home in readiness for a September debut over jumps.

OLD PAINLESS (IRE) 5 b g Imperial Monarch (IRE) – Baby Goose (IRE)
Trainer: Harry WHITTINGTON
Another five year old Irish pointing winner from the Doncaster May Sales, this athletic gelding was impressive in beating a big field at Dromahane on his career debut in early May, beating another debutant called Robin Des Fox (who made £60,000 at the same sale, joining Oliver Signy). Harry (Whittington) and I bought this lad for £50,000 and he should pay his way over jumps this time and is another chaser in the making.

O'TOOLE (IRE) 5 ch g Mahler – On Gallery Head (IRE)
Trainer: Stuart CRAWFORD

We bought this scopey Mahler gelding to stay in the yard soon after he had pulverised the opposition in a Fairyhouse bumper at the end of February. He then ran once more for the Double Green team of Munir and Souede at the Punchestown Festival. He had the option of going for the minor winners' bumper that week but Stuart was adamant he wanted to have a go at the Grade 1 Champion Bumper and how right he was. To split Kilcruit and Sir Gerhard by finishing second at level weights on only his second career start was a huge feat. Simon and Isaac have never had a bumper horse as good as him and, with a *Racing Post* rating of 131, he really is a very exciting novice hurdler for Stuart Crawford to have in the yard for the winter ahead. I suspect he will be best over further than two miles.

PULLING STUMPS (IRE) 4 b g Soldier of Fortune (IRE) – Pride of The Braid (IRE)
Trainer: Philip HOBBS

Back in the day, I bought Detroit City, Monkerhostin and Lacdoudal for their respective owners who then sent them to be trained by Philip Hobbs. Philip did a tremendous job with all of them and I was delighted when he asked me in the spring to find him some form horses. We purchased five horses at the two May sales, at Doncaster and Newmarket, including this UK bumper winner who beat a previous scorer at Ludlow in early May. He is only four and appears to have a large amount of improvement in him as he was only a shell of a horse this spring and raced greenly at Ludlow. Nicely related, he should do well for the Highclere Syndicate.

RATHMACKNEE (IRE) 5 b g Jet Away – Let's Park (IRE)
Trainer: Nicky HENDERSON

This attractive five year old Irish pointer missed the sales as he won on the last weekend of the season, a couple of days after the last organised auction. Whilst over at the Land Rover Store Sale, I arranged for a number of the Wexford trainers to bring some of these "last weekend pointers" up for us to inspect and one of the horses David Minton and I loved was this son of the up-and-coming sire Jet Away. Trained by Colin Bowe, who we've had a lot of success from, he was sick after his first race in the autumn and had spent the winter back at his owner's place before rejoining Colin in April, once pointing had resumed. By all accounts, it was a bit of a rush to get him to that last meeting and that probably explains why the Monbeg-trained Galunggung was able to join him and dead-heat on the line as he had made all and still held a two lengths lead at the last before blowing up. He has been bought for the Million In Mind Partnership.

RAYMOND TUSK (IRE) 6 b h High Chaparral (IRE) – Dancing Shoes (IRE)
Trainer: Alan KING

I bought this gorgeous entire horse from Middleham Park in February and Alan King has done a brilliant job in rejuvenating him this year on the Flat. Whilst he has not quite reached the heights of his 2019 season, when he peaked at 113, his excellent second at Royal Ascot in the Duke of Edinburgh Stakes has seen his mark return to 105. The plan is to give him a short summer break after that run before he goes jumping this Autumn/winter and he rates a very exciting prospect for novice hurdles with the target being hopefully one of the Grade 1 races at the spring Festivals.

ROCKY MAN (FR) 3 b g Doctor Dino (FR) – Lady Speedy (IRE)
Trainer: Dan SKELTON
This French-bred three year old by the top sire Doctor Dino was bought in April after an easy win in a long distance Flat maiden in the provinces for Henri Pantall. Whilst the depth of the race was not particularly strong, he was a class apart from his field that day and he has been gelded since arriving at Dan's (Skelton). He was bought by one of Dan's main supporters, Colm Donlon, someone I have known for many years having purchased the likes of Caid Du Berlais and American Trilogy for him and it is good to be working together again.

SCOTCH ON DA ROCKS (IRE) 4 b g Fame And Glory – Final Episode (IRE)
Trainer: Ben PAULING
This tall, well-bred four year old won a competitive English maiden point-to-point in what I considered to be the style of a really good prospect. I was particularly pleased that Highflyer's agent Tessie Greatrex and Ben Pauling agreed with me and bought him for 80,000gns at the Newmarket Sale in April. The form has already started to work out well with both the third and fourth winning since. I have a strong feeling that this will be a horse to follow over the next few seasons as he develops into his large frame.

SHARP SHADOW (IRE) 5 b m Fame And Glory – Sharps Express (IRE)
Trainer: Philip HOBBS
A decisive winner of her only mares' Irish point in early May at Dromahane beating Holly Hartingo, she ticked a lot of boxes at the sales and is the sort that Philip (Hobbs) will do well with in mares-only events this season.

SONIGINO (FR) 4 b g It's Gino (GER) – Soniador (FR)
Trainer: Paul NICHOLLS
It was tragic for all the connections this spring to lose two really exciting juveniles that I had sourced in France for Paul (Nicholls) in Houx Gris and Good Ball, but I was asked to find another horse for the owners of the latter and we hope that this one will prove lucky for them. Sonigino has won his last two races over hurdles in May and June making most of the running both times and, on his latest start at Auteuil, he gave plenty of weight away to some solid rivals. The French handicapper already has him on 140 after three career starts and I am confident that the Hales, Sir Alex Ferguson and Ged Mason Partnership have another very nice prospect in him.

THE CARPENTER (IRE) 5 gr g Shantaram – Just Another Penny (IRE)
Trainer: Nicky HENDERSON
Although this grey five year old was only second in his bumper at Navan, I believe he achieved as much as many of the winners who were sold this spring either at the sales or privately. There were plenty of horses with big reputations amongst the runners that day and the owners of the close third Corbeau turned down a bid of £280,00 in the sales ring at Tattersalls a few weeks later. I think The Carpenter looks another exciting youngster for Owners Group and I cannot wait to see him out over hurdles this winter.

TIGERS ROAR (IRE) 5 b g Leading Light (IRE) – Almnadia (IRE)
Trainer: Nigel TWISTON-DAVIES
An attractive five year old who did well to win his Irish maiden point at Dromahane in early May in soft ground, taking up the running from the fourth last and then battling back when headed on the run-in. He was in a ding-dong tussle that day with the Monbeg-trained Super Survivor who subsequently made £115,000 at the Doncaster May Sales (to join Jamie Snowden) and the front pair came nicely clear of the field. He should hopefully be competitive in two and a half miles novice hurdles this time around for the Million In Mind Partnership.

TIMEFORATUNE 5 b g Yorgunnabelucky (USA) – Timeforagin
Trainer: Paul NICHOLLS
Another new youngster for John and Lisa Hales, this scopey gelding was bought by David Minton at the Newmarket May Sales, whilst I was attending the re-scheduled Arqana Breeze Up Sale at Doncaster. He put up one of the visually most impressive bumper performances seen all spring when storming to victory at Ffos Las in May on good to soft ground. He is in the right hands to hopefully go on to the next level once he starts jumping this season.

HIGHFLYER BLOODSTOCK'S HORSE TO FOLLOW: O'TOOLE

For all the latest news and how to get involved in the
Million In Mind partnership, please visit
www.millioninmind.co.uk

Don't forget to read my Diary @
www.mhpublications.co.uk

CHANGING CODES

The following feature highlights a selection of Flat horses set to go jumping for the first time this winter who will, hopefully, prove profitable to follow and develop into smart hurdlers.

Having been purchased earlier this year by J.P.McManus, it is presumed the 102 rated **BENAUD** will go juvenile hurdling later this year. Trained by **Joseph O'Brien**, the Australia gelding has won 2 of his 8 career starts. Successful in a mile nursery at Leopardstown (Yielding/Soft) in October, he was gelded during the winter. His three year old career got off to the best possible start with a length three quarters win at Naas (1m 2f : Yielding/Soft) in May. Elevated in class and distance, he sported the famous green and yellow silks of the legendary owner for the first time and ran an excellent race to finish fourth in the Group 2 Queens Vase at Royal Ascot (1m 6f). Set plenty to do, he kept on well to fill fourth position less than four lengths behind Godolphin's Kemari. Twenty lengths in arrears of the top-class mare Tarnawa in the Group 3 Ballyroan Stakes at Leopardstown (1m 4f : Yielding/Soft) last time, he handles soft ground and stays well and should make an above average hurdler.

Dermot Weld doesn't have many jumpers nowadays but it is hoped he elects to send **CIEL D'AFRIQUE** over timber. Runner-up behind Zanahiyr and Mt Leinster in twelve furlongs maidens at Fairyhouse and Galway last year, he was gelded during the winter. Absent for 262 days, he was three and a quarter lengths second to the 147 rated chaser Zero Ten in a twelve furlongs maiden at the Galway Festival in July. The son of Sea The Stars shed his maiden tag at the sixth time of asking at Roscommon (1m 4f : Good/Yielding) the following month. His jockey Colin Keane said afterwards: **"He's a fine, big, strong horse. If he gave himself a chance, he might get further. Maybe in better races he might relax and there could be a good pot in him somewhere along the way."** The four year old, who is rated 82, is be tailormade for one of the maiden hurdles at Leopardstown's Christmas meeting.

Mick Halford trained Zanahiyr before he was sold and developed into a high-class juvenile hurdler last season for Gordon Elliott. The Co.Kildare trainer was also responsible for six race maiden **EBASARI**. A three year old gelding by Lope De Vega, he was a creditable third in a ten furlongs handicap at Roscommon (Good) in June off a mark of 72. Bought by **Willie Mullins** for **€47,000** at the Goffs Online Summer Sale in July, he is low mileage and ought to improve when tackling longer distances. Potentially well treated on the Flat, he has the attributes to make a decent juvenile hurdler, too.

Kevin Ryan is more likely to have his eye on decent middle distance handicaps on the Flat than eight flights of hurdles. However, it is not beyond the realms of possibility that the **FORZA ORTA** could pursue a career under National Hunt rules at some stage. A three year old by Fastnet Rock, he didn't race as a juvenile but has made up for lost time this season finishing second on his first four outings (1m – 1m 2f). Beaten a length and a quarter by Mahrajaan (won the Lanark Silver Bell at Hamilton since and rated 95) at Leicester (1m 2f : Good/Firm) in July, he was a ready winner at Hamilton (1m 3f) in early September. A four lengths scorer, he has yet to race on ground worse than good to soft. One could envisage him being ideal for juvenile hurdles at Musselburgh or Doncaster (ie. two miles on decent ground).

Veteran owner Hal McGhie, who tasted Grade 1 success when Noyan won the Heineken Gold Cup at Punchestown in 1997, is responsible for improving three year old **INNSE GALL**. Bred to stay well being a half-brother to 5 times winner Deauville Flyer and winning hurdler Taws, he cost 90,000gns as a yearling. A winner over a mile as a two year old at Ripon last season, he looked a well handicapped horse when scoring by two and three quarters of a length at Ayr (1m 2f : Good/Soft) off 68 in August – he was part of a 457/1 four timer for trainer **Iain Jardine** at the Scottish track. The subject of an ordinary ride next time at Hamilton (1m 3f), he should have followed up off a five pounds higher mark. While he still has unfinished business on the Flat, the Toronado gelding will make a lovely jumper once sent down that route. He has plenty more to offer.

It is hoped the connections of **TASHKHAN** decide to send the three year old over obstacles this winter. A gelded son of Born To Sea, he began his career with Emmet Mullins in Ireland winning by nearly four lengths at Navan (1m 2f : Heavy) on his handicap debut in March when rated 57. Bought privately to join **Brian Ellison**, his official mark has climbed from 70 to 96 for the Malton based handler. He beat the progressive Chalk Stream (won three times since and rated 105) by three and a quarter lengths at Haydock (1m 2f : Soft) in late May before registering another win at the same track (1m 6f : Soft) in early July. Fifth in the Melrose Stakes at York's Ebor Festival in August, he stayed on strongly less than two lengths behind Valley Forge. He has the credentials to make a high-class hurdler.

The Gredley Family have done very well in recent seasons with their odd runner over jumps. Allmankind is a dual Grade 1 winner and Stepney Causeway won four out of five over hurdles last season. The pair are trained by **Dan Skelton** and it would therefore be no surprise if the three year old **TOO FRIENDLY** went hurdling this Autumn. Previously trained by George Scott, the son of Camelot has been gelded and is rated 85 on the Flat. He beat the useful Dhushan (rated 99) by a length and a half in a ten furlongs maiden at Doncaster (Good) in late March. While he has failed to recapture that level of form in three starts since, he wasn't beaten far by subsequent Group winners Dubai Honour and Foxes Tales in a heritage handicap at Newmarket's July meeting (1m 2f : Good/Firm). Off since, he has only raced half a dozen times and is the sort Skelton excels with.

WILD DOLLAR is another J.P.McManus owned three year old who is expected to embark on a jumping career later this year. Trained by **Eddie and Patrick Harty**, the Zoffany gelding was well held on his first couple of runs at Leopardstown in the spring. However, he stepped up on those performances when 'winning' a ten furlongs maiden at the Curragh (Soft/Heavy) in late May. Beaten a short head, he was later awarded the race in the stewards' room having been bumped by Citronnade (won twice since) close home. Bought by McManus soon afterwards, he shaped well on his handicap debut over the same course and distance off 87 when a length and a half third behind Hell Bent. The same combination combined to win the 2008 Supreme Novices' Hurdle with Captain Cee Bee.

ZINC WHITE was acquired for a hefty £310,000 at the Goffs London Horses in Training Sale in June on the eve of Royal Ascot to join **Olly Greenall**. The Vadamos gelding held an entry in the Group 2 Queens Vase having won both his starts for Ralph Beckett during the spring. A wide margin winner of a couple of staying handicaps at Wetherby and Sandown (1m 6f) by an aggregate of over a dozen lengths off marks of 69 and 75, he revels in slow ground and stamina appears to be his strong suit. Rated 87, he is tailormade for juvenile hurdles and could return to the A1 track (13th October) for his jumping bow.

FRENCH REVOLUTION

In previous editions, the feature has highlighted subsequent Cheltenham Festival winners **A PLUS TARD, ARAMAX, BURNING VICTORY, DEFI DU SEUIL, ESPOIR D'ALLEN** and **KLASSICAL DREAM**. That trend continued last winter with **QUILIXOS** (Triumph Hurdle winner), plus **GAILLARD DU MESNIL** (Dual Grade 1 winner) and **MONMIRAL** (4 out of 4 including Grade 1 victory). Other noteworthy inclusions were **BLUE LORD, CAPODANNO** and **GAULOISE** (both Punchestown Festival winners) and **NASSALAM**. There were 30 winners from 118 runners (25%) during 2020/2021.

Having spent a lot of time watching races from France - both on the Flat and over jumps – I have put together an extensive selection of 42 horses who have been purchased to race in Britain and Ireland this season. Therefore the following will hopefully prove exciting recruits for their new connections. Largely unknown, some of them may develop into household names in years to come.

Similar to previous years, a number of the write-ups have been accompanied by comments from former French champion jockey **James Reveley** who has been in excellent form this year (Grade 3 & five Listed winners in 2021). Son of former trainer Keith, James has ridden 11 Grade 1 winners in France, including the Grand Steeple-Chase de Paris in three successive years (2016, 2017, 2018), plus the Grande Course de Haies d'Auteuil aboard the David Pipe trained Un Temps Pour Tout in 2015.

ALLEGORIE DE VASSY (FR) 4 b f No Risk At All (FR) – Autignac (FR)

One of a number of exciting purchases by **Rich and Susannah Ricci**, this daughter ought to be a real force in mares' novice hurdles this winter and beyond. Bought for €50,000 as a yearling, she raced four times over hurdles for Marcel Rolland improving with each start. Following a couple of indifferent performances at Compiegne (pulled up) and Auteuil (fifth), she produced a much better showing at the former track in April finishing second (2m 2f). Beaten five lengths, the No Risk At All filly chased home Hacienda but it was much closer between the pair when they met again at Auteuil (2m 2f) over three weeks later. Allegorie De Vassy stayed on strongly in a conditions hurdle behind Belle Promesse and the aforementioned Hacienda and was only beaten two lengths and a short head. The winner has subsequently won Listed and Grade 3 hurdles at the Parisian track. **Willie Mullins** appears to have another potentially smart filly on his hands. All four of her starts have been on testing ground.

Reveley's remarks: **"She has some top-class fillies' form. The winner at Auteuil is the best in her category. She ought to do very well for her new connections."**

BALKEO (FR) 4 b g Galiway – Hukba (IRE)

Bought by Highflyer Bloodstock on behalf of **Joe and Marie Donnelly**, he joins **Nicky Henderson** and will go novice hurdling. Placed in all three starts over hurdles when trained in France by Manon Scandella-Lacaille, he was beaten around ten lengths on his debut at Nimes (2m : Good) in September. Returning to action in the spring, he was three lengths second at Auteuil (2m 2f : Very Soft) – the third has won over fences since. A month later, the Galiway gelding filled the same position over C&D (Heavy) finding Sunseat two and a half lengths too strong with the Richard Kelvin-Hughes and Robert Waley-Cohen owned Piccadilly Lilly in third.

Reveley's Remarks: **"I rode him at Auteuil in May and he is a tough type. He ran a nice race and, while I don't think he is a world beater, he is capable of winning races in the UK."**

BRING ON THE NIGHT 4 ch g Gleneagles (IRE) - Brasileira
Featured in the *Top 40 Prospects* last year, the former Andre Fabre trained four year old has yet to race for **Willie Mullins** but is set to make his hurdles bow this winter. Speaking to Ruby Walsh at York's Ebor Festival in August, the chestnut was gelded soon after joining Ireland's champion trainer and was purposely left off until this season. A half-brother to Joseph O'Brien's dual Listed winner and Group 1 fifth Bolleville, he won two of his three starts for Andre Fabre in 2020. Unraced at two, the son of Gleneagles was slowly away on his debut on the all-weather at Chantilly in early March before staying on in eighth over an inadequate nine furlongs. Reappearing thirteen days later and switching to turf at Compiegne (1m 4f : Heavy), the son of Gleneagles relished the step up to a mile and a half and ran out an easy three and a half lengths winner (runner-up has won twice in 2021). Held up, he made good headway under Pierre-Charles Boudot before pulling clear in the homestraight. Back in action a couple of months later, he beat six rivals in a twelve furlongs conditions event at Deauville (Standard) in May. A three parts of a length winner, the second, third and fourth have scored since. Proven on testing ground, Bring On The Night looked a strong stayer on the Flat and his dam was a dual Listed winner. His sire produced Cabot Cliffs (3) and Tulin (2) to win over obstacles last season and he could develop into a high-class novice hurdler for owner **Joe Donnelly**.

DEMNAT (FR) 4 b g Doctor Dino (FR) – Sandside (FR)
Half-brother to the high-class Sceau Royal, he was bought for €64,000 at the Arqana Summer Sale in July and has joined **Venetia Williams**. He raced eight times for Francois Nicolle winning over hurdles and fences. Both victories were gained at Fontainebleau, including a twelve lengths win in April (2m 2f : Very Soft). Beaten half a length at Auteuil (2m 1f : Heavy) in June, the winner Youtwo Glass has finished runner-up in a Grade 3 chase at the same track since. Second at Compiegne on his most recent start later the same month, he is a bold jumper and likes to front run. Only four, he will be an exciting spectacle in two mile chases over here and could be ideal for something like the Castleford Chase at Wetherby (27th December). His stable won the race in 2012 and 2013.

DINOBLUE (FR) 4 b f Doctor Dino (FR) – Blue Aster (FR)
In training in France with Daniela Mele earlier this year, this daughter of Doctor Dino held entries but has yet to race. She is an interesting prospect nevertheless having been purchased by **J.P.McManus**. Having spent the summer at her own's Martinstown Stud in Ireland, she has joined **Willie Mullins** and will presumably start off in a mares' bumper this term. She is from a family Ireland's champion trainer knows well being a half-sister to Blue Sari, who finished runner-up in the Cheltenham Festival bumper in 2019. That gelded son of Saddex won at the first time of asking, so don't be surprised if this filly does likewise.

EL FABIOLO (FR) 4 b g Spanish Moon (USA) – Sainte Mante (FR)
Previously trained by Patricia Butel and Jean-Luc Beaunez, he was seventh in a maiden on the Flat at Clairefontaine (1m 6f : Very Soft) in August last year. Sent jumping the following month, he lined up in the Prix Finot at Auteuil (2m 2f : Very Soft), a Listed hurdle and shaped well in third. The Spanish Moon raced prominently jumping well and marginally led leaving the backstraight. Keeping on after the last, he lacked a change of gear suggesting he will be suited by two and a half miles. Bought by **Simon Munir and Isaac Souede**, he joined **Willie Mullins** last winter and has been given time. He is a half-brother to Tommy Silver, who won a Listed juvenile hurdle for Paul Nicholls.

FIL DOR (FR) 3 b g Doctor Dino (FR) – La Turbale (FR)

A half-brother to a Listed winner on the Flat and a chase winner at Auteuil, he was bought for €88,000 as a two year old at the Arqana Deauville Sale in November. Owned by **Andrew and Gemma Brown**, he made his debut on the Flat at Royan (1m 6f : Good/Soft) in June when trained by Hector de Lageneste and Guillaume Macaire. Racing in mid division, he moved into contention turning for home but couldn't reel in the winner In This World. Beaten two and a half lengths, he has been transferred to **Gordon Elliott** since and will go juvenile hurdling. Given his size, jumping will bring out the best in him.

GOT GLORY (FR) 3 b f Great Pretender (IRE) – Hideaway Girl

Owner **Audrey Turley** has enjoyed Cheltenham Festival glory in recent years thanks to Burning Victory and Galopin Des Champs. The same patron acquired this unbeaten filly during the summer having won on her debut on the Flat at Clairefontaine (1m 4f : Very Soft) in July. Trained by Francois Monfort, the daughter of Great Pretender was ridden by Maxime Guyon and, having raced keenly early on, she settled into a prominent position behind the leaders. Staying on strongly to lead inside the final furlong, she won going away by two lengths. The runner-up won next time and she looks a filly with a bright future. It remains to be seen whether **Willie Mullins** sends her juvenile hurdling this season, but she is bred for jumping being a half-sister to Oliver Sherwood's Listed chase winner Got Away. Either way, she is very much one for the future. She looks smart.

GOVEN (FR) 5 b g Poliglote – Sweeny (FR)

J.P.McManus paid €175,000 at the Arqana Mixed Sale in November for the five year old who is in training with **Willie Mullins**. Unbeaten in two AQPS Flat races for Alain Couetil, he won by four and a half lengths at Senonnes (1m 4f : Heavy) in October on his debut. Held up, he cruised into the lead with a furlong to run before pulling away without coming off the bridle – his rider spent most of the last 200 yards looking over her shoulder. Nineteen days later, the five year old followed up at Nantes (1m 4f : Heavy) under a hands and heels ride. Taken to the stands side in the homestraight, he was pushed out for a two lengths win. Set to go novice hurdling for his new connections this Autumn, he looks high-class.

GRIVEI (FR) 4 ch g Muhtathir – Stourza (FR)

By the same stallion as Envoi Allen, he is another unraced four year old to keep an eye on. Previously owned by Dungarven vet Walter Connors in France, he held entries at Auteuil during the spring. He now belongs to **Tim O'Driscoll**, who has enjoyed plenty of success with Dinons (8 wins) and Fakeira (Grade 3 winning novice hurdler last season) in recent years. Like that pair, Grivei is in training with **Gordon Elliott** and is expected to make his presence felt in a bumper this Autumn.

HADDEX DES OBEAUX (FR) 4 b g Saddex – Shifra (FR)

Gary Moore has taken charge of this former Nicolas Devilder trained four year old. He ran in three French bumpers winning at Chateaubriant (1m 5f : Soft) before finishing fifth in a Grade 2 event at Fontainebleau in September. Only tenth on his hurdles debut at Pau in January, he was a different proposition next time when making virtually all at Auteuil (2m 1f : Very Soft). Jumping well in front, he was headed between the final two hurdles but rallied strongly and was pulling away again at the finish to win by two and a half lengths. It was thirty lengths back to the third. Stamina looks his strong suit and he ought to be a force in handicap hurdles this winter before going chasing next season.

HALO DES OBEAUX (FR) 4 gr g Al Namix (FR) – Almeria Des Obeaux (FR)
A former stablemate of Haddex Des Obeaux, he was placed in two of his three races in AQPS Flat races – behind Horn Cape and Heross Du Seuil (both joined Nicky Henderson). The grey then went jumping for the first time at Auteuil (2m 1f : Very Soft) in March and beat the aforementioned Henn See by a length and three quarters with the pair a dozen lengths clear of the third. Bought out of Nicolas Devilder's yard, the Al Namix gelding has joined **Paul Nicholls** and remains a novice until the end of October. The Grade 2 Persian War Novices' Hurdle at Chepstow (8th October) is a possible target before going chasing.

HARDY DU SEUIL (FR) 4 b g Coastal Path – Pervenche Du Seuil (FR)
"He jumps beautifully and the plan is to follow a similar route to Ga Law last season and go novice chasing and use his four year old allowance. All being well, he will be running in October with a view to contesting the Grade 2 Rising Stars Novices' Chase at Wincanton (6th November)," reports **Jamie Snowden** who is training this gelded son of Coastal Path. Runner-up in AQPS Flat races at Vichy (the 130 rated hurdler Herbiers was fourth) and Vittel last year, the four year old was only eighth on his hurdles bow at Auteuil in September. Off the track until February, he returned at Fontainebleau (2m 1f : Very Soft) and made all. With the exception of a slight error at the last, he jumped well and the second and third have won since.

HAUTURIERE (FR) 4 ch f No Risk At All (FR) – Ocean Beach (FR)
Half-sister to dual hurdles winner Golfe Clair, she had one run in a French bumper at Fontainebleau (1m 6f : Very Soft) in February. Daniela Mele's filly was held up before being brought wide in the homestraight. Staying on, she was beaten five and a half lengths by Heros with a length and a half back to the third Henares (won twice at Auteuil since). She has joined **Willie Mullins** and belongs to **Dr Peter Fitzgerald**, who won the Galway Plate this summer with Royal Rendezvous. She is one for mares' novice hurdles.

HAWAI GAME (FR) 4 b g Diamond Boy (FR) – Rule of The Game (FR)
A seven lengths winner of his only start in an AQPS Flat race at Senonnes (1m 6f : Heavy) in late October, he led early on before being headed with a circuit to go. Moving to the front with a furlong and a half to run, he pulled away (slightly awkward head carriage) to score comfortably. The form looks solid with the second and fourth (Huflower – joined Paul Nicholls) winning twice since. Bought out of Gaeten Taupin's yard for €90,000 at the Arqana November Sale by **J.P.McManus**, he is trained by **Willie Mullins** and is another interesting prospect for novice hurdles.

HEAD LAW (FR) 4 b g Network (GER) – Law (FR)
Half-brother to Grade 2 winning chaser Ga Law, he was purchased for €150,000 by **J.P.McManus** at the Arqana November Sale and is in training with **Jonjo O'Neill**. The Network gelding won an AQPS Flat race at Le Mans (1m 3f : Very Soft) in November by two and a half lengths. Under the care of Gabriel Leenders, he made good headway turning for home before running on strongly. The second and third have franked the form by winning subsequently. A lovely big scopey four year old, he is a smashing addition to Jackdaws Castle and one to look forward to over hurdles.

HEIA (FR) 4 b f No Risk At All (FR) – Ulla De Montot (FR)

Featured in this section last year, the four year old filly has yet to race for **Kenny Alexander** and **Willie Mullins** and is therefore retained. By the increasingly popular sire, No Risk At All, she was a two lengths winner of her only appearance in an AQPS Flat race at Le Lion D'Angers (Left-Handed – 1m 4f : Good/Soft) in July 2020. In rear during the early stages, she challenged on the outside in the homestraight and won readily. Trained by Isabelle Gallorini (same source as Benie Des Dieux, Gaillard Du Mesnil and Klassical Dream), the runner-up has won since. She could be a similar type to the same connections' Gauloise and develop into a smart mare over hurdles.

HERCULE DU SEUIL (FR) 4 b g Saddler Maker (IRE) – Cibelle Du Seuil (FR)

Another **J.P.McManus** purchase from the Arqana November Sale, this gelded son of Saddler Maker cost **€185,000** and has been sent to **Willie Mullins**. Trained in France by Mickael Seror, he was beaten a short head on his hurdles debut at Strasbourg (2m 1f: Soft) in October. Attempting to make all, he was headed close home by the Guillaume Macaire trained Harowa (won twice over fences since). It was four lengths back to the third. Agent Hubert Barbe commented at the sale: **"Hercule Du Seuil is a little backward but is a powerful individual and will be given time over the winter before running next year."** The Saddler Maker gelding could be another very useful novice hurdler for the Closutton team.

HEVA ROSE (FR) 4 gr f Saint Des Saints (FR) – Wild Rose Bloom (FR)

Half-sister to a Grade 3 winning chaser, the daughter of Saint Des Saints is a maiden over hurdles and fences and has been bought to join **Venetia Williams**. A three lengths winner on the Flat for Guillaume Macaire at Pompadour (1m 5f : Good) in August last year, she was placed twice over hurdles at Auteuil and Pau. The four year old has also had a handful of runs over fences finishing runner-up twice at the former track in October and December. Her new connections have plenty of options for her.

Reveley's Remarks: "She is a canny filly who has run well at Auteuil. She has got ability and is certainly capable of winning races in the UK."

HOLLY (FR) 4 b f Voiladenuo (FR) – Righty Malta (FR)

Successful in three of her four races in AQPS Flat races for Erwan Grall, the **J.P.McManus** owned filly was moved to **Jonjo O'Neill** during the summer and is one to follow in mares' novice hurdles. She won one of the first bumpers of 2020 when leading close home at Vichy (1m 4f : Soft) in May. The daughter of Voiladenuo dead-heated with the prolific winning mare Harmonie Star in a Grade 3 at Le Lion D'Angers (1m 4f : Good/Soft) in July. She then beat Harderie by a length and three quarters in a similar event at Durtal (1m 4f) in late October. Fifth in the Grade 1 Prix Jacques De Vienne at Saint-Cloud (1m 4f : Heavy) last time – Epatante won the same race in 2017 – she was beaten a dozen lengths.

HORANTZAU D'AIRY (FR) 4 b g Legolas – Panzara D'Airy (FR)

A half-brother to Venetia Williams dual winner Enzo D'Airy (rated 127) and full brother to Ganzo D'Airy (bought for €300,000 by Barry Connell), he was trained by Hugo Merienne when making a winning start to his career in a bumper at Fontainebleau (1m 5f : Good) in September last year by three parts of a length. Keen early on, he showed good acceleration to lead close home and his jockey Jerome Claudic had sufficient time to wave his stick at the crowd as he crossed the line. The runner-up Hurrick Des Obeaux has won twice over hurdles at Auteuil and finished second in a Grade 3 hurdle at the same track since. Provided he learns to settle, **Rich and Susannah Ricci** and **Willie Mullins** have another potential top notcher on their hands.

HORS PISTE (FR) 4 b f Kapgarde (FR) – Valgardena (FR)

Willie Mullins bought Cheltenham Festival winners Al Boum Photo, Apple's Jade and Sir Des Champs out Emmanuel Clayeux's yard and Ireland's champion trainer has returned to the same source to buy this twice raced filly. Only fifth on her hurdles debut at Pau in January, she was beaten around thirteen lengths. The daughter of Kapgarde ran much better next time though when second eighteen days later over the same course and distance. (2m 1f : Heavy). Her jumping was very good and, having held every chance at the last, she ran on to finish second behind the unbeaten Roberta Has. Beaten three and a half lengths, the form has been boosted with the third winning a couple of times since. The first three pulled twenty lengths clear of the fourth. She now belongs to **Joe Donnelly** and could develop into a contender for the Grade 2 Dawn Run Mares' Novices' Hurdle at Cheltenham in March.

HUFLOWER (FR) 4 b g Saddex – Send Me Flower (FR)

Owned by **Chris Giles**, the four year old has reportedly pleased his new connections since arriving at **Paul Nicholls**' this summer. Adrien Fouassier trained him in France and the Saddex gelding progressed with each start in AQPS Flat races. Fourth and second at Senonnes (behind the aforementioned Hawai Game) and Craon in October and November, he made it third time lucky at Pornichet (1m 4f : Standard) when narrowly beating Heros (won next time) in December. Returning to action at Angers (1m 6f) in late February, he produced a good performance to follow up by a length from subsequent winner and Graded placed Guerrier Rose. The pair were thirteen lengths clear of the third. A tall scopey gelding with a white face, he is a fine prospect for novice hurdles.

IBERIQUE DU SEUIL (FR) 3 b g Spanish Moon (USA) – Tulipe Du Seuil (FR)

A half-sister to Nicky Henderson's Heross Du Seuil, she is a cracking juvenile hurdle prospect for **Bective Stud** and **Gordon Elliott**. Bought for €150,000 in August, she finished strongly on her debut in an AQPS Flat race at Vichy earlier the same month. Narrowly denied, she wasn't suited by the steady early gallop according to her rider Franck Blondel before finishing with a flourish. The third has bolstered the form by winning a Grade 3 bumper since. Formerly trained by Mickael Seror, she is another exciting youngster for Noel and Valerie Moran.

ICEO (FR) 3 b g Coastal Path – Rocroi (FR)

A five and a half lengths winner on his hurdles debut for the Lageneste/Macaire stable, he produced an impressive performance at Dieppe (2m : Soft) in late August. Prominent throughout, he led on the hometurn before pulling away after the last. Snapped up immediately afterwards by **Paul Nicholls** on behalf of **Chris Giles**, the form has yet to be tested but he looked Graded class and is one for the future.

Reveley's Remarks: **"I've never sat on him but was impressed with him having ridden in the race. I'd say it wasn't a bad race."**

IL ETAIT TEMPS (FR) 3 gr g Jukebox Jury (IRE) – Une Des Sources (FR)

A stablemate of Hors Piste, he is from the family of Arbre De Vie (rated 140 over fences) and has joined **Willie Mullins** and is owned by **Barnane Stud**, who are responsible for Grade 1 winning hurdler Echoes In Rain. Ten lengths fifth on his first start in a bumper at Moulins (1m 4f : Soft) in April, he stepped up on that performance next time when runner-up at Vichy (1m 4f) nearly a month later. Racing on the outside with no cover, the grey stayed on well in the homestraight a length and a quarter behind Il Est Divin (placed in a Grade 3 and won again since). It is hoped the Jukebox Jury gelding is sent juvenile hurdling this season.

ILLICO DES PLACES (FR) 3 b g Jeu St Eloi (FR) – Liliane Star (FR)
Tom Symonds' stable star Song For Someone began his career in France and the six year old is a triple Grade 2 winner. Nicky Henderson's former assistant has recruited another potentially very useful hurdler from across the English Channel in the wide margin winner Illico Des Places. Trained by Francois Nicolle, he won by eighteen lengths on his debut at Chateaubriant (2m 1f) in May. Leading early on, he galloped and jumped his rivals into submission stretching clear from an early stage. The fourth has won since. A bold jumping front runner, he will take some pegging back in British juvenile hurdles.
Reveley's Remarks: "The race was run at a small track but he was very impressive and should do well in Britain."

IN THIS WORLD (FR) 3 b g Saint Des Saints (FR) – Maia Royale (FR)
By the same sire as the stable's Grade 1 winning novice chaser Protektorat, the unbeaten In This World is set to take high rank in juvenile hurdles for **Dan Skelton** this campaign. Trained by Jean-Philippe Dubois, he looked a strong galloper when winning on his debut on the Flat at Royan (1m 6f : Good/Soft) in June. A two and a half lengths winner from the highly regarded Fil Dor, he has reportedly settled in well to his new yard and Dan Skelton spoke enthusiastically about the three year old when we chatted in August. Bought by Highflyer Bloodstock, he comes from a good family and has a bright future.

JUSTUS (IRE) 3 ch g Galileo (IRE) – Landikusic (IRE)
From the family of Zoffany and Rostropovich, he has been gelded since joining **Ian Williams** having been acquired for €80,000 at the Arqana Summer Sale in July. Previously owned by the Coolmore team, he raced four times on the Flat for Andre Fabre. Runner-up at Nancy (1m 4f) and Chateaubriant (1m 5f) in May, the son of Galileo appreciated the step up in trip at Dieppe (1m 7f : Very Soft) last time (third has won since). A neck winner, he led close home with stamina appearing to be his strong suit. Effective on testing ground, he was bought to go hurdling.

LA PRIMA DONNA (FR) 4 b f Saint Des Saints (FR) – Princesse D'Anjou (FR)
Owner **Kenny Alexander** has a terrific team of mares and this twice raced filly has been recruited. Out of the triple Grade 1 winner Princesse D'Anjou, she was trained by Sylvain Dehez and finished runner-up on both her starts over hurdles at Compiegne. Beaten ten lengths on her debut in October (2m 1f : Heavy), she stayed on well behind Starlet Du Mesnil (won twice since, including a Listed hurdle at Auteuil) having been held up during the first half of the race. Returning to the same venue three weeks later, she looked much more professional and caught the eye in finishing second to Hadaline. Third last turning for home, she was still fifth at the final flight but ran on strongly (third has won twice over fences subsequently). From a family who improve with age, La Prima Donna will take a lot of beating in mares' novice hurdles in Ireland.

LASKALIN (FR) 6 b g Martaline (FR) – Laskadya (FR)
Entered in the Paddy Power Plate at the Cheltenham Festival in March, the six year old was withdrawn on account of the drying ground. The six year old is the sort **Venetia Williams** will win a major staying handicap chase with over the next couple of years. Indeed, he looks tailormade for a race such as the Peter Marsh Chase at Haydock in January (the stable have won the race three times). Rated 143, he was bought for €77,000 at the Arqana Deauville February Sale having won five times for Mikael Mescam. A two and a half lengths winner at Pau (2m 7f : Heavy) in January, it was his fourth victory at the track. With only thirteen runs during his career, he is open to further improvement.

MAGISTRATO (FR) 3 b g Kapgarde (FR) – Franche Alliance (FR)
Bought for €92,000 as a yearling, he was trained by David Cottin when finishing runner-up on his hurdles debut at Auteuil (1m 7f : Very Soft) in April. The Kapgarde gelding attempted to make all jumping well and racing enthusiastically. Headed after the last, he kept on well and was only beaten three lengths by the aforementioned Porticello. The third Imprenable has won twice since and the seventh has scored subsequently, too. Purchased privately afterwards, he has delighted **Paul Nicholls** since moving to Somerset. He could make his UK debut at Chepstow (9ᵗʰ October) in a race his new stable have won six times in the last eleven years.

MESSAGE PERSONNEL (FR) 3 b g Saint Des Saints (FR) – Victoria Princess (FR)
Owned by **John and Lisa Hales** having been bought by Highflyer Bloodstock, he has joined **Dan Skelton** and is another juvenile hurdler to follow this winter (former stablemate of In This World). Over twenty lengths behind the aforementioned Illico Des Places on his debut at Chateaubriant in May when finishing fourth, the Saint Des Saints gelding was much sharper next time when coming from the rear to win decisively at Dieppe (2m : Heavy). Ridden by James Reveley, he jumped brilliantly and, having joined the leader at the last, the three year old pulled away to score by three and a half lengths.
Reveley's Remarks: **"He gave me a nice feel and is a typical Dubois horse improving a lot from his first start to his second. A chaser in the making, he should develop into a very nice horse for his new connections."**

OBSESSION (FR) 4 ch g Tin Horse (IRE) – So Good (IRE)
Only cost €5,000 as a yearling, he raced ten times on the Flat for Damien De Watrigant winning by eight and a half lengths at Toulouse (1m 4f : Heavy) in October 2019. The Tin Horse gelding was then transferred to Thomas Fourcy to go jumping and is unbeaten in two starts. Off the track for eleven months, he returned to Toulouse (2m 1f : Good) in September for his hurdles debut and scored by a length and a half under James Reveley. Both the runner-up and third have won since. The chestnut was even more impressive next time when winning by a dozen lengths at Auteuil (2m 2f : Heavy) in October. Always to the fore, he led at the first down the backstraight and dictated thereafter. James Reveley's mount raced along the far hedge and quickened clear after the second last to win eased down. Bought by **OTI Racing** since, he is believed to be in training with **Willie Mullins**. He could stay over hurdles or go chasing.
Reveley's Remarks: **"I liked him a lot. He hacked up on heavy ground at Auteuil and is the type to do very well for his new connections."**

OLYMPIC MAN (FR) 4 b g Martaline – Parcelle De Sou (FR)
Half-brother to the eight times winner Darwins Fox, he had a couple of runs over hurdles for Jean-Philippe Dubois. Sixth behind new stablemate Haut En Couleurs (third in the Triumph Hurdle) in the Prix Pride of Kildare at Auteuil in October, the Martaline gelding had a break before returning on the Flat at Machecoul (1m 6f : Very Soft) in March and won narrowly – the runner-up has won since. Back over hurdles at Compiegne (2m 2f : Heavy) the following month, he was given a patient ride by Felix De Giles before making headway leaving the backstraight. Marginally in front at the last, he found Kenadara two and a half lengths too good, but still pulled seven lengths clear of the third. Subsequently bought by **Willie Mullins**, the four year old is open to significant improvement. Winning a maiden hurdle should prove a formality before mixing it at a higher level. He's owned by **Audrey Turley**.

PARMENION 3 b g Soldier Hollow – Pearls of Passion (FR)
A younger sibling of Group 3 winner Pelligrina, he looked a high-class horse in the making when winning on his Flat debut for Edouard Monfort at Craon (1m 3f : Good/Soft) in mid June. Drawn wide, he raced handily before taking over in the homestraight. Drawing clear inside the final furlong, he won by three lengths from Laishann (bought by Gordon Elliott for €82,000). Not surprisingly, the son of Soldier Hollow attracted plenty of attention at the Arqana Summer Sale a few weeks later. **Willie Mullins**, on behalf of **Joe Donnelly**, purchased the three year old for €230,000. It remains to be seen whether he goes hurdling this winter or is saved for the 2022/2023 campaign. He is a horse with a big future.

ROCKY MAN (FR) 3 b g Doctor Dino (FR) – Lady Speedy (IRE)
A third juvenile hurdler for **Dan Skelton**, he raced twice on the Flat for Henri-Alex Pantall. A well beaten ninth on his debut at Machecoul (1m 4f : Soft) in February, he reappeared a couple of months later at Saumur (1m 7f : Good/Soft) and galloped his rivals into submission. Given a positive ride, he stretched clear turning for home and was never in danger thereafter winning eased down by four and a half lengths. Bought for **Colm Donlon**, he has been gelded and is sure to be well schooled. His front running tactics will make him a dangerous opponent in three year old hurdles this season.

T'ARAISON (FR) 4 b g Buck's Boum (FR) – Al Gane (FR)
Featured in this article last year, the full-brother to dual Cheltenham Gold Cup winner Al Boum Photo has still yet to run. However, the four year old has been sent to Jackdaws Castle and is in training with **Jonjo O'Neill**. He was bought for €150,000 as a two year old at Arqana Summer Sale in July last year by **J.P.McManus**. Like his older sibling, the Buck's Boum gelding was in training with Emmanuel Clayeux who commented last year: **"He worked with a three year old of mine and jumped better than him. He was incredible, so Charlie (Swan) bought him. At the same age he felt stronger than Al Boum Photo and I think he could be a very good horse."**

TRAPISTA (FR) 4 bl f Golden Horn – Quezon Sun (GER)
An interesting filly who finished an eyecatching third on her debut on the Flat at Clairefontaine (1m 4f : Good/Soft) in June last year. Beaten three lengths by Valia (dual Group 2 winner since and runner-up in the Group 1 Prix Royal Oak), Nicolas Clement's filly was very slowly away but she finished strongly. Subsequently sold for €22,000 at the Arqana December Sales, she joined Gabriel Leenders and was a seven lengths winner on her hurdles bow at Angers (2m 2f : Very Soft) in late March. Jumping well, she pulled away after the last and looked above average. A half-sister to the 2015 Prix du Cadran winner Mille Et Mille, she has reportedly joined **Jonjo O'Neill** and is expected to be aimed at mares' hurdles.

VADALY (FR) 3 b f Vadamos (FR) – Formerly (FR)
Trained by Daniela Mele, the Vadamos filly make a striking impression when winning at the first time of asking over hurdles at Dieppe (2m : Soft) in mid August. Partnered by James Reveley, she was held up before making ground before the final circuit. Taking the lead at the end of the backstraight, she kept on well to win by a length and a half from more experienced rivals. The fourth, who was beaten a dozen lengths, has won since. Subsequently sold to **Willie Mullins**, she is a juvenile hurdler to keep a close eye on.
Reveley's Remarks: **"Her victory wasn't a surprise. She jumped very well and I was impressed. She is a nice filly."**

YES INDEED (FR) 4 b g Martaline – She Hates Me (IRE)
Half-brother to the ill-fated 140 rated hurdler Never Adapt, the four year old raced eight times over hurdles/fences for the Lageneste/Macaire partnership. Runner-up behind Triumph Hurdle winner Quilixios on his jumping debut at Compiegne in March last year, he got off the mark at the fifth attempt a year later at Auteuil (2m 2f : Heavy). Switched to fences soon afterwards, the Martaline gelding was second at Auteuil before going one better in a Listed chase at the Parisian track (2m 6f : Very Soft) in late April. A three parts of a length winner from Hades (third in a Grade 1 chase since) under James Reveley, he was fifth in the Grade 1 Prix Ferdinand Dufaure in May (2m 6f : Heavy). Still eligible for novice chases this season, he was bought privately to join **Jonjo O'Neill** and is owned by **Michael O'Flynn and Roel Hill Farm**.
Reveley's Remarks: **"He is a very nice horse but has struggled to see out some of his races in the past. He has been a weak finisher but, if that can be rectified, he could be top-class. A superb jumper, he is capable of mixing it in the leading novice chases in the UK."**

YOU'RE THE BOSS (FR) 3 b g Karaktar (IRE) – Bleu Perle (FR)
Made a hugely promising start to his career when beaten a neck on his debut in a Listed hurdle at Auteuil (2m 2f : Very Soft) in September for trainer **Francois Nicolle** – he was the only debutant in the six strong field. Half-brother to Colin Tizzard's L'Air Du Vent, he was held up for much of the race before making his move in the homestraight. Not fluent at the last, he kept on well behind previous winner Imprenable (had finished third behind the aforementioned Porticello) with two lengths back to the third Igloo D'Estruval. His performance won't have gone unnoticed and the agents are likely to be tracking his progress.

Please see pages 183-194
for details of the
One Jump Ahead Updates

Don't forget to read my Diary @
www.mhpublications.co.uk

HANDICAP SNIPS

The following section includes 14 horses who are considered well handicapped for this season. Many of them are set to go chasing for the first time and are expected to graduate to a much higher rating over fences compared to their hurdles mark.

ASTIGAR (Rated 123) is one of three entries for the Pond House team of David Pipe. Bought privately out of Colin Bowe's yard in Ireland, the No Risk At All gelding remains a maiden having finished runner-up on three occasions. Beaten a head by the 134 rated hurdler Solwara One on his debut in a bumper at Uttoxeter in November, he chased home Patroclus at Exeter (2m 1f : Soft) on his hurdles bow before disappointing at the same track the following month. He filled the runners-up berth once again behind Smurphy Enki at Plumpton last time and has a wind operation since. From the family of stablemate Ramses De Teille, his owners The Angove Family fly over from the US to attend Cheltenham's Paddy Power meeting. With that in mind, the five year old looks tailormade for the **Conditional Jockeys' handicap hurdle (0-125) over two miles five (12th November)**. The stable have won the race four times in the last ten years. Long-term, he will jump fences but has unfinished business over hurdles in the meantime.

BASS ROCK (Rated 123) was raised eight pounds for winning a decent handicap hurdle at Ayr's Scottish National meeting (2m 5f). However, he looks set to develop into a useful staying chaser for Ray Green and Sandy Thomson and can stay ahead of the assessor. The Martaline gelding began his career with Dominique Bressou in France finishing fifth behind Arbarok (won four times since) at Clairefontaine in July 2019. Transferred to the UK, he was placed at Carlisle twice and Ayr. Runner-up to Tamar Bridge in a match at the latter venue in March (wind operation beforehand), he made his handicap debut the following month and stayed on strongly under champion conditional jockey Danny McMenamin to win by over three lengths. Three miles ought to be within his stamina range and it wouldn't be a surprise if his primary target is the **valuable staying novices' handicap chase at the Scottish National meeting next spring**. Decent ground appears to suit him.

DARGIANNINI (Rated 126), similar to a number of horses owned by Andrew and Kate Brooks, was transferred to Paul Nicholls during the summer. A half-brother to Grade 2 winner Keeper Hill, the Fame And Glory gelding won three times at Sedgefield last season, including a bumper by 20 lengths on his debut in October. Well held at Aintree over his hurdles bow, his stable were struggling at the time. Given a break, the six year old returned in the spring and won twice at the County Durham track. Making virtually all on both occasions, he won by aggregate of thirty six and a half lengths. Still eligible to run in novice hurdles until the end of October, he handles decent ground and is capable of reaching a much higher mark for his new yard. The **0-140 Paddy Power Intermediate Handicap Hurdle at Cheltenham (13th November) over two miles five** may be a suitable target. The champion trainer won it with Rangitoto (2011) and Morito Du Berlais (2014).

EASY AS THAT (Rated 130) is one of a trio of horses trained by Venetia Williams who are expected to progress still further over fences. From the family of Time For Rupert, he won both starts in bumpers during 2019/2020. Switched to hurdles last term, the Sans Frontieres gelding jumped poorly at Bangor and Chepstow (2 miles) before finishing second and fourth respectively. Granted an opening mark of 114, the six year old made a mockery of his rating winning a two miles three handicap hurdle at the Welsh track in February by nine lengths. Once again, his hurdling left something to be desired, but the longer trip played to his strengths and he went clear after the second last. Needless to say, the handicapper reacted with a steep rise of sixteen pounds. However, fences are expected to bring out further improvement. The Kate and Andrew Brooks gelding has only raced on soft or heavy ground and there is no reason why he won't stay three miles in time.

FRANCO D'AUNOU (Rated 124) was bought for €50,000 at the Arqana Sale in November 2019 having been placed over hurdles at Nantes behind Floureur (rated 140) for Thierry Poche. Absent for 395 days, the Saint Des Saints gelding raced a handful of times over hurdles for Venetia Williams last season. Placed twice at Chepstow, the six year old then produced a very good front running performance at Ffos Las (2m 4f : Heavy) to beat the well regarded Champagnesuperover by nine and a half lengths. Drying conditions may have found him out at Ludlow in late March, but he remains an interesting proposition. His trainer excels with ex-French horses once they go over fences and I don't expect that trend to change with this chasing bred gelding. Two and a half miles on testing ground appear to be his optimum conditions.

FRENCHY DU LARGE (Rated 120) is a stablemate and a similar type to Franco D'Aunou. Runner-up in three of his four bumpers, the Al Namix gelding went hurdling last season. Having run creditably behind the likes of Bear Ghylls and Fifty Ball at Lingfield and Sandown respectively, he gained a much deserved first win at Ludlow (2m 5f : Heavy) in February. Following his two and a half lengths victory, Venetia Williams commented: **"He's going to be one for fences next season, but we thought we'd pick up a hurdle race on the way."** One can envisage him winning his share of middle distance/staying handicap chases this winter.

GERICAULT ROQUE (Rated 126) was fourth in his only Irish point for Mary Doyle before being acquired on behalf of Professor Caroline Tisdall and Bryan Drew. Runner-up in a bumper at Newton Abbot last Autumn on his first start for David Pipe, the five year old proceeded to win twice over hurdles following a wind operation. A narrow scorer at Plumpton in January, the Montmartre gelding wasn't at home on the tight turns of Fakenham next time when only third of four. Regaining the winning thread on his handicap debut at Sandown (Good/Soft) in March, he pulled away to win by nearly ten lengths off a mark of 117. Both wins have been gained over two miles but his trainer expects him to stay three miles eventually. Look out for him in a novices' handicap chase because we haven't seen the best of him.

KILLER KANE (Rated 129) featured in the *Top 40 Prospects* last season, he has a lot more to offer. Bought for £300,000 having won a point-to-point for Donnchadh Doyle, he joined Colin Tizzard whose string were under the weather for much of last season. Runner-up at Aintree (2m 4f) in October, he weakened late on at Exeter (2m 2f) before finishing fourth in February. However, the half-brother to triple Grade 1 winner Go Native showed his true worth at the same track the following month. Dropped back to two miles one, he made all and galloped on strongly to win by five and a half lengths (runner-up won since). Expect similar tactics to be adopted over fences and he could be an exciting two mile novice chaser.

LECALE'S ARTICLE (Rated 125) was an expensive purchase (€320,000) out of Patrick Turley's yard having won his only Irish point-to-point. Forced to miss the whole of the 2019/2020 season due to injury, the Malinas gelding overcame an absence of 970 days to win on his hurdles debut at Newbury (2m : Soft) in December. Following his seven lengths win from Restandbethankful (won twice since), his trainer Nicky Henderson said: **"Lecale's Article is a nice horse. We had a problem in the autumn of last year, so he had to miss the season, but it probably hasn't done him any harm. He was a big baby then and is a big baby now. He jumps well and will jump fences and make a nice horse. He's quite good. We won't be that ambitious for the time being as I think he's more for chasing."** Runner-up next time at Warwick (2m 5f) behind Benny's Oscar, he spoilt his chance at Sandown (2m) last time by jumping and hanging to his left. Beaten over sixteen lengths, it is possible the seven year old will be at his best racing left-handed but it is worth remembering his point win was gained on a right handed track. A two or two and a half miles novices' handicap chase will be his first port of call and it will be disappointing if he doesn't take some beating.

NO ORDINARY JOE (Rated 133) won twice over hurdles at Southwell and Worcester in May and therefore is still a novice. Appreciating the step up in distance (2m 4f), he looked a smart prospect when winning a hotly contested bumper at Sandown in November. A three and a half lengths scorer, the Getaway gelding flashed his tail late on, but it didn't prevent him from winning decisively from some useful rivals. Fourth in the Grade 2 Kennel Gate Novices' Hurdle at Ascot next time, he was no match for Mr Drogo or Soaring Glory but wasn't disgraced. With his rating, it is possible he will take the 'Champ' route and contest the 0-150 handicap hurdle at Newbury's Winter Festival (27th November), a race his stablemate won in 2018. The Seven Barrows team also won the race with The Cashel Man the following year. There is a good staying handicap in the Nicky Henderson trained five year old before he goes chasing.

RED LION LAD (Rated 116) is the third and final entry trained by David Pipe. A ten lengths winner of his only point-to-point for Colin Bowe in Ireland, it is worth recalling Declan Phelan's comments in last year's edition of *OJA*: **"Barry O'Neill partnered and he was happy to sit off the leaders and during the closing mile, he nudged closer and without ever getting too serious, he moved between the two leaders as they faced the final fence and showed gears to settle the issue in a few strides, posting a comfortable ten length win. Those that chased him home may be limited, a remark that does not apply to this gelding as he is rich in potential."** An expensive store (€155,000), he was bought privately and moved to Somerset. Despite being placed in two of his three races over hurdles, the Flemensfirth gelding failed to live up to expectations. Third at Exeter (2m 1f) and Chepstow (2m 3f), he is another to have undergone wind surgery and, with a switch to the larger obstacles, the five year old could be a different proposition.

SHANG TANG (Rated 134) cost €80,000 as a store and, while it took him nine races to get his head in front, the seven year old developed into an above average novice hurdler last winter. By the ill-fated Shantou, he recorded victories at Ascot (2m 5f) and Fakenham (2m 4f). In between, Emma Lavelle's charge failed to stay three miles having travelled strongly in the Grade 2 River Don Novices' Hurdle at Doncaster in January. At his best on flat tracks, he goes chasing and could bid to emulate stablemate Killer Clown's win in the **novices' handicap chase at Kempton (26th December)**.

STARVOSKI (Rated 113) won her only Irish point by ten lengths for John Byrne in January 2020. Expert Declan Phelan wrote in last year's *Irish Pointers* section: **"She shared the lead for most of the race, jumping smartly: when given the office after jumping the final fence, she drew right away on the way to the winning post to record a dominant ten length win. The standard of her rivals may have been low, however I rated the style of her victory as comprehensive. She is very uncomplicated, and her slick jumping will be an asset going forward."** Bought for £35,000, the daughter of Aizavoski won one of her four races over hurdles for Kim Bailey last season. A fourteen lengths scorer at Southwell (2m : Soft), she was left clear at the last when Yauthym fell. The six year old was then still in front when blundering badly at the second last on her handicap debut at Sandown (2m) in March. That mistake knocked the stuffing out of the mare and she eventually finished fourth behind Gericault Roque. She is better than her finishing position suggests and ought to improve once switched to fences. Slow ground brings out the best in her.

THEME TUNE (Rated 125) didn't treat his hurdles with much respect but it didn't prevent him from winning twice over timber at Ludlow (2m 5f) and Carlisle (2m 3f). **"He's still got a bit to learn but he's a stronger stayer, so I fancied his chances over the last. Once his jumping improves he could be quite a nice horse, he's a strong stayer in the making. He's been schooling over fences at home and he's got a lot more respect for them. He's a lovely horse,"** commented Jonjo O'Neill jnr after the Fame And Glory gelding won by a neck at the Cumbrian track. Fourth at Uttoxeter (2m 7f) last time, the Jackdaws Castle inmate was still considered a big baby last year and has reportedly grown during the summer. From the family of Grade 2 winning chaser Supreme Prince, the 0-135 Gordon Richards Novices' Handicap Chase at Carlisle (31st October) over two and a half miles could be a suitable starting point for his chasing career before stepping up in distance later in the season.

www.mhpublications.co.uk

Please see pages 183-194
for details of the
One Jump Ahead Updates

IRISH POINTERS

Once again, point-to-point expert **Declan Phelan** has written his invaluable article regarding those horses who caught his eye 'between the flags' in the Emerald Isle last winter/spring. Last year's feature yielded **30 winners** at an impressive **strike-rate of 28%** and produced a £10 level stakes **PROFIT** of **£82.20** (following on from his **37 winners (PROFIT of £274.60) in 2019/2020** & **40 winners (PROFIT of £462.90) in 2018/2019)**). The headline acts included **VANILLIER** (Grade 1 Albert Bartlett Novices' Hurdle winner @ 14/1), **STAR GATE** (Grade 2 winner) and **EKLAT DE RIRE** (Grade 3 winner).

A FORTUNE OUT WEST (IRE) 4 b g Soldier of Fortune (IRE) – Western Road (GER)
Trainer: Gordon ELLIOTT   Form Figures: 1
Medium sized bay gelding, half-brother to a couple of fair chasers, dam at an advanced age when she delivered him. A £27,000 three-year-old store for Colin Bowe in 2020. Contested an eight runner four-year-old maiden at Punchestown (Yielding) in May. He knew his job, composed jumping and biding his time in third/fourth. Heading to the second last, the race was whittling down into a fight out between himself and Joyeux Machin: when that rival capsized at the obstacle, A Fortune Out West was left in front and he seized the initiative by stretching away entering the final bend and he galloped on to win by four lengths. The victory prompted Gordon Elliott to buy him for £90,000 at Tattersalls later in the month of May. He was professional on the day and well tutored: bound to win track races, I remain to be convinced he has the scope to sup at the highest altars of the jumping game. May win an ordinary bumper and in time may establish a track rating of 125-135 either over hurdles or fences.

ASH TREE MEADOW (FR) 5 b g Bonbon Rose (FR) – Alzasca (FR)
Trainer: Gordon ELLIOTT   Form Figures: 61
Well-proportioned bay gelding: French bred, his dam who won a Flat race and she is a half-sister to Foxhunters winner Pacha Du Polder. Acquired as a store in 2019 by Monbegs for £30,000, he commenced his stint pointing at Lisronagh (Yielding/Soft) in November. Nestled towards the rear and racing on the wide outside, he was within striking range three out and then he emptied heading to the penultimate fence, struggling home in sixth he scoped badly after this run: my suspicion is that he did not appreciate the testing ground. Given the opportunity to race on a lively surface, at Fairyhouse (Good) in April, he upped his game considerably. In a true run five-year-old maiden with sixteen runners, once he made his move and jumped to the lead at the third last fence, he put the race to bed: he powered clear to score by twelve lengths and galloped through the line with petrol left in his tank. He impressed Gordon Elliott, the handler paying £135,000 at Tattersalls a week later. He jumps neatly and possess a high cruising speed and therefore trips from two miles to three miles are within his zone and he will have plenty of options available to him. I would advance a case that a sound surface may be a vital ingredient to assist him to produce a premium performance. Hence his best pay days could be during the spring or summer Festivals rather than on heavy/soft during the winter. Until he illustrates otherwise, he can be viewed as a smart 125-135 borderline Graded jumper, with scope to scale loftier ratings. He would be an ideal candidate if one was to finger a horse to win one of the big jump races staged in the USA, such as the American Grand National at Far Hills (a timber race routinely run on good/firm). Gordon Elliott won that event previously with Jury Duty in 2018.

BALCO COASTAL (FR) 5 b g Coastal Path – Fliugika (FR)
Trainer: Nicky HENDERSON   Form Figures: 217
A light athletic dark bay French bred gelding, nothing of note on his continental based family tree. A €52,000 store purchase by the Monbeg Doyles, he was one of two horses representing the farm in a four-year-old maiden run at Curraghmore (Soft) in late October. Hidden towards rear of midfield for two miles, he crept through the pack and poked his head in front approaching the second last: tackled at that juncture by Gentlemansgame (the other Monbeg runner in the race), he was found wanting and he failed to find under pressure and, with his stamina reserves flagging, he was eventually all out to hold on for second place. Then secured at a tariff of £100,000 via the auction rooms, he moved to Nicky Henderson. He relished the combination of drop in trip (2 miles) and the all-weather surface, as he waltzed to a silky smooth seventeen lengths win in a bumper at Kempton in February. This winning performance earned him high ranking with the time figure analysts for bumpers, and accordingly he headed the market for the Grade 2 bumper at Aintree in April. This time, racing on good to soft, he moved to the lead with over a quarter of a mile to travel: once tackled he failed to respond and emptied to finish a disappointing seventh. Drawing a conclusion from all three of his starts, he has proven he does possess speed, he is doubtful on the question of stamina: moreover, whilst polished when racing on the bridle and in his comfort zone, he can be exposed if put under pressure. He will be effective racing at two miles up to two and a half miles over hurdles/fences, and his natural speed will be rewarded with successes; flat tracks like Kempton/Newbury may play to his strengths. Although connections may harbour hopes of top-level triumphs with this five-year-old, he may have to unearth significant improvement to fulfil those aspirations. For now, he is more of a 135 (Grade 3) standard hurdler/chaser, falling short of Cheltenham Festival Grade 1 level.

BALLYHAWKISH 5 b g Kayf Tara – Massannie (IRE)
Trainer: Neil KING   Form Figures: 1
Chunky bay gelding with a small white spot on his forehead: purchased by Graham McKeever for €24,000 as a three-year-old store. He made a successful point debut by landing a four-year-old maiden at Loughbrickland (Heavy) in November. On terrain placing a premium on stamina and character, Pa King anchored Ballyhawkish towards the back of the field until gradually improving their position on the final circuit. About five lengths down in fourth place approaching the second last, the partnership came round the outside with a potent challenge and edging to the front on landing over the final fence, he asserted to win by two and a half lengths. The performance was more substance over style and illustrated positive qualities, especially concerning his application to the job and appetite to please. Neil King, by spending the sum of £88,000 at the December Sales, will be hoping this young gelding can develop into a flagship horse for his stable. His dam was a four-times winner for David Pipe (rated 120s over hurdles) and I note she won on both soft and good/firm. Hence, Ballyhawkish, her first foal, may not necessarily be simply a mudlark. Over time he may be shy of top bracket ability, nonetheless with natural progress, he could become a 125-140 handicapper and contend in prestigious staying handicap hurdles/chases.

BARDENSTOWN LAD 6 ch g Black Sam Bellamy (IRE) – Pougatcheva (FR)
Trainer: John McCONNELL   Form Figures: 4 – 11 - 31
Compact chestnut gelding: his dam won three times over hurdles for Venetia Williams (2m to 2m 3f): raced twice in Irish points for midlands handler Adrian Murray: scoring on the second outing at Lingstown (Soft) in November. He arrived with a sustained run inside the final six

furlongs and leading three out, he was slow and cautious over the concluding fences, yet galloped resolutely on the flat to record his maiden win. Changed hands via the sales ring for £42,000 and rocked up at Tipperary (Soft) in March and bolted in by fifteen lengths in winning a point to pointers' limited bumper. He added to his track haul when overcoming the hinderance of a bumper winner's penalty, by staying stoutly to win his maiden hurdle at Wexford (Good) in July (3 miles). He may slot in now as a 120-125 rated hurdler/chaser and pay his way in those band of races at trip in excess of two and a half miles. In recent years, John McConnell has accomplished success at the early winter fixtures at Cheltenham with his experienced novice hurdles: Streets Of Doyen won staying novice hurdle last October at Prestbury Park, and Bardenstown Lad could be earmarked for the corresponding race in 2021, and he would have bright prospects of a stable repeat given good ground.

BARROWDALE (IRE) 6 b g Cloudings (IRE) – Tanya Thyne (IRE)
Trainer: Donald McCAIN　　　　　　　**Form Figures: 1**
Testify and Wymott carried the silks of Trevor Hemmings to success, so when their younger sibling (eventually named Barrowdale) sold as a young store, it was no surprise that the Isle Of Man based owner acquired him for a price of £50,000 in 2018. The horse was then dispatched to Mr Hemmings' farm in Cork and, as a late developer, only joined Mick Winters as a five-year-old. The horse has been troubled by a few niggling issues, and he made a belated debut in a winners' of 2 point at Boulta (Soft/Heavy) in December. It is an odd spot to drop a newcomer into a race mixing with experienced maiden winners. Kicked into the lead from the start, he displayed the habit of jumping out to the right at most fences: he lost ground in the process, yet he had too much ammunition for his rivals, in the end galloping out through the line to record a ten lengths win. Boulta is a left-handed circuit and I wonder if he may prefer racing right-handed. A tricky client to draw conclusions on, until more evidence is presented: for now, he ticks the boxes of (1) powerful galloper, (2) handles heavy, and (3) stays three miles at his leisure.

BILL BAXTER (IRE) 5 gr g Milan – Blossom Rose (IRE)
Trainer: Warren GREATREX　　　　　　　**Form Figures: 214**
A medium grey gelding, a sibling to three ordinary winners, cost Denis Murphy €31,000 as a store. He gave an excellent account of himself in defeat on his only point appearance: at Moira (Yielding/Soft) in October, he was one of three runners who forced a slick pace from the outset: he looked like a horse who loved jumping fences: by the second last fence, along with Dreams Of Home, the race was reduced to a match, and Bill just did not have the extra gear to get past a classy rival, going down in honour by a length. A winter switch to Warren Greatrex produced instant success: as he made light work of landing a moderate bumper at Fakenham (Soft) in January. Although only fourth at Newbury in a Listed bumper in February, there was plenty to admire about the effort in defeat. He has the traits of an honest, consistent and reliable jumping prospect: he is effective on soft/heavy and trips from two and a half to three miles are within his comfort zone. He can figure up to Grade 3 level as a novice hurdler and a chase mark of 140 is achievable. He is capable of winning a decent handicap as he has natural fight in his belly.

BOLD ENDEAVOUR 5 b g Fame And Glory – Araucaria (IRE)
Trainer: Laura MORGAN   Form Figures: 1 - 1
Bulky bay gelding: his dam was a four-time winner for John Kiely (2 bumpers/ 2 hurdles). Under then amateur, Jordan Gainford, he popped out and jumped neatly and asserted his superiority by drawing clear from the second last fence to score on his debut at Necarne (Yielding/Soft) in late September. He was one of the sales toppers at Goffs UK auctions in November, heading to Ms Morgan courtesy of a £190,000 transfer fee. It came as a surprise that he lined up at Sedgefield in May (Good) to make his UK/track debut in a bumper. He made light work of that task, winning easily by ten lengths. In victory, he wore a hood, which could hint that this gelding may have been keen/excitable at home and the hood was deployed to keep a lid on him. For now, he retains a 100% record, a win on soft over three miles and another over two miles and 178 yards on good: evidence rates him versatile on the counts of trip/ground. Bigger examinations await, and his class or limitations may not be revealed until he encounters proper 130+ rivals. As a young exciting five-year-old, he could prove over time, to be a rock-solid standard bearer for an upwardly mobile and ambitious stable.

BROOMFIELD BURG (IRE) 5 br g Sageburg (IRE) – Somedaysomehow (IRE)
Trainer: Nicky HENDERSON   Form Figures: 17 - 11
Medium sized near black gelding, his dam won a maiden hurdle. Sported the colours of Cork owner Ray Fitzgerald when winning on his first appearance at Castletown (Soft/Heavy) in October. In a steadily run contest (timed at 23 seconds slower than preceding maiden), this lad was restrained out the back for two miles and then gradually progressed towards the front end and swept to lead on the downhill run to the final fence and kept on to score by four lengths. The placed horses won later in the season to give some substance to the form. Fitzgerald secured a nice profit, as having purchased the horse for €23,000 as a store, he was then positioned to resell to team McManus for £90,000 in November. Broomfield Burg ran twice in bumpers in 2021: he refused to settle on his track debut at Newbury and had used his fuel with a quarter of a mile to travel (seventh of nine). He then recorded comfortable back-to-back wins in the month of May, in a bumper at Southwell (Good) and over hurdles at Warwick (Good/Soft): again, keen in both races, he settled sufficiently to allow him to utilise his gears to prevail. He is quite talented and versatile (trip/ground): at Castletown he sweated freely pre-race and at Newbury he boiled over. If team Henderson can get this horse to relax and conserve his energy for racing positively, then he can promote himself as a fine 140+ jump prospect. Some horses can be tutored out of bad habits, if he falls into this category, he can win at Graded standard.

CHAMP KIELY (IRE) 5 b g Ocovango – Cregg So (IRE)
Trainer: Willie MULLINS   Form Figures: U - 1
A relatively cheap foal (€5,800): not much of appeal in his pedigree, his dam pulled up in all four of her outings in Irish points. Physically, he filled my eye when I saw him in the parade ring prior to his sole point run for the Pat Doyle camp. A strong well-proportioned bay gelding with plenty of scope. In that point race, at Dromahane (Soft/Heavy) in December, Pa King settled him towards the rear, moving away from the fourth last and heading towards the homestraight, the partnership eased closer and they were looming up as a big threat when his rear end seemed to slip on landing over the third last: the horse regained his balance, but Pa King went sideways, unseating. On balance, he was travelling so smoothly, victory appeared to be at his mercy. Snapped up by Willie Mullins for the Masterson family, the horse proved his worth in a bumper at Limerick (Yielding/Soft) in May. This time ridden prominently by Jodie Townend, they gradually upped the ante, and from the two furlong pole, he drew away with Bellaney Lord

from the other sixteen runners, and in the private battle, Champ Kiely was not found wanting as he battled to score by half a length. He has plenty of class and winning Graded hurdles/chases should be a formality. He has natural speed and he may be more potent held up and conserved rather than gunned from the front. He has the capacity to figure in 2m 2f and upwards, Graded hurdles in 2020/21 and connections can optimistically dream of realistic Festival aspirations. Comfortably a 140+ graduate from the pointing code. He has raced to date on soft/heavy, given his physique, such conditions may be his cup of tea.

CHIANTI CLASSICO (IRE) 4 b g Shantou (USA) – Ballinderry Lady (IRE)
Trainer: Kim BAILEY   **Form Figures: 1**

Sturdy bay gelding: a €37,000 store out of an unraced dam. Bowled along at the head of affairs on his only point start at Tipperary (Good/Yielding) in April. Running for Colin Bowe with Barry O'Neill in the saddle, the champion point jockey controlled the race from the beginning. On the final circuit, he put the squeeze on his rivals by upping the tempo from four out: he had the race in the bag approaching the final fence: he was lucky to survive a bad mistake at this fence, he recovered his momentum to win by two and a half lengths. Sold to Kim Bailey for £105,000, he will win races for his new trainer. He is a sharp horse capable of scoring from 2m 2f and upwards and might win a bumper, if that is his opening salvo in track racing. Apart from that late error at Tipperary, I noticed he got in tight to some fences: there may be question of his scope as a chaser unless he grows his frames and improves his jumping technique. Doubtful if he is equipped with the talent to become a Cheltenham championship horse. He can slot in as an above average 125-140 track performer.

COBBLERS DREAM (IRE) 5 br g Yeats (IRE) – Miss Parkington (IRE)
Trainer: Ben CASE   **Form Figures: P1**

Small bay gelding: his dam (a full sister to 140 rated chaser Tornado Bob) won a Punchestown bumper: raced in one point for Cork handler Paul O'Connell (his brother, a farrier for Colin Bowe, had purchased the animal for €15,000 as a three-year-old store). At Turtulla (Soft) in November, he failed to make any impact inside the last half mile and pulled up prior to the final fence. That outing qualified him to contest the Easter Monday pointers limited bumper at Cork (Good) over 2m 3f. Sited in midpack until the home turn, once asked to improve by James Hannon, he suddenly took off and waltzed away for a smooth win. A date 18 days later at Tattersalls sales resulted in an £85,000 transfer to Ben Case. His size may eventually count against him, if the plan is to develop him into a chaser. He is a sharp individual with speed and he will more than pay his way as a 2m to 2m 6f novice/handicap hurdler in the coming winters. If given time to build his confidence as a hurdler and carefully plotted along the way, a race like the Lanzarote Hurdle at Kempton, as a 125-135 hurdler, might be a contest to aim at. Flat, speed biased tracks may favour him and good/soft likewise.

CONSTITUTIONAL HILL 4 b g Blue Bresil (FR) – Queen of The Stage (IRE)
Trainer: Nicky HENDERSON   **Form Figures: 2**

Rangy bay gelding with a white spot between his eyes: first foal of a mare who won a couple of minor hurdle races in England (rated 125): purchased as a foal by Barry Geraghty at a cost of €16,500, and retained by that ex-jockey and prepared in conjunction with Warren Ewing for a four year old maiden at Tipperary (Yielding): Ridden with a degree of confidence by Ben Harvey, he led or shared the lead from the beginning, and set a slick tempo. At the second last, with rival Anyharminasking blundering, he had the race at his mercy. He met the final fence on a wrong stride and landed awkwardly: Harvey was almost unseated, and to maintain the partnership, he was forced to wrestle the horse to regain balance: the manoeuvre cost momentum and he surrendered the lead: once back on an even keel, he rallied, alas the winning post came too soon for him, as he lost out by a head in a photo finish. I would have no doubt that he was the best horse in the race. Nicky Henderson paid £120,000 for this youngster at Goffs UK Spring sales, no doubt encouraged by Geraghty. He has some tactical pace and will win a maiden/novice hurdle at his ease (130+). Entering his first track campaign this winter, he is not star material, yet he warrants attention as one with the capacity to upgrade from his current category standing of 'above average'.

COOL SURVIVOR (IRE) 4 b g Westerner – Pale Face (IRE)
Trainer: Gordon ELLIOTT   **Form Figures: 1**

Medium sized bay gelding with a white blaze on his face: a €15,000 foal, he hails from a German family most associated with Flat racing. Racing for the Monbegs, he was the second leg of the farm winning both divides of the four-year-old geldings maiden at Cork (Good/Yielding) in April. Held up and racing out deep on the track to get a view of his fences to halfway, he moved into second place with four to jump. He came through on the bridle to lead at the third last and thereafter readily held off the attentions of the runner up Serious Charges. He was foot perfect at the last fence and scored by four lengths in a quick time. The Flat biased pedigree and limited size could channel one to the obvious conclusion that he may find a home over hurdles, as a possible lack of scope could limit him when he enters the chasing ranks. He is a straightforward honest individual assessed on his day at Cork: he will unfold into a 130+ novice hurdler and it is conceivable his best trips could be around the 2m 4f distance. Only time and racing action will solve if he can handle winter conditions. Another to be snapped up by Gordon Elliott (£175,000) during his restocking process.

CURTAIN TIM (IRE) 4 b g Curtain Time (IRE) – Flemenslass (IRE)
Trainer: Gordon ELLIOTT   **Form Figures: 1**

Sturdy bay gelding from the family of Tullymurry Toff: he made the running to win a very slowly run four runner maiden on testing ground at Necarne (Soft/Heavy) in May. Representing the Monbegs, he did clout some fences, his long stride assisted him to maintain a three to four lengths advantage: his three rivals moved to his tail heading to the second last: pestered throughout the last two furlongs, he kept finding enough for a two lengths win. The tight turning nature of this circuit inside the closing half mile doing him no favours: I suspect his honest gallop will gain extra reward on a stiff galloping track such as Navan. Another four-year-old added to Team Elliott for the coming winter session (cost £100,000): his sire was responsible for the 2021 Irish Grand National winner and this youngster may find his forte this season in staying novices hurdles and in later campaigns, stamina testing handicap chases.

DONNY BOY (IRE) 5 b g Westerner – Lady Roania (IRE)
Trainer: Nick ALEXANDER   **Form Figures: 1**

There was much to like about his debut win at Dromahane (Soft/Heavy) in December: saddled by the Aidan Fitzgerald team, he nestled at the back for two miles, then made a move rounding the homebend: with Champ Kiely (a big threat) exiting three out, this stout bay gelding powered on and recorded a composed four lengths success. It was a polished almost professional first outing for a youngster. Vanillier won a division of the corresponding race in 2019, and Donny Boy won here in a faster time in 2020. He has a bright future and aspirations of progressing into a 135+, even Graded class jumper can be entertained. He did enjoy the testing ground and therefore he may prefer winter style conditions, and he may be in his pomp racing at 2m 4f and upwards, though winning a two mile bumper on heavy ground is an avenue with potential. The UK based owner Lynn McClennan paid £32,000 for this five-year-old when he was a store and she could have chased in for multiples of that investment had she so wished. One could imagine him figuring in the staying Grade 2/3 novice hurdles and earning a shot at the Albert Bartlett, and eventually becoming a more than decent handicap chaser. His dam was a dual winner for Peter Bowen (both wins on good ground), and Ebony Jewel is a full brother.

DREAM IN THE PARK (IRE) 4 b g Walk In The Park (IRE) – Old Dreams (IRE)
Trainer: Emma LAVELLE   **Form Figures: 2**
Light framed athletic bay gelding with a white face: from a successful family of winning jump mares associated with Robert Tyner (I Can Imagine, Byerley Babe). Dam a dual track winner. He was a €27,000 foal and joined the Monbegs for pointing. He tasted action once, at Dromahane (Yielding/Soft) in May and signalled that he had sufficient talent to succeed as a track horse. Held up off the pace, he made a move rounding the home bend to take a hand in the finish. Jumping the third last, his jockey attempted to squeeze through inside the leader (Frontier General): with no room at the inn, the move inflicted momentum damage on both horses, with Dream In The Park forced to rein back and switch around for his challenge. He held every chance from two out and he could not match a superior rival, losing by under two lengths. In defeat, he posted a commendable run and, having been bought privately to join Emma Lavelle, he strikes me as a project who might enjoy a good pay day in an upper market handicap hurdle as a 130 handicapper. One to respect and keep on your side. He is owned by Paul Jacobs, of Limato fame.

EMMA BLUE (IRE) 4 b f Mahler – Rhapsody In Blue (GER)
Trainer: Oliver GREENALL   **Form Figures: 1**
Robust bay mare with a white spot on her forehead and one white rear sock: her dam, a Flat winner is a half-sister to Group winner and stallion Norse Dancer: represented Harley Dunne in a late season four-year-old mares maiden at Ballingarry (Good): from the start, she composed herself towards the rear of the pack. Entering the last half mile with three to jump, with little persuasion, she moved into third and on the bend heading to the final fence, she put on a spurt, took command and won with a swagger. She has inherited the Flat speed in her clan and has stamina to boot: I was not surprised that she made a price of £82,000 at Tattersalls May sale and she will be one of the upper-class mares in the novice hurdle division housed in a north of England stable. Winning a mares' maiden hurdle will be a stroll in the park when Oliver Greenall has her ready, and depending on how she is campaigned, she may be a candidate for the mares' novice hurdle series final at Newbury in the spring.

FABLE (FR) 6 b m Coastal Path – Toscane Des Fleurs (FR)
Trainer: Nicky HENDERSON   **Form Figures: 1211**
A nice big athletic bay mare: an expensive three-year-old as a store, costing Monbeg €45,000: her debut was delayed until she was late in her five-year-old age bracket: the patience was rewarded as she finished up the steep hill at Oldcastle (Yielding) with purpose and won a mares' maiden by a dozen lengths. A French bred and a sibling to 120 rated Dom Dolo, she sold to Nicky Henderson for £60,000 via the November auctions and he ran her three times over hurdles in the spring. She lost narrowly at Wincanton to the talented Rose Of Arcadia, before rattling off a brace of wins at Huntingdon and Haydock: she looked above average on the latter track, as she enjoyed the three miles and toyed with her rivals. She has raced exclusively within her own sex, and now rated 128 over hurdles, her future may now focus on novice chases, again

the mares' only type. As a heavy topped mare with a Gallic background, some cut in the ground will enhance her prospects and she can add further wins to her tally in 2m 4f+ mares novice chases. She may fall short of Grade 1 standard in the mares' code, though she is liable to win a Grade 3 mares' chase, if placed to effect.

GANDHI MAKER (FR) 5 b g Policy Maker (IRE) – Thellya D'Arc (FR)
Trainer: Phil KIRBY   **Form Figures: 1**

A £34,000 store, this imposing rangy bay gelding was housed with Monbegs for his sole point at Tipperary (Yielding) in April. Setting out his stall from the start, he led and pinging his fences, he was able to maintain relatively high revs: this knocked his rivals out of their comfort zones. Squeezed rounding the hometurn, in a few strides he was a dozen lengths clear. Eased down in the closing stages, his official winning margin of six lengths underscores his superiority. Visually it was one of the most impressive wins by a five-year-old in the spring campaign and there is no doubting that he is an exciting prospect. In terms of raw facts, he won the seventh race on a 9-race card and clocked the slowest time, although the difference between the fastest/slowest was only fourteen seconds. By the same sire as Chacun Pour Soi, this lad hails from a French family with a mix of jumps/Flat winners. He is the best progeny of his sire I have seen race between the flags in Ireland. If he evolves, he could develop into a classy and aggressive chaser at the shorter (2m to 2m 4f) distances, as he possesses loads of natural toe. Undoubtedly one of the smartest Irish pointers to have entered the gates of the Kirby establishment and he may be a northern based jumper who could shake up the better class southern rivals or Irish raiders at a big Festival sometime into the future.

GINTO (FR) 5 b g Walk In The Park (IRE) – Tina Rederie (FR)
Trainer: Gordon ELLIOTT   **Form Figures: 121**

Tall attractive bay gelding, a €60,000 store. French dam was a winner and he is a sibling to another Irish point winner. Strolled with a majestic debut win at Tattersalls (Soft) in October. He jumped cleanly in the hands of Jamie Codd, with the normal fences in the home stretch omitted there was an extended run in, and once on the level he powered clear for a twelve lengths win, clocking the fastest time on the card. He won that point racing for team Elliott and upon heading to the auctions, a price of €470,000 saw him knocked down to the Morans and retained by the Elliott barn. His track debut at Fairyhouse in January was underwhelming: he never travelled with conviction and laboured home in second: that afternoon all of the Elliott runners failed to fire, so in the case of Ginto, the form may be meaningless. He then recorded a bumper win at Navan in February, rather workmanlike. To date, Ginto has not repeated the poise and authority of his point win on the racecourse proper. He could benefit from father time to muscle up his impressive frame. He may establish himself as a Graded class staying novice hurdler this winter, and he has a bright future as a 140+ staying chaser to look forward to. He has raced exclusively with dig in the ground and it remains to be seen if he will be risked on a livelier surface.

GIVEGA (FR) 5 b g Authorized (IRE) – Sivega (FR)
Trainer: Gary MOORE   **Form Figures: 1**

Thick set bay gelding: French bred, his dam is a full sister to Quevega. Racing for owner Walter Connors and trainer Colin Bowe (they teamed up previously with Envoi Allen in his pointing days), this horse made a belated debut at Tralee (Soft/Heavy) in May in a five-year-old maiden. There may have been a lack of depth to the quality of the race: by the finish, one was able to recognise that Givega was in a different league to his dozen rivals. His jockey, Barry O'Neill decided to give him plenty of daylight by taking the widest route: in a race run at a dawdle, he jumped neatly and ambled along in midfield until striking the front at seven from home. Gradually stepping on the gas from three out, Barry was barely moving a muscle as his partner defeated his rivals with contempt. The runner up was fully exposed as an ordinary pointer and hammering such an opponent was no big deal. Givega is the owner of potent equine blood: winning a slowly run point to point recommended he can jump and gallop to a fair level and functions on testing terrain. Bigger tests await him in his track career, he may thrive in a high-class battlefield like his aunt. Bought privately and new connections could have a proper 'Saturday Ascot style chaser' on their hands.

GRAND JURY (FR) 5 b g Tiger Groom – Saboum (FR)
Trainer: Henry De BROMHEAD   Form Figures: 11 - 4
Tall athletic bay gelding: French bred, dam dual jumps winner, half-brother to expensive Irish point winner Fiston Des Issards. Competing for Pat Doyle, he recorded a comprehensive win on his debut at Turtulla (Soft) in November. In victory, he was landing the same maiden for the Doyle team for the second season on the spin: in 2019, Bob Olinger came up trumps, he posted a faster time in 2019, albeit on nicer ground. In his own right Grand Jury clocked the fastest race on the card in 2020. He sat close to the lead throughout and surged away from three out to win handsomely by five lengths in a decent race which has unearthed three bumper winners. He jumped accurately and stayed the three miles and had the vital extra kick inside the last half a mile. Sold privately to join Henry de Bromhead, he scored on the track proper at Punchestown (2m 1f : Heavy) in March, landing a pointers only bumper. Ridden with a deal of confidence by Paddy Mullins, he launched his bid for gold about two furlongs out: when first encouraged to exert his class, he appeared to either hang or jink left for a few strides: however, once balanced, he injected some pace to prevail by under five lengths. He lost his pristine record when rather one paced from the quarter mile pole in a good quality winners' bumper at the Punchestown Festival (4th). Either the drier ground or the possibility that he was over the top, were reasons for the defeat. He will be a competitive 2m 2f+ novice hurdler in 2021/22: he has a gear change that may allow him to operate at Graded level, though he may be a tad shy of reaching the peak (Grade 1) in the novice hurdling ranks. He may require soft/heavy to help bring out the best in him, and when he embarks on a chasing career, he will be a 135+ merchant.

GUILY BILLY (FR) 5 gr g Coastal Path – Ukie (FR)
Trainer: Henry De BROMHEAD   Form Figures: P - 1
I included this grey gelding in the 2019/20 edition purely on his home reputation for the Monbegs. To recap, in March 2020 he pulled up at Borris on his debut, in mitigation the Monbeg inmates at that moment in time were suffering from a viral issue and the run could be ignored. A four-year-old maiden at Tinahely (Soft/Heavy) in November was used as the launchpad to get his career and reputation back on the rails. Positively ridden at the head of affairs, he upped the tempo leaving the third last and proved too good for his ordinary rivals, scoring by four lengths from Captain Quint. He did clout some fences, getting in deep and low and that aspect needs remedying. There was a whiff of style and class in the manner of his galloping through the race: he could look super against weak opposition, a flat track bully type, and I wonder how he will respond when pitted against tough high-ranking rivals, might he down tools easily? Another of the horses David Thompson (Cheveley Park) purchased at December sales, his tariff £310,000. Now housed with Henry de Bromhead, he will win a maiden/novice hurdle this winter and is likely to figure at a Festival meeting. Can become a 135+ 2m 4f and upwards chaser with genuine aspirations of Graded success in the chase discipline: from a successful line of French jumpers, most of whom operated best on soft/heavy.

HAPPY D'EX (FR) 4 gr f Saddler Maker (IRE) – Soiree D'Ex (FR)
Trainer: Gordon ELLIOTT   Form Figures: 1

Tall, lean steel grey lady: a French bred, her dam won four Flat races: secured by Rob James for a chunky €57,000 as a three-year-old store: it proved to be a wise investment, as a debut win in her point, added an extra £138,000 to her price tag inside of ten months. James, under suspension, posted the mare to Denis Murphy to train and she faced two rivals in a mares' maiden at Dromahane (Good/Yielding) in May. In a slowly run event, Luke Murphy in her saddle relaxed her last of three: she drew alongside the leader three out: moving to two out Murphy nudged her into the lead and once shaken up approaching the final fence, she quickened right away to score by fifteen lengths. It was one of those races without depth and clocking a poor time, yet one could identify Happy D'Ex as a classy mare. She joins team Elliott at a cost of £195,000 via Goffs spring sale at Doncaster. The family genes, especially the Flat speed she has inherited aligned to her ability to jump slickly, ought to stand to her and she is one of the more exciting four-year-old mares emerging from the spring pointing session of 2021. A confident selection to win a bumper and likely to make her presence felt in Listed/Graded bumpers for her sex. When she muscles up her frame, she is liable to become a Graded class novice hurdler and chaser within her own sex. Her stamina was not really tested in this race at Dromahane, the way the race unfolded certainty highlighted that she would have no trouble operating over shorter trips.

HARRY DES ONGRAIS (FR) 4 gr g Crillon (FR) – Lola Des Ongrais (FR)
Trainer: Henry De BROMHEAD   Form Figures: 1

Light framed grey gelding who will muscle up with time: a French bred, a sibling to a French jumps winner: Henry De Bromhead invested €60,000 in him at the 2020 Land Rover Goffs Sale and farmed the horse to Colin Bowe for a pointing education. He left a positive impression by posting a ten lengths win on fast ground at Fairyhouse in April. Despite a field of six runners, the gallop was generous enough to develop the event to the fastest run on the card. Harry Des Ongrais sat fourth/fifth until making ground to challenge three out and landing in front away from that fence, he asserted and strode away like an honest horse with an appetite for the game. The form was subsequently boosted by the runner up recording a maiden win on his following run. Harry has a natural aptitude to jump fences, he illustrated that he could fiddle them and by-times gain ground at the obstacles. Now returning to Henry de Bromhead with this vital experience in the locker, he could be a diamond if he polishes up with more time and racing. He will harvest a few races at 2m 4f-3 miles as a hurdler and could earn a crack at Graded novice hurdles. He can be an exciting novice chaser whence he turns to that discipline. He coped with the lively sod at Fairyhouse, his pedigree recommends softer conditions ought to pose no problems.

HARRY DU BERLAIS (IRE) 4 b g Shirocco (GER) – Theatre Mole (IRE)
Trainer: Nick KENT   Form Figures: 1

Chunky bay gelding with one white rear sock: his dam, Theatre Mole (a sibling of 150 rated chaser Mr Mole), won a mares' maiden point for Colin Bowe and Kavanagh family (owners). Harry Du Berlais is the first produce of that mare and he represented Bowe and Kavanagh in a four-year-old geldings maiden staged at Dawstown (Yielding) in May. Ridden with confidence by Barry O'Neill, his precision jumping was a sight to behold: he disputed the lead until a spring heeled leap at the third last gained him a three to four lengths advantage and, on the uphill climb to the finish, he extended away to record a ten lengths win, clocking the fastest time at the fixture. Harry is an individual with an exciting future, if he retains his hunger to please as a racehorse. If anything, he may prefer racing over trips in the two miles to two and a half miles range and his accurate jumping will be a key asset in his locker. The race he won lacked for strength in depth and therefore when stiffer examinations are presented to him, further clues to his ability level will unfold. Evaluating him judged on this one performance is tricky: he can advance to become at least a 130-track practitioner, and there is the potential under his bonnet to transform into a higher class Graded jumper, especially over fences. More than likely the most expensive recruit purchased by the Kent yard in Lincolnshire.

HEREWEGOHONEY (IRE) 5 b m Sageburg (IRE) – Knappogue Honey (IRE)
Trainer: Fergal O'BRIEN   **Form Figures: 1**
Athletic black mare with a white blaze on her face: sibling of four track winners: raced once for Paurick O'Connor, at Necarne (Soft) in May: took time to relax and, with a circuit to travel, she had dropped the bit and sat last of a field of ten runners. Halfway down the backstraight, she cruised up into contention. The race had been run at a strong gallop and given the testing conditions, those that forced the pace were beginning to tread water. In a matter of strides, she assumed the lead away from the second last and rocked on home for a four lengths win. Fergal O'Brien (Middleham Park Racing), via a £62,000 purchase, added her to his stable: he has worked the oracle with lower class Irish pointing mares and this mare with scope may win a bumper and most certainly will record hurdle wins within her sex and have a fair crack of placing (and maybe more) in Graded mares' novice hurdles. She enjoyed the soft/heavy testing terrain at the County Fermanagh circuit and she can operate in the depths of winter on this showing.

INGENIOUS STROKE (IRE) 5 b g Jet Away – Just For Jean (IRE)
Trainer: Henry De BROMHEAD   **Form Figures: 1**
Compact bay gelding, owner of three white socks: dam placed in two bumpers for Donald McCain: raced for Waterford handler Rosemary Connors at Cork (Good/Yielding) in April and he produced a lovely front running effort, which yielded a two lengths success. He was crisp at his fences and he enjoyed the act of jumping: he clocked a decent time, all his own work, which suggests he has a smart cruising speed. The runner up and third won their own maiden points in the following weeks to frank the form. Connors, apart from handling some pointers, also helps to pre-train young stock for Henry de Bromhead, and it is a positive sign, that Henry privately purchased Ingenious Stroke straight after this win. His sire is making an impact on the track proper, complementing his impressive strike rate with pointers. Ingenious Stroke could be an uncomplicated front runner in novice hurdles this season and he can win in the category and down the line, a chase rating of 125-135 is within his reach, and a drop down in trip to 2m 4f will not be a problem.

LIFE IN THE PARK (IRE) 4 b g Walk In The Park (IRE) – Jeanquiri (FR)
Trainer: Donnchadh DOYLE / Rob JAMES   Form Figures: F
Rangy bay gelding with a white stripe on his forehead: a half-brother to 2021 Punchestown Festival winner, Lifetime Ambition: secured by Rob James at a cost of €28,000 at the 2020 Land Rover Goffs store sale. Amateur jockey/handler James received a 12-month suspension in March and this gelding switched to the Monbegs for his point racing. In a nine runner four-year-old maiden at Fairyhouse (Good) in April this young horse almost posted a copybook debut. Settled off a frantic early gallop, he edged closer during the closing mile: by the second last, he mastered the long-time leader Gris Majeur, and he had drawn twenty lengths clear when he over jumped at the final fence and fell. Whilst recorded as a faller from this sole point run in

the spring, his performance merited a position amongst the top 5 in his age group (4-year-olds). When he bulks out his frame, he will be a sizeable chaser in the future. More than capable of winning a bumper, he has the ability and talent to advance to become a competitive Graded hurdler/chaser, and a mark above 140 may be within his range. He coped with the lively terrain at Fairyhouse and softer conditions should not unduly bother him based on offerings from other members of his family.

LOUGHDERG ROCCO (IRE) 5 br g Shirocco (GER) – Banaltra (IRE)
Trainer: Laura MORGAN   **Form Figures: 21**

Pat Coffey from Nenagh in Tipperary was a big point-to-point consigner and supporter: he sadly lost his life in a freak accident last October. His business plan was purchasing young unbroken stock and putting them through their paces in points and hoping to then sell for a profit. Over the years he teamed up with trainer Denis Murphy and they enjoyed some fruitful equine projects. Pat picked up Loughderg Rocco as a foal for €15,500 and posthumously his patience with this gelding was rewarded. A tall, unfurnished bay, he navigated his way from fifteen lengths off the pace at the fourth last, to place a challenge at the final fence on his Cork (Good/Yielding) debut. Once positioned to win, the counter of long-time leader, Ingenious Stroke proved too much, and he finished an honourable second. The sense that he had placed a deposit on a point win materialised at the end of the same month of April. In a lesser five-year-old maiden at Fairyhouse (Good), from four out he toyed with inferior rivals and galloped clear to win by a dozen lengths in a commendable time. The upwardly mobile lady trainer Laura Morgan was happy to secure him for £75,000 at Doncaster May Sales. If campaigned on the northern circuit, he may reward in novice hurdles and eventually operate as a fair 120-130 handicapper: he has raced to date on a relatively sound surface.

MAGIC DAZE (IRE) 5 b m Doyen (IRE) – Magic Maze (IRE)
Trainer: Henry De BROMHEAD   **Form Figures: 1312 - 4**

Tall bay mare, amongst her kinfolk is Kicking King: clocked the fastest time on a busy card at Curraghmore (Soft) in October, a fixture which included the maiden success of Gentlemansgame: granted this mare ran in the first race on fresh ground and conditions churned up thereafter. She posted a polished business-like triumph, always to the fore, she stretched away on the run and won with a bit up her sleeve. Regarded by handler Colin Bowe as his smartest mare of the autumn session, she changed hands for €92,000 at the Tattersalls November sales. She was pitched into an upper-class maiden hurdle (2m4f) at the Leopardstown Christmas fixture and prominent from the start, she collected a commendable third of twenty. A drop back into her own sex was rewarded with a smooth all the win at Clonmel (Heavy) in January. She brought her game to a new level on her following start: in the Grade 2 mares' novice hurdle at the Cheltenham Festival, she was able to sit at ease in the first four, then led as they advanced to the final hurdle and only succumbed to stablemate Telmesomethinggirl in the last hundred yards. It was a mighty performance from such an inexperienced hurdler. She was over the top when failing to repeat the same standard at the Punchestown Festival. No mare who debuted in an autumn point campaign has won a race at the Cheltenham Festival inside six months, and in finishing second Magic Daze came closest and was going against the grain. This winter she has the scope to excite in the mares' novice chase division because judged on Curraghmore she has an appetite for jumping fences.

MARVEL DE CERISY (FR) 4 ch g Masked Marvel – Midalisy (FR)
Trainer: Henry De BROMHEAD   **Form Figures: 1**
Compact chestnut gelding with a broad white face: French bred half-brother to three winners: in the care of Pat Doyle when he lined up for a four-year-old maiden at Tipperary (Good/Yielding) in April. Sent out to make the running, save for a blunder four out, he jumped with speed and from the home turn when he cranked up the pace, his rivals had no answer, as he won by five lengths. The performance was commendable as he clocked the fastest time on the card. Bought privately to join Henry de Bromhead, he is an exciting addition because he can use his natural gears to compete at a decent level over shorter trips. There would be a seed of doubt in my mind about his sire, and whether his stock train on: nonetheless this gelding is the sort of raw material Henry has in the past built into a 140+ chaser and he needs to be respected, especially in races when he can dominate from the front.

MINELLA COCOONER (IRE) 5 b g Flemensfirth (USA) – Askanna (IRE)
Trainer: Willie MULLINS   **Form Figures: 2 - 1**
John Nallen's Minella brand enjoyed a memorable spring of 2021, with Nallen point graduates winning the Gold Cup and Aintree Grand National. Minella Cocooner was one of the team's elite soldiers from the 2020/21 pointing squad. A fine, big robust bay gelding, if he can replicate his dam, he will be the business. His mother, Askanna, was a remarkable mare: handled by Colin Bowe, she completed the full menu of jumps wins: landing two points, a bumper win, four hurdle wins (including a Grade 2) and 2 chase wins (one at Grade 3 level). Minella Cocooner has a high bar to reach to match those exploits: he cost John Nallen €82,000 as a store. He raced at Turtulla (Soft) in November and gave a commendable account of himself. He moved with comfort through the race and, once the field wheeled into the home straight for the final time, he was contesting the lead with Grand Jury: he gave it his best shot, which was not enough and he was defeated by a classy rival, claiming the runner up spot. Bought privately to join Willie Mullins, a Kilbeggan (Good) bumper in June was the setting for his track debut: a race a few leagues beneath the Turtulla point presented him little trouble and he won with the minimum of fuss. I gather he has excited the Mullins camp since he moved to them. He is now proven over two miles and three miles, acted on good and soft, and therefore has all sorts of possibilities open to him. He has bright prospects of gaining a Graded win over hurdles and he may condition into a 140+ middle distance chaser of note in a year or two.

MONTY'S STAR (IRE) 4 b g Walk In The Park (IRE) – Tempest Belle (IRE)
Trainer: Colin BOWE   **Form Figures: 2**
Chunky bay gelding sporting a white spot on his head: half-brother to Monalee, which no doubt accounts for the fact that he fetched a price of €60,000 when sold as a foal. Done precious little wrong in his only point run, at Tattersalls (Good) in May: he bided his time, attacked after two out and came out the wrong side of a late battle with Supreme Gift. He would be one of the highest rated maiden four-year-olds judged on this performance. He jumped neatly, illustrated tactical speed and coped with a sound surface. If he muscles up and develops, he will unquestionably harvest plenty of track races and his engine can measure up as a Graded class hurdler/chaser. Remains with Colin Bowe and can bag his maiden point in the autumn before an inevitable big money sale.

MY MATE MOZZIE (IRE) 5 b g Born To Sea (IRE) – Leo's Spirit (IRE)
Trainer Gavin CROMWELL　　　　　　　　　**Form Figures: 1 – 1 (2)**
Stout bay gelding: from a family of Flat racers: a cheap €7,500 store purchase by Mags Mullins. He landed his maiden win in comfortable style at Tattersalls (Soft/Heavy): run in a fog, he appeared out of the gloom producing a challenge: landing in front over the last he won untaxed by eight lengths. The ease of victory enticed plenty of fanciers and it took a bid of £205,000 to wrestle the gelding for Team Cromwell at Goffs sales. He repaid his first instalment by routing a field of 24 rivals in winning a bumper at the Punchestown Festival: surging clear, displaying a change of gear to score by eight and a half lengths. With so much Flat blood in his genes, he ran in a 1m 5f maiden on the level at Ballinrobe and failed by half a length to retain his pristine record. He is an exciting young horse: he is capable of mixing it in Graded novice hurdles and earning a crack at a Cheltenham Festival championship novice hurdle.

PIMLICO POINT (IRE) 4 ch g Flemensfirth (USA) – Royale Flag (FR)
Trainer: Kerry LEE　　　　　　　　　　　**Form Figures: 1**
Sturdy Chestnut gelding with a white stripe on his forehead: first foal of a classy French based mare who won five jump races, including a Grade 1: hence Pimlico cost €95,000 as a three-year-old store. Represented Colin Bowe in a four-year-old maiden at Ballindenisk (Yielding/Soft) in May. Barry O'Neill settled him close to the pace and he pottered along in a relaxed stride and jumped accurately. He moved up to lay his claims at the second last: he had to be rousted along to master Glencorrig Sky: green at the final fence, he opened up a three lengths winning margin by the finish. He suggested that he may be a canny horse who will only do as much as is necessary and he may prefer racing behind a fast gallop and arriving late to challenge. Kerry Lee paid a big fee of £160,000 at Tattersalls May Sale to recruit this gelding and she will be hoping that he may become a new flag bearer for the stable. I doubt if he will scale lofty heights as a hurdler: when he matures, he is liable to beef up into an individual capable of competing in highbrow 'Saturday' feature handicap chases over trips beyond 2m 4f.

QUEENS RIVER 5 b m Kayf Tara – Follow My Leader (IRE)
Trainer: Nicky HENDERSON　　　　　　　**Form Figures: 1**
The most expensive mare to emerge for the 2020/21 point academy: a broad bay mare, she has a masculine appearance. Originally sourced as a store by Scobie Fitzgerald at a price of €20,000 in 2019: her dam failed as a track racer and is a sibling of Master Of The Hall and Pairofbrowneyes. She turned up at Boulta (Soft/Heavy) in mid-December for a four-year-old mares' maiden and she was primed and had her homework done. Derek O'Connor allowed the mare to dispute the running: popping her fences neatly, she was one of a quintet in contention approaching two out. Between the last two fences, she took control for minimum pressure from the saddle, and a change of gear close to home was perceptible as her margin of victory stretched to over three lengths with O'Connor relaxed in the saddle. The time of the race was slow enough compared to other races that day, and it was the visual impression created that boosted her sales price to £330,000 at Goffs December Sales, J.P. McManus making the successful bid. In 2018, Minella Melody won the corresponding maiden (20 seconds faster time) and she has moulded into a proper 135+ Graded jumper. Queens River has bright prospects of matching the achievements of Minella Melody: she will be a smart player in mares' novice hurdles and she has loads of scope to excite as a future chaser. I find it tough to call if she has the class to mix it in a race like the mares' novice hurdle at the 2022 Cheltenham Festival, for now an open minded rather than dogmatic approach to her future is fairest. When she is faced with a proper battle, only then will her other characteristics be revealed. Given her size, she may prefer ground with cushion (soft/heavy), almost the opposite of the typical Henderson jumper.

REE OKKA 5 b g Getaway (GER) – Presenteea (IRE)
Trainer: Harry FRY   **Form Figures: P1**
Attractive athletic bay gelding: dam a sibling of Identity Thief. Bought by the Halsall family for
€60,000 as a three-year-old store. Stationed with the Crawfords for two spring points. The fast
pace of the five-year-old maiden at Cork (Good/Yielding) in April troubled him, and he could
never recover from sloppy jumps on the first circuit and pulled up after two miles. Four weeks
later and with his belt tightened, he was up to speed: kicked out to lead from the start, jumping
crisply he had little trouble recording a three lengths win at Broughshane (Good/Yielding). If
he can continue along the road of incremental improvement, then Ree Okka may accomplish
a chase rating in the 125-135 zone in due course, the type to be at home on a flat circuit like
Wincanton.

SUPREME GIFT (IRE) 4 b g Getaway (GER) – Prairie Call (IRE)
Trainer: Henry DALY   **Form Figures: 4 - 1**
Strapping bay gelding with a white mark on his face and white socks: his dam won a two miles
maiden hurdle: a €23,000 foal. Fourth on his debut, he recorded a win in a six-runner maiden at
Tattersalls (Good) in May: the race was run at a fair clip and concluded with a proper drawn out
three furlongs battle: this gelding showed gears between the last two fences to head the field
jumping the last fence, and driven right out, he held on from a talented rival in Monty's Star. He
was ridden by Jamie Codd, who retired from point-to-point riding after this victory. An exciting
prospect, he can win a maiden hurdle (2m to 3m), and a key to his future will be once physically
mature, can he unlock extra improvement: if he does, his competitive landscape will feature
Graded hurdles and chases. It is easy to nominate him as a decent 120+ handicapper in the
making, his early track performances may be the indicators, if he has the capacity to operate at
higher levels. A private addition to the Daly yard.

TANGO TARA 5 b g Kayf Tara – Bling Noir (FR)
Trainer: Paul NICHOLLS   **Form Figures: 1**
Powerfully built bay gelding, British bred, a €72,000 store and sibling to 135 rated chaser
Rapper. Hailing from the James/Mary Doyle yard, he left a fine impression when prevailing at
Ballindenisk (Soft) in November: jumping like a professional, he was in the mix from the third
last: the race whittled down to a competitive match from the second last and he secured a
two lengths victory by knuckling down for the battle and mastering Upping The Ante. He has
a pounding action and a long stride and soft/heavy may be his required ingredients in track
races. Bought by Paul Nicholls for £120,000 (Middleham Park Racing), he is liable to become a
130 hurdler with the likelihood that chasing will allow him to advance his standing.

THE KING OF RYHOPE 5 ch g Malinas (GER) – Eleven Fifty Nine
Trainer: Dan SKELTON   **Form Figures: 1**
Medium sized chestnut: his dam won three races for Anthony Honeyball, including a Listed
bumper, and earned a hurdles rating of 125: a €21,000 three year old store, and that price
qualified him for the auction maidens: he won such a race for four year olds at Lingstown (Soft)
in November: his race position chopped and changed frequently during the three miles: the 16
runner field were covered by a spread of a dozen lengths with four to jump: when the tempo
increased, The King Of Ryhope was most comfortable: he took the measure of his rivals when
accelerating into a four lengths advantage racing to the last: he blundered at that fence and,
for a few strides, lost his momentum: to his credit when rebalanced, he found again to score by
a length and a half, a margin not doing justice to his superiority. He won that point in the care

of Cian Hughes, a handler who previously produced Chantry House. The King of Ryhope is blessed with natural speed and is bound to be a fair prospect for Team Skelton who he joined via a £75,000 transfer fee. Given that his dam preferred good ground, his ability to quicken may be magnified on a sound surface: he will win his maiden/novice hurdle and middle distances could be his niche, and he may be close to Graded class as a hurdler and chaser (120-135).

TIGERS ROAR (IRE) 5 b g Leading Light (IRE) – Almnadia (IRE)
Trainer: Nigel TWISTON-DAVIES　　　　**Form Figures: 9 - 1**

Angular bay gelding with broad white face: a €16,500 foal, his dam won 7 times (5 hurdle races). Raced for East Cork based Pat Collins in the spring of 2021. With the point season between January and March cancelled, handlers were permitted to race point qualified stock in track races, and Tigers Road received an educational spin in a maiden hurdle at Punchestown in February. As long as they did not win track races, such pointers were permitted to return to race between the flags when the action restarted in April and May. Tigers Road encountered his first point run at Dromahane (Yielding/Soft) in May. With the benefit of his track outing in the locker, and obviously super fit, he was bucked out in front and enjoying the task of jumping, he held the call until tackled at the third last by Super Survivor. In a sustained battle in horrible weather conditions, he emerged on top by a head in a photo finish. He liked the soft ground and is the type that should have no bother dropping down in trip as he has a decent cruising speed.

UNDERSUPERVISION (IRE) 5 ch g Doyen (IRE) – Dances With Waves (IRE)
Trainer: Nigel TWISTON-DAVIES　　　　**Form Figures: 1142**

A big chestnut unit sporting a white star on his head: a £22,000 store for the Monbegs, his dam has bred two other jumps winners. There were signs of greenness on his sole point run at Loughanmore (Yielding/Soft) in October: he had to be rousted along to tag the leader Banbridge on the approach to the final fence: He clocked the fastest time of the day on an above average card: the visual impression may not have screamed star material, it did identify him as a hungry young horse with a great attitude and one you could trust in a battle. I felt the £130,000 Nigel Twiston Davies paid at Goffs November sales was a smart piece of business. He enjoyed the 3m 2f marathon at Hereford when winning a novice hurdle on his track debut with a bit in hand. He then ran an honourable fourth under a penalty when upped in class at Kempton and then failed by less than two lengths against seasoned handicappers off a mark of 125 at Warwick. Nigel has a tradition of nurturing long-distance chasers, premium class ones, and in Undersupervision he has the raw material to develop into a 140+ staying chaser, who could win an elite handicap, perhaps one of the Grand Nationals.

UP FOR PAROL (IRE) 5 b g Flemensfirth (USA) – Clarification (IRE)
Trainer: Jamie SNOWDEN　　　　**Form Figures: P1411**

Athletic bay gelding, year younger full brother to quality treble bumper winner Letsbeclearaboutit: Wexford handler Matty O Connor paid close to a personal high fee of €30,000 when deciding to buy him as a three year old store. He raced twice in the autumn: he was moving with menace on the coattails of the leaders when his saddle slipped after two out at Loughrea and promptly pulled up. He had laid the solid foundations in that race, and three weeks later he recorded an emphatic win at Damma (Soft/Heavy): jumping sweetly and kicked for home after three out, he waltzed home by 18 lengths from two subsequent maiden point winners. Rumour was he changed hands for a price in the £250-300,000 range and became Jamie Snowden's most expensive recruit. He probably was not 100% tuned in when fourth on his track debut at Doncaster in January. He atoned by posting two hurdle wins over the two mile trip, at Wetherby (making all) and Ffos Las (chore simplified when a threat fell at the last). He is a classy individual capable of delivering over a variety of trips and is now proven on heavy and good ground. He owns an engine with the ability to change gears and he can continue to win races when novice chasing beckons on his horizon. Rated 131 at season's end over hurdles, with maturity and progression he could increase that sort of rating by fifteen pounds. When a seasoned chaser in a few years, he may become a player in those valuable 2m 4f/2m 6f handicap chases held before Christmas at Cheltenham, or even one to note in his second season as a chaser, if earmarked for the Ladbrokes Trophy at Newbury in November: his class/speed can count on a Flat galloping track such as Newbury.

VIVA LAVILLA (IRE) 5 br g Getaway (GER) – Viva Forever (FR)
Trainer: Dan SKELTON   Form Figures: 1
Medium bay gelding, dam a dual-purpose winner: he cost €8,500 as a foal. Housed with Denis Murphy, he pointed once, at Lingstown (Soft) in November: confidently ridden, he gradually crept closer under Jamie Codd and set his sights on the leader landing away from two out. He hit the front at the last fence and was always holding the persistent Gateau De Miel, winning by a length clocking the fastest time at the fixture. He moves fluently at gallop and looks a fine jumper with scope. A six-figure private acquisition for Team Skelton, they will be hoping he can prosper as a novice hurdler and advance to earn a crack at one of the Cheltenham championship novice hurdles. One, not to be under-rated, if brought along steadily and allowed to find his feet and gain confidence, he could attain a hurdles rating north of 140, and can become a high end handicapper, if he stays sound in the fullness of time.

DECLAN PHELAN'S
NATIONAL HUNT SERVICE 2021/22

If you would like to join the winter jumps service
contact via **mrdeclanphelan@hotmail.com** for full details.

The service includes a complete Irish Point Dossier on the 2020/2021 academy (246 horses) and the popular weekend and Festivals preview package.

For Irish (only) clients, Declan's nightly views on the next day's action are available from 10pm on **1560 111 112**.

Don't forget to read my Diary @
www.mhpublications.co.uk

Sunday 30th May 2021

"Ralph Beckett continues to send out an endless amount of winners (9 from 31 during the last 14 days), including Kinross (5/1) in the Group 3 John of Gaunt Stakes. The son of Kingman, who had contested three Group 1 events earlier in his career, had been gelded following two lacklustre performances at Meydan during the winter and looked right back to his best under Frankie Dettori in the seven furlongs event. Taking over at the two pole, he stretched clear to win in the manner of a smart performer. With his confidence restored, the four year old will hopefully tackle the top seven furlongs events this summer, including the Lennox Stakes at Goodwood and the Hungerford Stakes at Newbury - he doesn›t seem to mind some give in the ground and could be one for the Group 1 Prix de la Foret at Longchamp›s Arc meeting in early October. Seven furlongs looks his trip." **KINROSS won the Group 2 Lennox Stakes at Goodwood (27/7/21) @ 6/1**

Friday 18th June 2021

"I was disappointed by the performance of Suesa who lost her unbeaten record in eighth. The Night of Thunder filly spoilt her chance by racing too keenly early on - I feared the worst after two furlongs and it was no surprise to see her fade during the latter stages. She is better than she showed here and it will be interesting to see if she is dropped back to five furlongs. Despite this reversal, she could still emerge as a Prix de L'Abbaye candidate in the Autumn." **SUESA won the Group 2 King George Stakes over five furlongs at Goodwood (30/7/21) @ 7/1**

Thursday 29th July 2021

On Thursday, I nominated Perfect Power in the Group 2 Richmond Stakes and, while the formbook tells us that Richard Fahey›s Royal Ascot winner only finished fifth of the seven runners, those facts don't do his performance justice though. Granted the rub of the green, I am convinced Paul Hanagan's mount would have won. Slowly away, the son of Ardad was immediately on the backfoot but he was in contention at halfway. However, he then met trouble in running on two occasions with the former dual champion jockey being tightened up at crucial stages. Beaten a length and a quarter, it is hoped he gains compensation in the Group 2 Gimcrack Stakes at York next month. **PERFECT POWER won the Group 1 Prix Morny at Deauville (22/8/21) @ 3/1**

APPENDIX

As in previous years, I have attempted to highlight a number of horses, in various categories, who are expected to contest the major prizes during the 2021/2022 campaign.

Two Mile Chasers

It promises to be a tremendous division with real strength in depth on both sides of the Irish Sea. **PUT THE KETTLE ON** extended her unbeaten sequence at Cheltenham (4 out of 4) when claiming some notable scalps in the Champion Chase in March. A half length winner, Henry De Bromhead has indicated that the Stowaway mare will begin her campaign in the PWC Champion Chase at Gowran Park (2nd October). A dual Festival winner, she has won 7 of her 10 starts over fences but one can't help thinking she met Chacun Pour Soi on an 'off day' last spring.

Beaten a length and a half in third in the Queen Mother, **CHACUN POUR SOI** was flawless otherwise last term winning four times. The nine year old recorded his fifth Grade 1 victory at Punchestown in April when defeating stablemate Allaho by five and a half lengths. **"That was the real Chacun. We were all disappointed at Cheltenham. They're horses, not machines and he didn't fire there. That was the proper performance we were hoping for. His jumping kept me in my comfort zone. Jesus, he was electric. He was a joy to ride,"** enthused Paul Townend afterwards. Rich and Susannah Ricci's gelding will continue to be hard to beat 'in his own back yard' but, at the age of ten, is likely to be vulnerable at Cheltenham next March. It is possible he's at his best on flatter tracks. Incidentally, Willie Mullins is now training his half-sister, **HISTORIQUE RECONCE**, a four year old filly by Lauro.

Ireland's champion jockey may be faced with a few tricky decisions over the winter such is the strength in depth in the two mile chase department within Willie Mullins' yard. **ENERGUMENE** was ruled out of the Arkle Trophy at Cheltenham having been found to be lame a few days beforehand. The seven year old was back in action at Punchestown though and made it four wins from as many outings over fences. The former Tom Lacey trained winning UK pointer won his second Grade 1 when trouncing stablemate Janidil by sixteen lengths. Making all, his jockey said: **"That was class. Chacun Pour Soi was unbelievable at the start of the Festival and, for a novice to put in a display like that, is special as well. From day one, he's been electric over fences. It's hard to resist giving him a squeeze everywhere because it's just so much fun on his back."** His trainer added: **"He's going to go down the Champion Chase route now. We'll keep going that way until he tells us he needs to an extra half mile. If Chacun Pour Soi and himself, and Shishkin get there, it's going to be a hell of a race."** The Denham Red gelding hasn't raced in the UK since winning a maiden point at Larkhill in January 2018.

In all likelihood, **ALLAHO** will be kept to longer distances having produced arguably the performance of the Festival at Cheltenham in March when winning the Ryanair Chase. However, his front running style would lend itself to the Champion Chase and he is the 'dark horse' of the division. Following his twelve lengths win, Mullins commented: **"That was awesome. He's so slick and fast, it wouldn't be a big leap of faith to think he could be a Champion Chase horse."** Five and a half lengths runner-up behind Chacun Pour Soi at Punchestown the following month, he may not have been at his best that day. The Cheveley Park Stud owned gelding has an excellent record at Cheltenham (331) and has only raced twice over the minimum trip (42).

Nicky Henderson has won the QM Champion Chase on six occasions and **SHISHKIN** heads the ante-post market following his unblemished first season over fences. The former *Sky Bet Supreme Novices' Hurdle* winner won all five of his races last term, including a twelve lengths victory in the Arkle Trophy. Front runners Allmankind and Captain Guinness played into the seven year old's hands by setting a strong gallop and he could be called the winner along way from home. Workmanlike, rather than spectacular, in victory at Aintree, his trainer said: **"He was probably just getting a bit lonely in front. Nico (De Boinville) felt they weren't going quick enough down the back. He's very laid back and has a wonderful temperament."** The 169 rated chaser will be tested fully this season but there is no disputing his class and he is unbeaten at Prestbury Park. The Grade 1 Tingle Creek at Sandown (4th December) is expected to be his first port of call.

Champion trainer Paul Nicholls has also won the two mile crown at Cheltenham half a dozen times and **GREANETEEN** doesn't have to improve too much to better last year's fourth. Only beaten a couple of lengths, the Great Pretender gelding started the season on a mark of 151 but is now rated 168. Successful in the Haldon Gold Cup at Exeter in November, he came good on the final day of the campaign when beating Altior by three and three quarters of a length in the Grade 1 Celebration Chase at Sandown. **"It's not surprised me that Greaneteen has run a huge race. I thought he could possibly do something like that next season. He's always had huge potential but he's starting to settle now. That's the big thing. He'll become a proper racehorse and the obvious race will be back here for the Tingle Creek."** His record on right-handed tracks is 6111121 compared to 101434 on left handed ones. Expect the seven year old to be a major player in both the Tingle Creek and Clarence House Chases, in particular, this season.

Nicholls has always had huge belief in stablemate **HITMAN**, too, and we almost certainly haven't seen the best of the five year old. Twice a winner over fences last year, the ex-French gelding seemingly got outstayed by Protektorat in the Grade 1 Manifesto Novices' Chase at Aintree (2m 4f) last time. With his rating of 151, **the Falco gelding looks tailormade for the Grade 2 Haldon Gold Cup at Exeter (2nd November), especially if Greaneteen heads the weights off 168**. Team Ditcheat are seeking their eighth win in the race. Don't be surprised if he makes similar progress this term and develops into a Grade 1 chaser over the minimum trip.

At a lower level, **MALYSTIC** is capable of winning a good two miles handicap chase according to former champion jockey Brian Hughes. The seven year old, who is trained by Peter Niven, is rated 146 having won two of his four novice chases. His two defeats were suffered at the hands of the Dan Skelton pair Protektorat and Allmankind. Pencil him in for something like the Castleford Chase at Wetherby (27th December). The fact he handles good and soft ground is a bonus.

Two and a half Mile Chasers:

For the majority of last season, the previously unbeaten **ENVOI ALLEN** was one of, if not, the hottest properties in National Hunt racing. That all changed when Cheveley Park Stud elected to remove their string from Gordon Elliott and distribute them amongst Henry De Bromhead and Willie Mullins. The five times Grade 1 winner hit the floor at the fourth fence in the Marsh Novices' Chase on his first start for the former, but worse was still to come at the Punchestown Festival. Found to be lame on his near hind joint after pulling up in the Grade 1 staying novices' chase – his first run over three miles – De Bromhead commented: **"Rachel (Blackmore)** said he was leaning out the whole way through the race. There's obviously something bothering him." A subsequent CT scan at Fethard Equine Hospital revealed the seven year old had chipped a joint. Chris Richardson, managing director for Cheveley Park, commented in late May: **"It took a while for the swelling to go down. But surgery has now been performed, and he can now have a nice holiday and hopefully come back later in the year."** His trainer issued a positive bulletin in late August saying: **"He had a nice break, is back cantering and seems really good now."** Rated 163 over fences, he begins his second season over fences with a few questions to answer.

Dan Skelton is believed to be aiming his Grade 1 winning novice chaser **PROTEKTORAT** at the £135,000 Paddy Power Gold Cup at Cheltenham (13th November). The Saints Des Saints gelding, who is unbeaten on the Old course over fences at Prestbury Park, won 3 of his 5 races last season, culminating in a three and three quarters of a length win in the Manifesto Novices' Chase at Aintree (2m 4f : Good/Soft). The six year old had a wind operation beforehand and was fitted with a tongue tie for the first time. His first time out record is 221 and, with his rating of 154, he looks set to play a leading role in the two and a half miles handicap in November.

ALLART lacks chasing experience but showed what he is capable of when winning the Grade 2 Noel Novices' Chase at Ascot (2m 3f : Soft) in December on his fencing bow. Following his two and three quarters of a length win, Nicky Henderson said: **"He's got gears. He showed he stayed, but he's got natural pace."** A faller at Haydock next time, the seven year old is rated 152. Fifth in the Sky Bet Supreme Novices' Hurdle the previous season, he could be aimed at a Graduation chase. Alternatively, the Grade 2 Chanelle Pharma 1965 Chase at Ascot (20th November) could be an option.

That event could also be consideration for stablemate **ANGELS BREATH** (3 from 3 at Ascot) who is reportedly back in training having been absent since December 2020. Ironically, the seven year old also won the Grade 2 Noel Novices' Chase (returned with a cut to his tendon) and is unbeaten in two races over fences. The former Irish pointer won by an aggregate of 31 lengths and is rated 153. Only seven, he has time on his side and is a superb jumper, although he has yet to tackle a field bigger than four over fences.

Staying Chasers:

The top staying chase division looks set to be dominated by the usual suspects. Cheltenham Gold Cup winner **MINELLA INDO**, who missed the Punchestown Festival due to a bruised foot, is set to reappear in the Grade 1 Champion Chase at Down Royal (30th October), while runner-up and stablemate **A PLUS TARD** will return in the Grade 1 Betfair Chase at Haydock (20th November). Unexposed over three miles plus and still only seven, it will take a very good horse to beat the Cheveley Park Stud owned gelding at the Merseyside track. His form figures since arriving from France on left-handed tracks are 11213212.

Even though he blotted his copybook and lost his unbeaten record over fences at the Punchestown Festival, **MONKFISH** remains a staying chaser of immense potential. The former Albert Bartlett Novices' Hurdle winner looked a natural over fences last winter winning three Grade 1 events. A three lengths winner of the Neville Hotels Novice Chase at Leopardstown (3m) over Christmas, Willie Mullins stated: **"He looked hugely natural over fences, he looked like a handicapper. He's a real old fashioned chaser with lots of scope, he loved it every** time he saw a fence – he just wanted to jump it." Even more emphatic in victory in Flogas Novice Chase at Leopardstown's Dublin Racing Festival (2m 5f) when beating old rival Latest Exhibition by eleven lengths, his trainer remarked: **"I was more impressed with him today than any other day. It looks as though he might be getting better with each run. Everything is just so effortless. He jumps, gallops, seems to be in the right position and he has huge scope no matter where he is, he just comes up. Paul (Townend) looked like he was on a lead horse turning for home. Absolutely no effort."** A six and a half lengths winner of the Brown Advisory Novices' Chase at the Festival, the Stowaway gelding wasn't as convincing as in his previous starts with Mullins explaining: **"Chatting to Paul Townend, he said he was idling on the first circuit, watching the jeep with the camera and the men at the fences. Anything bar concentrating on his jumping. The lack of concentration, I think, was down to the lack of runners in the race and, once you go into a Gold Cup field, they'll be going much faster. He certainly seems like a Gold Cup type."** Eight lengths in arrears of stablemate Coolreevy at Punchestown last time, he made a mistake at the third last and came under pressure soon afterwards. The dual Festival winner is a major threat to the De Bromhead pair.

Below is a selection of staying chasers with nominated targets.

ASK ME EARLY – Welsh National (27th December)
The Harry Fry trained seven year old looks tailormade for the marathon event with course form figures of 311. A three times winner over fences last season, he is rated 140 and proven in soft/ heavy ground (3311P1). Following his two and a half lengths win at Uttoxeter (3m) in March, his trainer said: **"He was very sore through his back after Sandown and was diagnosed with a kissing spine, so we treated that. He's an out and out galloper. He'll be a lovely second season chaser."** Expect the Ask gelding to have one run before heading to Chepstow over the Festive period.

CAPODANNO – National Hunt Chase (15th March 2022)
Willie Mullins has won the race twice (Back In Focus (2013) & Rathvinden (2018)) and this five year old looks set to develop into a live contender for the three miles six event. Featured in the *French Revolution* section of *OJA* last year, the Manduro gelding won twice over hurdles at Clonmel (2m) and Punchestown (3m : Yielding). Relishing the step up to three miles at the Festival on the latter occasion, he won a competitive 25 runner handicap by upwards of a dozen lengths off 132. His trainer remarked: **"Capodanno was impressive. He's a fine big horse, a real chaser in the making. I think a bit of nicer ground has made a huge difference to him. He's one I think we'll be looking forward to over fences. Jockeys will be queuing up to ride him over fences."** Rated 147 over hurdles, he stays well and has only raced six times. Available at 25/1 (Bet365 & Unibet), the J.P.McManus owned gelding is worth supporting.

ENRILO – Ladbrokes Trophy (27th November)
The champion trainer has won the Newbury showpiece on three occasions (Strong Flow (2003), Denman (2007 & 2009)) and he has the race in mind for the 147 rated chaser. Twice a winner over fences, the seven year old crossed the line in front in the Bet365 Gold Cup at Sandown only to be placed third following a stewards' enquiry. Raised four pounds since, his record at the Berkshire track is 31 and his first time form figures are 112. Unexposed over three miles plus (21P13), he is the type to improve with age and has plenty more to offer. He is currently available at 14/1 with Unibet.

ESPOIR DE ROMAY – King George (26th December)
Kim Bailey's progressive young chaser was still in front when falling at the second last in the Grade 1 Mildmay Novices' Chase at Aintree. **"He's a big baby and we hoped he would be good enough to come here and it looked like we might have been right. He's a talent but we've known that all season,"** said his trainer afterwards. David Bass, who was on board, added: **"I can't say we would have won but we were going well enough. He just knuckled on landing but he's a very good horse to be going forward with. He's still very raw and green and has so much to learn."** Rated 160, the seven year old has only raced four times over fences. He is expected to reappear in the Listed Colin Parker Memorial Chase at Carlisle (31st October), a race his stable won with Imperial Aura last year. The Kap Rock gelding's record racing right handed is 3111.

THE FERRY MASTER – Rehearsal Chase (27th November)
Sandy Thomson won the Listed three miles contest with Yorkhill (66/1) last season and the Berwickshire based handler is reportedly aiming this 133 rated chaser at the contest this time around. The Elusive Pimpernel gelding is unbeaten at Gosforth Park having won over C&D in November. Fourth in the Scottish National at Ayr last time off 133, he was beaten seven and a half lengths having been committed for home a long way out. The handicapper has left him alone and he is expected to have a prep run in the Autumn beforehand. His form figures second time out are 3121.

GRAND NATIONAL

Following the victory of Minella Times (advised in the Aintree *Update*, plus Any Second Now, who was unlucky in third), that success must have gone to my head because I like the prospects of a couple of horses for this season's renewal.

GALVIN won five out of five over fences last term, culminating in a length and a half win in the National Hunt Chase at Cheltenham under the guidance of Ian Ferguson. Jack Kennedy (1 from 1) was on board and said afterwards: **"I think he could be a National horse. He stays well and has a bit of class."** Following his seven lengths win at the same track in October, his jockey Robbie Power said: **"I think the step up in trip will bring more improvement – I think he'll stay all day."** Unbeaten over three miles plus, he has run nine times over fences and is rated 154. Davy Russell, who fractured his C6 vertebrae when falling on Doctor Duffy in the Munster National at Limerick in October, will be keen to renew his association with the seven year old. He has won 4 times on the Gold Well gelding and Gordon Elliott is seeking his fourth win in the race.

SECRET REPRIEVE was the second reserve in the race in April but missed the cut. However, the seven year old has time on his side and, having only raced six times over fences, he has scope for more improvement. Twice a winner at Chepstow last season, including the Welsh National by three lengths off a mark of 134, he is now rated 142. **"I think he showed all the tools to be a Grand National horse. Everytime we challenge him to step up to higher levels he does, as we saw at Chepstow last time. I had a horse underneath me last weekend who could take me anywhere I needed to be in that race. When I needed to go for a gap, he was already in the gap. I had so much in hand and could put him wherever I wanted to,"** remarked Adam Wedge in mid January. Evan Williams trained State of Play to be placed three times in the Grand National and he has a prime contender for the 2022 version.

The pair are available at 33/1 (Galvin (Bet365, William Hill), Secret Reprieve (Skybet, Unibet)).

Two Mile Hurdlers:

HONEYSUCKLE remains the one they all have to beat following her spectacular season, which saw her extend her unbeaten career record to thirteen races. Eight of those wins have been achieved at the highest level, including a couple of breathtaking performances last winter. Following her ten lengths win in the Irish Champion Hurdle at Leopardstown in February, she was similarly impressive when beating Sharjah by six and a half lengths in the Champion Hurdle at Cheltenham. The Sulamani mare is set to stay over timber with the Grade 1 Hatton's Grace Hurdle at Fairyhouse (28th November), a race she has already won twice, her first target.

The only horse to have beaten Bob Olinger is the former Festival bumper winner **FERNY HOLLOW**. The six year old beat Henry De Bromhead's gelding by a length in a thrilling two miles maiden hurdle at Gowran Park in November. Unfortunately, the Westerner gelding hasn't been seen since with Willie Mullins commenting in December. **"It looks like he has a bit of a stress fracture. He was a bit lame after his last run and he didn't recover. We can't find it on an x-ray but he's lame and that usually means there's a little fracture. Those things will recover 100%."** The good news is that the ex-pointer is back to full fitness with Patrick Mullins explaining in late August: **"Ferny Hollow is fine. He was back in training at the end of the season but he wasn't going to be ready for Punchestown. We just got him back up to speed and he went out then a couple of weeks after the other horses went out. He's back in again now. He falls into the could be anything category and you have the option of going for a Champion Hurdle route or going chasing."** It is hoped he continues over hurdles because the six year old is blessed with plenty of speed and a turn of foot. The manner in which he gave Appreciate It a healthy head start and still beat him readily at Cheltenham in March 2020 will live long in the memory.

Stablemate **ECHOES IN RAIN** never stopped improving last year winning four of her five races. Ex-French, the daughter of Authorized was too keen when first arriving but got better with practice and ended her season with a Grade 1 win at the Punchestown Festival. An eight lengths winner from subsequent County Hurdle and Grade 1 novice winner Belfast Banter at Naas in February, Willie Mullins said: **"She's improving all the time. She's learning to settle. She has a lovely turn of foot and, if we could teach her to settle better and use that, she could turn into a very smart two miler."** The five year old then beat stable companion M C Muldoon by fifteen lengths in a Grade 2 at Fairyhouse's Easter Festival. Following her three and a quarter lengths win in the Grade 1 Champion Novice Hurdle at Punchestown (2m : Yielding), her trainer remarked: **"She's now won at the top level and hopefully that's where she'll stay for the next couple of years. She's learning how to pace herself jumping now. She's improving every day, with every run."** A winner on heavy and yielding ground, Barnane Stud have a top-class filly on their hands.

It will be interesting to see what Mullins can achieve with **FRENCH ASEEL**, who has yet to race for the Closutton outfit. A mile winner on the Flat in France, the four year old was subsequently bought for €62,000 and joined Ellmarie Holden. A 22 lengths winner of a maiden hurdle at Leopardstown's Christmas fixture on his first run over obstacles, he was purchased privately shortly afterwards on behalf of Joe Donnelly. Entered in the Triumph Hurdle, the French Fifteen gelding didn't run again but Mullins stated in late February: **"We've done a huge amount of schooling with him and he's been very good. He's a horse who is going to keep improving with age."** Visually, he was impressive at Leopardstown but is a real unknown quantity.

Compatriot **ZANAHIYR** looked a top-class recruit to hurdles when winning his first three starts for Gordon Elliott. The Nathaniel gelding was explosive in victory at Fairyhouse in November beating Saint Sam by fourteen lengths. **"He is a big horse who will get stronger. We thought he was nice at home. I thought it was a very good performance, he did everything very easily. He's not just a juvenile, he's big and strong and only going to get better,"** remarked his trainer. The ex-Mick Halford trained four year old was similarly impressive in Grade 2 company at Leopardstown on St Stephen's Day. Following his three and three quarters of a length win, Jack Kennedy said: **"I think Quilixios is very good, but this horse might edge it over him."** Unfortunately for those who backed him ante-post at fancy prices for the Triumph Hurdle, the wheels fell off thereafter. Fourth at Cheltenham and second at Punchestown (Denise Foster's runners at the latter Festival produced 0 from 36), he ran well but nowhere near to the level he had produced during the first half of the season. I fear there is something ailing him, possibly his wind. If that can be resolved then his connections will be back in business.

The Champion Hurdle may prove beyond him, but I will be surprised if there isn't some mileage in **BOOTHILL**'s mark of 137 over timber. A bumper winner at Kempton the previous season, he was restricted to one outing over hurdles last year. Harry Fry's former pointer won by nine and a half lengths at Taunton (2m : Good/Soft) in December with his trainer saying: **"I think he has the potential to be very good."** Unfortunately, he had a problem with a splint, which forced him to miss the remainder of his novice season. Races such as the Sidney Banks and Dovecote Novice Hurdles had been under consideration. Chasing is where his future lies, but he is more than good enough to win a big handicap hurdle before then. The **£105,000 Betfair Exchange Trophy at Ascot (18th December) could be a suitable target** – Paul Nicholls' former assistant won it with Jolly's Cracked It in 2015.

Two and a half Mile plus Hurdlers:

Gavin Cromwell's **FLOORING PORTER** proved a revelation last season winning four of his seven races with his official rating escalating from 122 to 164. The Yeats gelding progressed through the handicap ranks before winning two Grade 1 events, including the Stayers' Hurdle at Cheltenham by three and a quarter lengths. **"He is not long back and his season will be all around Leopardstown at Christmas and Cheltenham. Punchestown just didn't suit, we'll keep him to left-handed track. He won't be over raced,"** reported the six year old's trainer in late August.

THYME HILL was forced to miss the Stayers' Hurdle at Cheltenham having pulled a muscle behind the saddle. The seven year old gained compensation though when narrowly taking the Grade 1 Liverpool Hurdle at Aintree from Roksana. Philip Hobbs' gelding, who is rated 162, is to continue down the stayers' route and will continue to be a major player having only had seven runs over hurdles.

It remains to be seen whether they enter the stayers' hurdle picture, but last year's two outstanding juveniles are set to remain over timber. **MONMIRAL** is unbeaten in five career starts and is rated 153. Previously trained in France by Francois Nicolle, he joined Paul Nicholls during the summer and has been expertly campaigned. Following wins at Exeter, Doncaster (Grade 2) and Haydock, the Saint Des Saints gelding purposely skipped Cheltenham and was aimed at Aintree instead. A seven and a half lengths winner of the Grade 1 juvenile, his rider Harry Cobden said afterwards: **"He's a proper Grade 1 horse and the best juvenile I've sat on. He travels well and jumps great. He's top class."** While connections have the option of going down the Champion Hurdle route, it is debatable whether he will be fast enough. Stamina looks his strong suit and he is a hugely exciting horse for the future. He looks every inch a King George horse in the making.

QUILIXIOS is a former stablemate of Monmiral and has a similar profile. Bought by Cheveley Park Stud having won by a dozen lengths on his hurdles debut at Compiegne in France, he proceeded to win his first three starts for Gordon Elliott, including a Grade 1 at the Dublin Racing Festival at Leopardstown in February. Transferred to Henry De Bromhead, he stayed on powerfully to win in the Triumph Hurdle by three and a quarter lengths. His trainer said: **"We knew he jumped really well. He's just a lovely horse to do anything with. He's a gorgeous looking horse with loads of size and scope. He'll be a lovely chaser in time."** The Maxios gelding lost his unbeaten record at the Punchestown Festival – De Bromhead was 1 from 32 at the meeting – but was evidently over the top by that stage. **"He has grown and strengthened into a gorgeous horse. We haven't any firm plans for him and, while it hasn't been discussed, I'd imagine he will stay over hurdles,"** reported the four year old's trainer in late August.

Former Cheltenham Festival winner **KLASSICAL DREAM** overcame an absence of 487 days to win the Grade 1 Champion Stayers' Hurdle at the Punchestown Festival. The Dream Well gelding was tackling three miles for the first time and was fitted with a hood, but it didn't prevent him from routing the opposition by nine lengths. **"This horse has missed a year and to come back with a performance like that, he could stay hurdling or go novice chasing. Looking at the size of him there in the parade ring, I'd say anyone would love to ride him down to a fence. Staying hurdling is very hard on horses. I'd rather go chasing and, if it doesn't work out, you can always come back,"** explained Willie Mullins afterwards. Rated 165 over hurdles, he looks the pick of the Irish challenge at present, although it has yet to be decided whether he pursues a chasing career instead. A four times Grade 1 winner over hurdles, he will be eight at the turn of the year.

HAUT EN COULEURS is a stablemate of Klassical Dream and he is another youngster with a bright future. By the same sire as Monmiral, he won on his debut at Auteuil in October when trained by Gabriel Leenders. Purchased by Mullins for Joe Donnelly, he had his first run for his new connections in the Triumph Hurdle at Cheltenham and ran a cracker in third. Three and a half lengths behind Quilixios, he filled the same position in the Grade 1 juvenile hurdle at Punchestown next time. Crying out for a step up in distance, he can win Graded races over hurdles this winter before embarking on a chasing career in twelve months time. He is smart.

Please see page 195
for details of
Ahead on the Flat 2022

INDEX

SELECTED HORSE = BOLD   *Owners' Enclosure & Talking Trainers = Italics*

ONE JUMP AHEAD UPDATES

I shall be producing **5 One Jump Ahead** *Updates* throughout the 2021/22 National Hunt season. Each *Update* comprises information about the horses in *One Jump Ahead*, Ante-PostAdvice (recommendations for the major races), **Big-Race Previews, News from Ireland** from one of the most informed Irish experts Declan Phelan and **Significant Sales. Please note, the** *Updates* **are ONLY AVAILABLE VIA EMAIL (Not Post).**

It is £8 per *Update* (except £10 for the Cheltenham Festival version and £6 for the February one) or £40 for ALL 5 via **EMAIL**.

Summary of the 2020/2021 *Updates*:

What The Clients Said:

"Just want to pass on my thanks for the inclusion of GDS in the November Update. Luckily, I took the any race option. The Top 40 had a very good Cheltenham. Great work." **M.C.**

"Just wanted to join the others who have thanked you for the winners from the Top 40 Prospects list. I'd backed all of them at big prices in the autumn so was very pleased when they came good." **D.S.**

"Many thanks for your great work with the recent OJA Update for Cheltenham and as always your fantastic book One Jump Ahead, they are both great companions to guide us through the week of The Festival." **P.W.**

"I just wanted to drop you a line for the excellent pointers in the various book/ updates culminating in an excellent week for myself thanks to my ante post bets. You offer real value for money. I have had an excellent week and it's all down to reading your publications. The last race was great after you named the horse in your Update (Galopin Des Champs) I backed it 25/1 with William Hill to win any race at Festival. It certainly came good as did Sir Gerhard 14/1 and others throughout the week." **M.H.**

"Mark, brilliant. I have won a packet. Backed Galopin at 33s, 25s and 16s and I am grands in front. We are having a good booze at home and its due to you." **T**

"Just a message to thank you for the continued fabulous information that has yet again proved invaluable with tasty ante post positions on Zanahiyr (50/1) and Quilxios (20/1) in The Triumph allowing a healthy cash out / winner profit. Sir Gerard was another valuable pointer alongside Galopin Des Champs who I had backed at 50s for the Supreme and Ballymore but because of that had a nice end to the Festival in the Martin Pipe. I have been a follower and customer of yours for some years now and its information such as has been highlighted here that shows why you are at the top of your profession." **K.E.**

"Another very profitable and enjoyable week at Cheltenham thanks to your update. A few near misses but had a number of wins and places and Galopin Des Champs victory in the last was the icing on the cake! Many thanks for your info." **R.J.**

"Cheers Mark, more great information. Backed GDC at 33/1 a few weeks ago." **I.R.**

"Had Gallopin at 25s to win any race at Cheltenham thanks to you. That one bet has made it a great Festival. I just wanted to say thank you very, very much you are the top man." **S.M.**

"Just a quick line to say thanks and well done for highlighting Sir Gerhard in OJA - 25/1 in the ante post book was a trophy price too - what can I say, just brilliant." **S.H.**

"Your work is outstanding. This week's Update is absolutely awesome. I dont subscribe for selections -so don't judge you on that alone - but for the analysis and guidance. I will be a lifetime supporter" **D.M.**

"Well what can be said about the update except SENSATIONAL - Terrific advice from one who must be and is one of the best in the business and to top it all the NATIONAL advice. Three brilliant days of racing and enjoyed every minute." **A.H.**

"Well done with your selections for the Aintree festival. A profit every day culminating with the big race winner. Long may it continue." **C.D.**

"Congratulations on a successful Grand National meeting, especially with Abracadabras and Livelovelaugh winning. How unlucky were you not to have a 1-2 in the National itself. Given the same luck in running as the winner, Any Second Now must have prevailed. But hey, a 12/1 winner isn't to be sniffed at." **A.M.**

"Top class updates throughout the season, especially for both Cheltenham and Aintree. You obviously have some great sources of information, long may it last." **D.B.**

"Thanks for a very enjoyable and rewarding Aintree via the Update. It's paid for the next book and updates (already ordered) and then some. Fantastic." **D.D.**

The PADDY POWER MEETING 2020

WINNERS: THE BIG BREAKAWAY (4/9), PUT THE KETTLE ON (Advised @ 2/1)
Ante-Post Advice
GALOPIN DES CHAMPS – Any race at the Cheltenham Festival @ 25/1

Quote: **GALOPIN DES CHAMPS** *"Has reportedly impressed his new connections since arriving from France during the summer. Described as a 'beautiful horse' by Willie Mullins, he won his only start at Auteuil in May when handled by Arnaud Chaille-Chaille before being snapped up by Ireland's champion trainer. Entered in the Grade 1 Royal Bond Novice Hurdle at Fairyhouse (29th November), the Timos gelding is expected to develop into an exciting novice and I suggest backing him for next March's Cheltenham Festival."* **WON the Martin Pipe Conditional Jockeys' Handicap Hurdle at Cheltenham (19/3/21) @ 8/1**

FRENCH REVOLUTION – Part II: WINNERS: GOOD BALL (9/4, 2/1), KALKAS (2/1), SHENTRI (7/4), TEAHUPOO (4/1, 4/9)

Quote: **TEAHUPOO:** *"Gordon Elliott is training the unbeaten Teahupoo having been purchased on behalf of **Robcour**. The three year old by Masked Marvel beat Good Ball by a length and a quarter in the Prix Emilius (conditions hurdle) at Auteuil last month. Leading on the approach to the final furlong, the Gab Leenders trained gelding stayed on strongly after the last and looked a smart sort. His new stable already have the likes of Quilixios, Zanahiyr and Duffle Coat in the juvenile hurdle department and this once raced three year old looks another useful addition to the squad."* **WON on his Irish debut at Fairyhouse (16/1/21) @ 4/1**

Plus: **ALBORKAN (9/1), ASHINGTON (4/1), BELLATRIXSA (Evens), CAPE GENTLEMAN (5/4, 5/2), ELYSIAN FLAME (5/2), HILL SIXTEEN (2/1 & 11/10), IMPERIAL ALCAZAR (5/1), IMPERIAL STORM (8/13), L'AIR DU VENT (2/1), MY DROGO (4 wins – 100/30, 9/1, 2/1, 5/4), SAGE ADVICE (7/4), ZANAVI (25/1)**

Quote: *"Speaking to Dan at Aintree last Saturday, he passed on news of another highly promising youngster, namely **MY DROGO**. A five year old by Milan, he was sent off 50/1 on his racecourse debut in a hotly contested bumper at Cheltenham's showcase meeting last month. Making good headway coming down the hill, the Richard Kelvin-Hughes owned gelding stormed home to finish a length and three quarters second behind the highly regarded I Am Maximus. Dan described the once raced gelding as '**exceptional**' and the plan is for him to make his debut over hurdles at Newbury's winter Festival (27th November). There is a two miles* maiden hurdle, which the stable introduced French recruit Captain Forez to finish third in 2016." **WON at Newbury @ 100/30 – he went on to win all 4 of his starts over hurdles, including a Grade 2 at Ascot (9/1) and Grade 1 at Aintree (5/4).**

Quote: "***ZANAVI*** *was acquired at the same sale by Denis Hogan for* ***€34,000***. *A three year old gelding by Champs Elysees, he was trained by Dermot Weld and, having shown little on his belated racecourse debut at Roscommon (1m 2f : Heavy) in early July, he ran considerably better next time. Reappearing at the Curragh (1m 4f : Soft) over three months later, he stayed on well in second behind the Jessica Harrington filly Flor De La Luna conceding five pounds. Lightly raced, he could prove a fine dual purpose horse for his new connections."* **WON over hurdles at Fairyhouse (22/2/21) by 13 lengths @ 25/1**

Quote: "*I have got a lot of time for Emmet Mullins as a trainer and he is set to unleash* ***CAPE GENTLEMAN*** *over obstacles this winter. Previously trained by Nicolas Clement in France, he won over a mile and six at Clairefontaine last season before being purchased for €80,000 at the Arqana Sale in October 2019. The four year old has only run twice for Mullins finishing five lengths runner-up to Mt Leinster at Listowel (1m 6f : Soft) in September. He then won the Irish Cesarewitch at the Curragh (2m : Soft) by a couple of lengths off a mark of 85. Bought as a dual purpose horse, he has only had five runs during his career and couldn't be in better hands."* **WON twice over hurdles, including the Grade 2 Dovecote Novices' Hurdle at Kempton (27/2/21) @ 5/2**

Quote: "***HILL SIXTEEN*** *is a horse I have followed since Declan Phelan included him in his Irish Pointers section in OJA during the 2018/2019 season. Even though he won a couple of times over hurdles and fences, the former Trevor Hemmings owned gelding never quite lived up to expectations. A winner at Sedgefield in January, he is rated 126 over fences and could have more to offer. Sold for £46,000 at the Goffs UK September sale as part of Trevor's dispersal, he is now owned by Million In Mind and in training with* ***Nigel Twiston-Davies***. *The Court Cave gelding was placed behind the likes of One For Rosie and Windsor Avenue as a novice hurdler and has plenty of ability but still looked raw. If his new trainer can find the key to him then he could have a progressive young chaser on his hands."* **WON his first two starts for Nigel Twiston-Davies @ 2/1 & 11/10.**

CHRISTMAS SPECIAL 2020

KAUTO STAR NOVICES' CHASE: SHAN BLUE (Advised @ 2/1)

Quote: "***SHAN BLUE*** *won his only Irish point for Andrew Slattery before being bought privately to join Dan Skelton. A six year old by Shantou, he won over hurdles at Southwell last season before chasing home Shishkin in the Listed Sidney Banks Memorial at Huntingdon. Beaten 27 lengths in sixth in the Ballymore Novices' Hurdle at Cheltenham in March, he has improved since sent chasing recording two emphatic victories at Wetherby in October. A fourteen lengths winner on his fencing bow (2m 3f), he was even more impressive next time at the same track 16 days later. Following a terrific round of jumping, he pulled sixteen lengths clear of Snow Leopardess conceding thirteen pounds – the runner-up has won a decent handicap at Haydock since and is rated 135. He was due to run at Huntingdon at the beginning of the month (meeting abandoned) and therefore arrives here fresh (off 57 days). Unbeaten over three miles, his record racing right-handed is 12 (won his point-to-point) and he has won on good and heavy ground."* **Advised @ 2/1 - WON the Kauto Star Novices' Chase at Kempton (26/12/20)**

Quote: **ADRIMEL**: *"His trainer has entered him in the Grade 1 Challow Hurdle at Newbury (29th December) but I am hoping he will wait for the Grade 2 Leamington Novices' Hurdle at Warwick (16th January). The two miles five event is invariably run in a bog and that will suit him. Don't be surprised to see him sport cheekpieces at some stage."* **WON the Grade 2 Leamington Novices' Hurdle @ 7/2 (wearing cheekpieces for the first time)**

Quote: **BOB OLINGER**: *"Henry De Bromhead once again has a strong team of youngsters but few are more exciting than this Sholokhov gelding. A wide margin point and bumper winner last season, the five year old had the misfortune to bump into the Cheltenham Festival bumper winner Ferny Hollow on his hurdles debut at Gowran (2m) last month. Beaten a length by Willie Mullins' winner, he ran very well though and was thirty one lengths clear of the third. Stepped up half a mile at Navan last week, he trounced his rivals by upwards of fourteen lengths making all and never looking in danger. Scruffy over the last two flights, his jumping was largely good and he is a horse with a huge amount of ability. He looks tailormade for the Ballymore Novices' Hurdle at Cheltenham."* **WON the Ballymore Novices' Hurdle at Cheltenham (17/3/21) @ 6/4**

Quote: **METIER**: *"Rated 88 on the Flat for Andy Slattery, he was acquired for 150,000gns over a year ago and his new connections have been rewarded for their patience. Harry Fry has a high-class novice hurdler on his hands, if his two performances at Newton Abbot and Ascot are anything to go by. The gelded son of Mastercraftsman has shown a real aptitude for his new discipline producing a good round of jumping to win at the West Country track in late October. Leading at the third last, Sean Bowen's mount breezed clear to win easily. Three weeks later, he made it two out of two in an Introductory hurdle at Ascot making all and beating Tile Topper by five and a half lengths conceding five pounds to the runner-up. Both wins have been gained on heavy or soft ground which bodes well for his next target the Grade 1 Tolworth Novices' Hurdle at Sandown (2nd January), which is invariably run in testing conditions. It represents a significant rise in class but he looks ready for it with his stable in tremendous form (5 winners from their last 16 runners (31%) during the last 14 days)."* **WON the Tolworth Hurdle by 12 lengths @ 7/4**

The IRISH ANGLE by Declan PHELAN: WINNERS: GINTO (5/6), JOURNEY WITH ME (4/7), KILBEG KING (7/4), STAKER WALLACE (4/7)

Quote: *"**KILBEG KING** (an impressive physical specimen) joins Anthony Honeyball and, if he can remain injury free (a problem up to now), the purchase fee of £45,000 earlier this month may prove to be a shrewd piece of business (another requiring soft/heavy)."* **WON by seven and a half lengths at Uttoxeter (20/3/21) on his Rules debut @ 7/4**

Quote: *"The banker of the Limerick Festival is **STAKER WALLACE** in the hunters' chase on **Sunday December 27th (1.30)**: he has a brace of point wins to his name and some smart hunter chase form. He was placed second in two Opens already this winter, and his form is head and shoulders above the rest of the entrants in this hunter chase. I expect him to win this race at his leisure, though the odds of reward are likely to be in the 4/6 range."* **WON @ 4/7**

THE HORSE I AM MOST LOOKING FORWARD TO SEEING OVER CHRISTMAS: ANTHONY BROMLEY: GOOD BALL – WON at Newbury (29/12/20) @ 9/4

FRENCH REVOLUTION – Part III : WINNERS: HOMME PUBLIC (11/8), RIVIERE D'ETEL (8/15)

Quote: **RIVIERE D'ETEL**: *"Well bred, she is a full-sister to Listed hurdles winner Ria D'Etel and a half-sister to Paul Nicholls' 135 rated winning chaser Kapcorse. Trained by Yannick Fouin, the grey daughter of Martaline finished fifth on her only start on the Flat at Clairefontaine (1m 4f : Soft) under Pierre-Charles Boudot in late July. Switching codes, she made her hurdles debut in the Prix Finot at Auteuil (2m 2f : Very Soft) in September, a Listed event for fillies. Attempting to make all, she jumped well and was still in front at the last. Headed on the run-in by Obeone (see page 149 of OJA), she was beaten a length and a half with the pair pulling twenty lengths clear of the third. Both fillies looked smart. Purchased since by big spending owners **Noel and Valerie Moran,** she is now in training with Gordon Elliott and will presumably go juvenile hurdling in the New Year and will make a fine broodmare one day, too."* **WON by 12 lengths on her Irish debut at Punchestown (31/12/20)**

Talking Trainers with EVAN WILLIAMS

Quote: **SECRET REPRIEVE**: *"The Welsh National at Chepstow on Sunday (27th December) is his target and I have thought for sometime that he is the right type of horse for the race. I have always liked him, but he suffered with sore shins last year and we could never get into a rhythm with him. We sorted his shins out and have given him plenty of time. Having only had a handful of runs over fences, he lacks chasing experience which could count against him. However, if everything stays right and things fall into place on the day, I wouldn't swap him for anything else in the field. A faller at Haydock on his reappearance, I wanted to run him in a good race but he got caught out and hit the floor. He was good at Chepstow last time though winning by a dozen lengths and, while he incurs a four pounds penalty, he is set to race off a twelve pounds higher mark in future. Adam (Wedge) will ride him at Chepstow and he is in very good form at home."* **WON the Welsh National at Chepstow @ 5/2**

Quote: **SILVER STREAK**: *"It is a quick turnaround but we are going to run him in the Christmas Hurdle at Kempton on Saturday (26th). Runner-up in the race last year, it won't be easy with Epatante in the field once again, but the ground is likely to suit him and he has a good record at the track."* **WON the Grade 1 Christmas Hurdle at Kempton (26/12/20) @ 13/2**

WINNERS: BASS ROCK (17/2), BEAR GHYLLS (10/11), BOB AND CO (11/8, 1/5, 3/1), CADZAND (5/2), EILEENDOVER (11/8), EKLAT DE RIRE (11/4), SIRWILLIAMWALLACE (6/4)

Quote: *"As stated in the November Update, owner Ray Green is a great planner when it comes to his team of horses and he is certain to have an end of season target in mind for the ex-French trained **BASS ROCK**. Fifth on his only start over hurdles for Dominique Bresou, he was beaten seven and a half lengths at Clairefontaine (2m 1f : Very Soft) in July 2019, in a race which has worked out well – the first four home have all won since. Transferred to the UK this year, he joined Sandy Thomson and has finished runner-up on both occasions at Carlisle this Autumn. Beaten three lengths by Stoner's Choice (won again since and now rated 139) in October, he filled the same position in arrears of the 90 rated Flat racer Severance over three weeks later. Yet to race beyond two miles one, the Martaline gelding will be suited by a step up to two and a half miles and an opening mark of 117 underestimates his ability."* **WON on his handicap debut at Ayr (18/4/21) @ 17/2**

Quote: "**BOB AND CO** is already a dual hunter chase winner registering victories at Bangor and Fontwell in February. Rated 146 over fences, the nine year old had spells with Emmanuel Clayeux, Francois Nicolle and Gabriel Leenders in France before joining Paul Nicholls last year. A strong stayer, the Dom Alco gelding has reportedly undergone wind surgery since his last run and ought to be a force in the leading events this season." **WON 3 hunter chases, including the Champion Hunters Chase at Punchestown (30/4/21) @ 3/1**

Quote: "Provided the ground isn't too testing at Kempton on Sunday, **CADZAND** doesn't look overburdened on his handicap debut in the concluding **Watch Racing Free Online At Ladbrokes Handicap Hurdle (3.40)**. Rated 129, Dan Skelton's gelding has always had a lofty reputation since winning a UK point-to-point for Tom Lacey in March 2019. Placed in two bumpers at Newbury and Warwick, he underwent wind surgery soon afterwards and has run twice over hurdles this term. Beaten nine and a half lengths behind Do Your Job (runner-up in a Listed race since) at Ayr in late October, he may not have appreciated the testing conditions. He had no trouble going one better at Warwick (Good/Soft) the following month when readily seeing off Twominutes Turkish by five and a half lengths in receipt of six pounds. This will be his first run on a right-handed track but Kempton ought to play to his strengths given his high cruising speed. Good to soft is ideal with form figures on such a surface being 1321." **WON at Kempton @ 5/2**

Quote: "**EKLAT DE RIRE** is one of Declan Phelan's Irish Pointers in OJA (page 155) and the big strapping Saddex gelding made a splendid start to his chasing career when galloping his six opponents into submission at Punchestown (3m 1f : Heavy) this month. Rachel Blackmore's mount jumped well and was always towards the forefront of the field. Taking over at the fourth last, he stayed on strongly to beat the 134 rated School Boy Hours, who had also finished runner-up behind Latest Exhibition at the same track in October. Henry De Bromhead indicated afterwards that a **Grade 3 at Naas over three miles (31st January)** is likely to be his next target – stablemate Chris's Dream finished runner-up in the race in 2019." **WON at Naas @ 11/4**

FEBRUARY 2021

BETFAIR HURDLE: SOARING GLORY (Advised @ 12/1 WON @ 17/2)

Quote: "**SOARING GLORY** is another very good novice amongst the field and the six year old's trainer Jonjo O'Neill sent out Get Me Out of Here to win this during his first season over hurdles in 2010 (rated 135). The same trainer was also responsible for Vicario Di Bray who finished runner-up in 1989 when sent off 4/7 favourite. Twice a bumper winner last season, the six year old has only won once over hurdles but is the only horse to have beaten subsequent Grade 1 winner Bravemansgame over obstacles this season. He got the better of Paul Nicholls' 150 rated hurdler at Chepstow in October. Runner-up behind the sidelined Dusart over C&D in November conceding six pounds, he then fell at the second last at Wetherby when seemingly going strongly. Six lengths third behind My Drogo in a Grade 2 at Ascot before Christmas, this has been the plan since (off 57 days). Well handicapped off 133, he is a big threat provided his jumping stands the test and the ground isn't too demanding. His record on good and good/soft is 112F compared to 123 on soft/heavy. **Best Price: 12/1 (Bet365).**" **ADVISED @ 12/1 WON at Newbury (21/2/21) by three lengths @ 17/2**

Quote: "Olly Murphy sent out Thomas Darby to finish third in this event last season and Gordon Elliott's former assistant plans to run another of his stable stars, namely **BREWIN'UPASTORM** *in the two and a half miles event later this month. Despite winning a couple of times last season, things haven't gone to plan over fences for the eight year old. The former pointer lost his jockey at the fourth last in the Arkle Trophy last spring and he finished last in both the Colin Parker Memorial Chase and Tingle Creek Chase at Carlisle and Sandown respectively earlier this term. Reverting to hurdles at Taunton (2m 3f) last time, he defied top weight and a rating of 148 to beat nine rivals by upwards of eleven lengths. Now rated 155, he looked much happier over hurdles and it is worth remembering the Milan gelding was fourth in the Ballymore Novices' Hurdle at Cheltenham and runner-up in Grade 1 company at Aintree during the 2018/2019 season. Despite the fact all five of his wins under Rules have been gained on right-handed tracks, he won his Irish point going left-handed and, as stated, he produced career best efforts at Aintree and Cheltenham. I confirmed with Olly on Saturday that this is his target and he will hopefully take plenty of beating."* **BREWIN'UPASTORM WON the Grade 2 National Spirit Hurdle at Fontwell (28/2/21) @ 3/1**

Quote: **EASY AS THAT**: *"If his jumping frailties can be remedied, the dual bumper winner is favourably handicapped over hurdles off 114. From the family of Time For Rupert, he looks ready for a step up in trip, which would also give him more time over his obstacles. The ability is there but his jumping technique requires more fine tuning. He is in the right hands to exploit such a lenient looking mark (entered at Chepstow (3.50) on Friday (5th February) in a 2m 3f handicap hurdle)."* **WON at Chepstow (5/2/21) by 9 lengths @ 85/40**

Quote: **GALOPIN DES CHAMPS**: *"Yet to race beyond two miles two, a step up in distance won't go amiss and I am hoping Ireland's champion trainer will also enter him in the Martin Pipe Conditional Jockeys' Handicap Hurdle at the Festival."* **WON the Martin Pipe Conditional Jockeys' Handicap Hurdle at Cheltenham (19/3/21) @ 8/1**

Talking Trainers with DONALD McCAIN: WINNERS: BAREBACK JACK (5/2), DREAMS OF HOME (4/5, 2/5), FIVEANDTWENTY (6/4), FRUIT N NUT (3/1), GAELIK COAST (85/40), MACKENBERG (5/6, 5/4), MILANS EDGE (11/10), MINELLA DRAMA (13/8)

Quote: **GAELIK COAST**: *"Even though he has been running over two miles, I think he will be suited by stepping up to two and a half miles. With that in mind, we might also enter him in the Frodon Novices' Chase at Musselburgh on Saturday (6th February). He is a very good jumper."* **WON at Musselburgh @ 85/40**

Quote: **MILANS EDGE**: *"She is a nice mare who I like and she has sharpened up a lot since arriving. We will aim her at a mares' bumper."* **WON a mares' bumper at Wetherby (23/2/21) by nine and a half lengths @ 11/10.**

The CHELTENHAM FESTIVAL 2021

6 WINNERS: SHISHKIN (1/2), HONEYSUCKLE (Advised @ 5/2), BOB OLINGER (Advised @ 2/1), MONKFISH (1/4), SIR GERHARD (85/40), GALOPIN DES CHAMPS (Advised @ 14/1)

Quote: *"**HONEYSUCKLE** is another top-class mare in the line-up as she bids to emulate African Sister (1939), Dawn Run (1984), Flakey Dove (1994), Annie Power (2016) and Epatante (2020), who landed the prize for the fairer sex. Unbeaten throughout her career, including ten times over hurdles, six of which have been at Grade 1 level, she won the mares' hurdle at the Festival* last year. Half a length separated her and Benie Des Dieux and the seven year old has continued in a similar vein this season. The daughter of Sulamani claimed her second win in the Hattons Grace Hurdle at Fairyhouse in November when beating Ronald Pump by half a length. She then produced arguably a career best effort when annihilating her rivals in the Irish Champion Hurdle at Leopardstown last month. A ten lengths scorer from Abacadabras, she pulled away after the second last. It was a devastating display and one hopes it doesn't leave the same mark as it did to Apple's Jade, who produced a similar performance in the same race a couple of years ago. Otherwise, Henry De Bromhead's mare has outstanding claims." **Advised @ 5/2 WON the Champion Hurdle @ 11/10**

Quote: "**BOB OLINGER (Top 40)** won his only point-to-point for Pat Doyle (yielding ground) before joining Henry De Bromhead. Ironically, he won the same point bumper at Gowran Park which First Lieutenant landed in 2010 before winning this event the following season. The Sholokhov gelding has won two out of three over hurdles suffering his only defeat on his reappearance in November. Beaten a length by Ferny Hollow at Gowran over two miles, he has improved since stepped up to middle distances. A wide margin winner at Navan in December, he then produced a career best when readily brushing aside Blue Lord in the Grade 1 Lawlor's of Naas Novice Hurdle in January. Staying on strongly after the second last, he was pushed out to win by six and a half lengths. Envoi Allen won the same race before following up here. This has been his target since and it will take a very smart novice to beat him." **Advised @ 2/1 WON the Ballymore Novices' Hurdle @ 6/4**

Quote: "**SIR GERHARD (Top 40)** was a high profile purchase out of Ellmarie Holden's yard having won his only Irish point (beat Listed novice hurdle winner Minella Drama by 12 lengths). Bought for £400,000, the Jeremy gelding has looked a top-class prospect in both his starts in bumpers for Gordon Elliott this term. The six year old streaked fourteen lengths clear at Down Royal in October (second and third won since) before providing his trainer with his sixth win in the Listed bumper at Navan in December during the last ten years. The heavy ground may not have played to his strengths but Jamie Codd's mount quickened smartly to beat three previous winners by four and a half lengths. Elliott has won the race in the past with Don Cossack (2011), Samcro (2016) and Envoi Allen (2018). Transferred to Willie Mullins this month, he threatens to be an even better horse on quicker ground. He has a lethal turn of foot and is the one they all have to beat provided he has settled in well to his new surroundings." **WON the bumper @ 85/40**

Quote: "**GALOPIN DES CHAMPS (Top 40)** has had multiple entries this week but looks tailormade for this. A winner at Auteuil (2m 2f) in May 2020 when trained by Arnaud Chaille-Chaille, he has raced three times for Willie Mullins and has been given a mark of 142 by the UK handicapper. Runner-up behind Sea Ducor at Gowran Park (2m) in November, Willie Mullins won the same two miles maiden hurdle with the likes of Douvan and Sharjah in previous years. Sent off evens favourite for a Grade 2 hurdle at Limerick over Christmas, the Timos gelding pulled up and was found to be suffering with irregular abnormalities. Back in action in early February, the five year old ran well in sixth in a Grade 1 at the Dublin Racing Festival at Leopardstown. Beaten less than ten lengths by stablemate Appreciate It, he has only raced on soft or heavy ground but it would be no surprise to see him improve on a sounder surface. He is crying out for this step up in trip – he looked a stayer when winning at Auteuil and he is a half-brother to a 2m 6f winner. His trainer has won this three times (Sir Des Champs (2011), Don Poli (2014) & Killultagh Vic (2015)), two of which were five year olds." **Advised @ 14/1 WON the Martin Pipe Conditional Jockeys' Handicap Hurdle @ 8/1**

The AINTREE GRAND NATIONAL MEETING 2021

7 WINNERS: MONMIRAL (10/11), ABACADABRAS (5/1), CHANTRY HOUSE (11/8), LIVELOVELAUGH (15/2), MY DROGO (Advised @ 5/2), SHISHKIN (1/8), MINELLA TIMES (Advised @ 12/1)

Plus: SULLY D'OCC AA (Advised @ 25/1 – 2nd @ 12/1), JOHNBB (Advised @ 16/1 – 2nd @ 9/1), ANY SECOND NOW (Advised @ 10/1 – 3rd in the Grand National @ 15/2)

Quote: *"**MINELLA TIMES** has yet to race beyond three miles but is bred to stay longer distances and could excel over this marathon trip. From the family of Borders National winner Rambling Minster, the eight year old doesn't look overburdened off 146 and remains lightly raced over fences (only 10 starts). A faller in his only Irish point when handled by John Nallen,* expert Declan Phelan commented in the 2017/2018 edition of One Jump Ahead: **"A beautifully structured bay gelding: may have the ability to match his looks. Moved through from third, five out, to lead three out and had the race put to bed only to fall at the final fence on his one run at Belclare (R) (Yielding) in April: he was on his way to a 10 out of 10 first effort until trapped by the final fence. He relaxed and travelled as asked during the race and showed gears to inject pace in gaining control. On this evidence he could develop into a very classy horse: over many years, I have noted last fence "unfortunate" fallers tend to be horses worth following from pointing ranks....Gold Cup winners such as Mr Mulligan and War Of Attrition were also last fence fallers in points. John Nallen sold this four year old's older brother to Tom George in 2016, Cruiseaway, he too is talented but with issues. Nallen cashed in with a private sale of this four year old to J.P. McManus (six figures) and I gather that Henry de Bromhead is training him. Hopefully Minella Times will mature into a proper straight forward racehorse and, if he does, he would be one you would expect to see competing in decent races at future Cheltenham Festivals."** *A dual winner over fences, including at Listowel (2m 6f) in September off 130. Rachel Blackmore (1122) was on board and remarked:* **"He's a real stayer. He's a typical one of Henry's and it makes a jockeys life easier when they can jump as well as him."** *Four and a half lengths second in the Paddy Power Chase at Leopardstown in December off 136, he was staying on at the death. The eight year old completed his preparation at the Dublin Racing Festival when half a length second to the same owner's Off You Go in another competitive handicap chase (2m 5f). That event has produced subsequent winners Goose Man (6th), Bapaume (11th) and Myth Buster (12th). Effective on any ground, his record over three miles is F22. He has major claims with the jockey of the moment on top.* **Best Price: 12/1 (Bet365, Paddy Power, William Hill).**" Advised @ 12/1 WON the Grand National by six and a half lengths @ 11/1

Quote: *"**ABACADABRAS** tackles the trip for the first time but he is a half-brother to a 2m 3f winner. The sharp track and decent ground will play to the strengths of the dual Grade 1 winner. The seven year old won the Morgiana Hurdle at Punchestown by a neck in November before disappointing at Leopardstown in late December when his stable were under a cloud. Beaten ten lengths by Honeysuckle in the Irish Champion Hurdle over the same C&D in February, he was an early faller in the Champion Hurdle last time. The Davidoff gelding hit the floor at the third flight. He hasn't raced on good to soft or better ground since October 2019 (1R21) and is a high-class horse on his day. A proven Grade 1 performer, he likes drying ground and has speed. This track should play to his strengths. There have been nine Irish trained winners this century."* **WON the Aintree Hurdle @ 5/1**

Quote: *"**LIVELOVELAUGH** has been targeted at this race all season and, despite being an eleven year old (Always Waining was the last winner from his age group in 2012) and only winning one of his eighteen races over fences, he has leading claims. Willie Mullins has won this twice with Its Time For A Win (2002) and Cadmium (2019). The Beneficial gelding ran well for a long way in the Grand National in 2019 until his stamina gave way after the third last. Without a win since January 2018, he has been placed four times this season, including twice at Leopardstown. Third behind Off You Go at the Dublin Racing Festival in February off 135, he jumped brilliantly next time only to get collared close home by Mitchouka in a similar event over the same C&D (2m 5f) last month off 137 (runs off 145 here). Decent ground is ideal."* **WON the Topham Chase @ 15/2**

Quote: *"**MY DROGO** chased home I Am Maximus on his debut in a bumper at Cheltenham in October but hasn't looked back since winning three out of three over hurdles. A well bred gelding by Milan, he is out of seven times winner My Petra (won a Grade 2 chase over 2m 3f). Following his win at Newbury's Winter Festival, he then landed the Grade 2 Kennel Gate NH at Ascot before Christmas by nearly three lengths (Soaring Glory was third). Given a break of 78 days, Dan Skelton purposely missed the Cheltenham Festival, instead he reappeared in the Grade 2 Premier Novices' Hurdle at Kelso (2m 2f) last month. Staying on strongly after the last, he beat Do Your Job by nine and a half lengths conceding five pounds. His racing style and pedigree suggests he will be even better over this trip."* **Advised @ 5/2 WON the Grade 1 Mersey Novices' Hurdle @ 5/4**

Quote: *"**SULLY D'OC AA** is another horse who has benefited from a wind operation. A three times winner over hurdles in France, the Konig Turf gelding beat the aforementioned Editeur Du Gite by nearly lengths five lengths at Ascot (2m 3f) in October off 125 (now rated 136). Third at Newbury behind Clondaw Castle off 135, he was then absent for 111 days. Anthony Honeyball's lightly raced chaser contested the Paddy Power Plate at the Cheltenham Festival and, while the seven year old ran well for a long way, the trip may have stretched his stamina. A strongly run two miles on drying ground – his trainer is adamant he doesn't want soft ground – will suit."* **Advised @ 25/1 finished 2nd in the Grade 3 Red Rum Handicap Chase @ 12/1**

Quote: *"**JOHNBB** could be an interesting proposition stepping up in trip. From the family of Operation Houdini (won over 3m 1f) and Tommy Rapper (won over 2m 7f), the Stowaway gelding is bred to stay and is lightly raced this campaign. Rated 137, he won by four and a quarter lengths at Wetherby (2m 3f) in November – and had the subsequent Grand Sefton Chase winner Beau Bay back in fifth. A faller next time at the same track, he is very good fresh (105 days) and his record on good or good to soft ground is 231. It is worth recalling Tom Lacey's comments on page 93 of One Jump Ahead:* **"Successful over fences at Sandown in December, he doesn't want over racing because he appears to be best fresh and hasn't always backed up next time. I also think he will benefit from some nicer ground. Despite his win at Sandown being gained over two miles, he needs further. Two and a half miles handicap chases will be on his agenda and I would love to try him over the National fences at Aintree one day."** *The Herefordshire trainer has also entered him in the Bet365 Gold Cup (3m 5f) later in the month and he won this with Thomas Patrick in 2018."* **Advised @ 16/1 finished 2nd in the Grade 3 Betway Handicap Chase @ 9/1**

SPRING WATCH:

2.25 CORAL SCOTTISH CHAMPION HURDLE (Grade 2) – 2 miles

*"**MILKWOOD** doesn't look too badly treated either off a mark of 142, provided the ground isn't soft. Suited by flat, left handed tracks on decent ground, Neil Mulholland's charge won at Ffos Las in October before finishing fourth behind Sceau Royal in the Welsh Champion Hurdle over the same C&D when rated 141. Unlucky in the Gerry Feilden Hurdle at Newbury, the Dylan Thomas gelding was badly hampered at the second last. Robbie Dunne is his regular partner, but the Irishman hasn't excelled on either of his last couple of rides aboard him. Firstly, he was positioned too far back in the Betfair Hurdle in February and then, secondly, he made his move much too soon in the County Hurdle at Cheltenham last month. Beaten two and a quarter lengths by Belfast Banter, he travelled strongly but his rider should have sat and waited longer. Raised two pounds since, this has been his target since with his trainer commenting:* **"With hindsight, I think Robbie (Dunne) wishes he'd held on to him a bit longer, but I'm happy with his run. We rode him a bit handier today and he settled well, so I was pleased about that, but something has struck into him and taken a hind shoe off. We'll look now at the Scottish Champion Hurdle, where the track will suit him."** *Available at* **10/1 (generally)**, *he is expected to go well, provided the heavens don't open."* **Advised @ 10/1 WON the Scottish Champion Hurdle at Ayr (18/4/21) @ 3/1**

BROOMFIELD BURG: *"A four lengths winner on his debut for Richard Harding in early October, he was purchased the following month by J.P.McManus for £90,000. Much too keen on his Rules bow in a bumper at Newbury in January, he weakened and only finished seventh. However, his homework since has reportedly been out of the top drawer – there is every chance he will wear a hood on his next outing. Provided he settles, it will be well worth waiting for."* **WON by eight and a half lengths at Southwell (4/5/21) @ 3/1**

It is £8 per Update (except £10 for the Cheltenham Festival version and £6 for the February one) or £40 for ALL 5 via EMAIL.

Don't forget to read my Diary @
www.mhpublications.co.uk

ONE JUMP AHEAD UPDATES 2021/2022
ORDER FORM (EMAIL ONLY)

AVAILABLE AT £8.00 EACH (£10 Cheltenham & £6 February) OR £40 FOR ALL 5

- **CHELTENHAM PADDY POWER MEETING 2021**
(Will be emailed on Thursday 11th November 2021)

- **CHRISTMAS SPECIAL 2021**
(Will be emailed on Wednesday 22nd December 2021)

- **FEBRUARY 2022**

- **MARCH 2022 - CHELTENHAM FESTIVAL PREVIEW**
(Will be emailed on the Sunday before the Festival)

- **APRIL 2022 – AINTREE PREVIEW**
(Will be emailed on the Tuesday before the Meeting)

Total Cheque / Postal Order value £............. made payable to MARK HOWARD PUBLICATIONS Ltd. Post your order to: MARK HOWARD PUBLICATIONS. 69 FAIRGARTH DRIVE, KIRKBY LONSDALE, CARNFORTH, LANCASHIRE. LA6 2FB.

NAME: ....

ADDRESS: ....

....

....POST CODE: ....

Email Address: ....

If you have not received your *UPDATE* via email 24 hours before the meeting starts, please contact us immediately.

Available to order via **www.mhpublications.co.uk**

AHEAD ON THE FLAT 2022

The 22nd edition of *Ahead On The Flat* will be published in early April for the 2022 Flat season. It will be formulated along the same lines as previous years with a **Top 40 Prospects, Ballydoyle Juveniles, Handicap Snips, Maidens In Waiting, Significant Sales** & **Unraced Three Year Olds**. In addition, there will be the usual stable interviews with some of the top trainers in Great Britain (this year's included **Andrew Balding, Ralph Beckett, George Boughey Roger Charlton, Clive Cox, Tim Easterby, William Haggas, James Tate & Roger Varian**). Ahead On The Flat will contain 152 pages and the price is £10.99.

I shall also be producing **three** *Ahead On The Flat Updates* **(EMAIL ONLY)**. There will be a **Royal Ascot Preview** (**6 winners** in 2021 including **KEMARI (Advised @ 11/1)** & **SUREFIRE (Advised @ 10/1)** plus **NICEST (Advised @ 66/1 – 3rd)** & **RAYMOND TUSK (2nd @ 25/1))**, **York Ebor Preview** and an **Autumn** *Update*. The Royal Ascot version is £10 with the other two £6 or £19 for the ALL THREE.

ORDER FORM

•   **AHEAD ON THE FLAT 2022 (Book ONLY)**   **£10.99**

AHEAD ON THE FLAT UPDATES 2022 (can be ordered individually at £6.00 EACH (£10 ROYAL ASCOT) or ALL 3 updates for £19.00):

•   **ROYAL ASCOT PREVIEW 2022**   **£10.00**

•   **YORK EBOR MEETING PREVIEW 2022**   **£6.00**

•   **AUTUMN PREVIEW 2022**   **£6.00**

•   **ALL 3** *UPDATES* **(EMAIL ONLY)**   **£19.00**

•   **AHEAD ON THE FLAT + 3** *UPDATES*   **£28.99**

Total Cheque / Postal Order value £............. Made payable to MARK HOWARD PUBLICATIONS Ltd. Please send to: MARK HOWARD PUBLICATIONS Ltd. 69 FAIRGARTH DRIVE, KIRKBY LONSDALE, CARNFORTH, LANCASHIRE. LA6 2FB.

NAME: ....

ADDRESS: ....

....

....POST CODE: ....

Email Address: ....

Value Racing Club

"Winning Together"

Our aim at Value Racing Club is to introduce new people into the world of horse racing. We provide a cost effective and simple way of becoming a racehorse owner. There are never any hidden costs or extras. Once the initial purchase has been paid, no further monies are required during the entire racing season.

What we offer and benefits:

- An opportunity to become involved in racehorse ownership.
- What we pay for a horse is what you pay, there are no added fees of any kind.
- A one-off cost covers the entire racing season.
- Stable visits arranged to watch your horse work on the gallops.
- Free owners badge every time your horse runs guaranteed.
- Each syndicate keeps 100% of all prize money won.
- 68% overall strike rate of our runners finishing in the first three places.
- Horses in training with David Pipe, Mick Appleby, Jamie Snowden, Tom Lacey & Tristan Davidson.
- Racing TV pundit Mark Howard is our Club Ambassador.
- We are members of the ROA "Racehorse Owners Association" & RSA "Racehorse Syndicates Association" to ensure good practice.

Big race wins include the £70,000 Imperial Cup, £30,000 Betfred Summer Hurdle, £30,000 Durham National, £20,000 Lincolnshire National. Valuable flat winners at York, Newmarket & Haydock.

Over £700,000 of prize money won for owners.

Website: www.valueracingclub.co.uk email: contact@valueracingclub.co.uk Twitter: @valueracingclub

Call James for more information: 07939800769